Contents

To Janet

Acknowledgements
I should like to express my thanks to the many students and teachers who have allowed me to observe and video-tape their teaching and who have discussed with me the views offered in this book. I am also grateful to Bill Rogers for the insights he has offered on his annual visits to Cambridge and whose influence is apparent in the later chapters of this book.

Especial thanks go to Janet Parkinson whose research assistance, typing and enthusiasm were so helpful.

Introduction

I once overheard a headmaster remarking to a friend at a conference that he couldn't understand how a 'slip of a girl' on his staff should have no difficulty in controlling her classes, whereas a hefty male colleague was like putty in their hands. This book attempts to provide some explanations for this paradox. It is usually the case that difficult students only present extreme problems for some members of staff, whereas others seem to be able to cope with them fairly easily. The approach adopted in the following chapters is, therefore, 'teacher-centred'. Rather than being primarily concerned with why certain children are more disruptive than others, an attempt is made to explain why some teachers experience less difficulty than others in managing their classes.

We must perhaps acknowledge that a normal day school may not be the most appropriate educational setting for those students who create difficulties for even the most experienced of staff. However, research into coping with emotionally disturbed children in normal schools suggests that they respond to techniques of good classroom management in the same way as non-disturbed children (Kounin and Obradovic, 1968). It may seem to some readers that to focus on the problems facing teachers is somewhat callous. Should we not concentrate on the problems facing the individual child, problems which explain why he needs to behave as he does? This approach has certainly not been neglected; indeed, there is a wealth of literature concerning early experiences, learning difficulties and emotional maladjustment in children. These factors are referred to in Chapter 5, but no attempt is made to provide a comprehensive description of the association between environmental factors and behaviour problems. Such an approach usually offers little to the teacher by way of practical advice in classroom management, though it may have wider implications for social and educational changes. The questions most teachers are concerned with are how to reduce the unwanted behaviour and how to deal effectively with it when it occurs, and this book aims to offer practical advice in these respects.

Unfortunately, the use of the word 'control' offends some teachers, as it smacks of an authoritarian regime which denies children any rights or respect. Nevertheless it is often a more appropriate term than alternatives such as 'management' or 'discipline', as the context is frequently one of controlling communication and interactions as well as one's own responses. It will become clear that there are no authoritarian connotations intended by using the term, as the emphasis is largely on understanding the nature of authority in teacher-student relationships with the aim of avoiding, if possible, the need to force students to comply with the demands made on them. There is an attempt to clarify what is entailed in maintaining co-operative relationships based on the teacher's authority so that conditions can be established in which learning can take place. Students are not the victims of classroom control, they are the beneficiaries. Furthermore, without their co-operation classroom control is not possible – as with any relationship both partners must work to maintain it.

There continues to be a growing number of articles and books devoted to various aspects of classroom discipline and disruptive behaviour and some of the more relevant findings have been included. A rigorous and exhaustive analysis has been avoided in favour of offering the reader some coherent, practical advice although, naturally, only the teacher can decide if any particular course of action is appropriate. Special attention is given to the hidden messages conveyed in non-verbal and verbal communication. Gestures, vocal variations, facial expressions and other bodily movements can reveal a teacher's insecurity or boredom, his confidence or enthusiasm. Unlike words, their meaning is often ambiguous and can only be interpreted reliably if we have other information, such as the status of the speaker and what he is saying. Nevertheless, when there is any discrepancy between the meaning of the words being spoken and the non-verbal behaviour accompanying them, it is the latter which we take to reveal the true feelings of the speaker. For example, we know whether we are really welcome when we call unexpectedly on a friend, regardless of what is actually said. When non-verbal behaviour is consistent with the meaning of the words used, it may even pass unnoticed, though its message will still be received by the listener. Non-verbal communication and language also feature strongly in the expression of authority and power but, surprisingly, there have been few attempts to describe their role in detail in practical situations such as teaching. This will be a major focus throughout the book as it is essential that teachers understand the way they exchange unspoken messages with students.

Rather than present a series of theoretical perspectives and attempt to show their educational relevance, the opposite approach has been taken. Illustrations and transcripts taken from video and audio-taped lessons are presented, which hopefully all teachers will be familiar with, and interpretations of the significant features of the interaction are offered.

Non-verbal behaviours, in the form of the actions we carry out, are particularly significant in the expression of status and power and the first chapter considers this in some detail. Various features of behaviour are illustrated and the underlying messages about relationships being claimed are discussed. The second chapter gathers together the points established and attempts to describe the process whereby authority is negotiated and how it is affected when teachers use persuasion or resort to power. The view developed in the first chapter is that teachers who wish to establish their authority should behave as if they were already *in* authority. This is not as simple or as obvious as it sounds. Teachers, by virtue of their higher status and the role they have to perform, have certain rights to behave in ways denied to students, and in exercising those rights they reinforce their authority. This does not mean that they should be repressive or authoritarian, but rather that their behaviour should be consistent with their status. Students are less likely to question teachers' authority if, by their behaviour, they define the situation as one in which their authority is legitimate. It is particularly important for a teacher to do this in the first meetings with a new class, and it is mainly within this context that ways of conveying status are discussed in the third chapter.

The major bases for legitimacy, as far as teachers' long-term authority is concerned, are not simply the ascribed powers, institutional status and role, but more the personal qualities they possess which contribute to their effectiveness as teachers. In this respect, Chapter 4 considers the role of non-verbal behaviour in effective teaching and influencing the emotional climate of the classroom.

Chapter 5 presents an analysis of unwanted behaviour based on three different perspectives. These have been chosen to help teachers understand why some children are prone to misbehave and what can be done to reduce the opportunities and encouragements for them to do so. The first two perspectives consider the causes and motives for unwanted behaviour and the third deals with various aspects of classroom management. Proficiency in this aspect of teaching contributes to the legitimacy of the teacher's claim to be in authority. There is clearly a close link between preventing unwanted behaviour and dealing effectively with it, and the emphasis in the first five chapters is mainly on creating conditions in which it is least likely to occur.

However, prevention is not always possible and most teachers have to deal with low-level disruptions from students such as calling out and hindering other students on a daily basis. Chapter 6 presents ways in which teachers intervene with low-key reminders and more direct measures but in non-confrontational ways.

Many schools are adopting more comprehensive whole school approaches to behaviour management and Chapter 7 discusses the important features of such schemes at a classroom and school level. Chapter 8 presents some of the ways in which teachers can work with individual students or small groups who are the more persistent or serious offenders to help them improve their behaviour, and finally as a summary, a checklist of behaviours associated with various aspects of teaching and teacher-student relationships is presented. This is indexed to the main text to facilitate reference on specific problems and enhance the practical value of the book. It is hoped that the practical activities included will also give teachers the opportunity to practise aspects of self presentation and plan for some of the more predictable problems.

Status differences have diminished steadily in our society in the past forty years and professional groups such as doctors, lawyers and teachers are no longer held in the same high esteem. At the same time, the status of young people has risen and much of the fashion and entertainment industries are focused on them so that when they attend school they are far less likely to accept teachers' authority without good reason. Whether we like it or not, teacher-student relationships are becoming more informal, reflecting this diminishing status difference, and the approach throughout this book, therefore, is to give teachers some insight into why conflicts arise and how we can best work *with* students to avoid them.

1 Expressing Authority

This chapter looks at aspects of our behaviour which characterise authority relationships and it is important to explain some of the distinctions which will be made. Mehrabian (1972) carried out research on how status differences are conveyed and the two dimensions of bodily behaviour which he identified will be referred to in the subsequent discussion.

The first dimension, which he termed *immediacy*, includes those behaviours which 'increase the mutual sensory stimulation between two persons'. To put this another way, immediacy behaviours tend to focus or intensify communication between people, so that they have greater impact on each other. Included in this dimension would be touching, closer position, forward lean, eye contact and more direct body orientation. Immediacy behaviours seem to be particularly involved in communicating the extent that one person likes or feels aggressive towards another. The second dimension, which is involved in the communication of status, Mehrabian termed *relaxation*, as evidenced by bodily posture. Relaxation is conveyed by an asymmetrical positioning of the limbs, openness of arm position, a sideways lean and tilt of the head or, if the speaker is seated, a more reclined position.

In any hierarchical organisation some members have different degrees of status and for the purpose of this discussion they will sometimes be referred to as *superiors* and *subordinates*. In school, a teacher may be a superior in his status relationship with a student, but a subordinate with the headteacher. In some cases, authority relationships may operate between students, even though they are nominally of the same status, by virtue of particular attributes which one possesses and others value. Some readers may find the terms offensive because of other connotations they have, but they will be used here only to denote differences in 'rank' or to label any behaviour which expresses status differences. A more neutral term, 'superordinate', is used in the same way.

Argyle (1975) stated that 'Dominance relationships occur when there are no clear differences of power or status between people. Dominance signals are used to establish status differences where there is no objective basis for such differences, as in groups of primates'. It could be argued that there are clear and objective differences of power and status between students and teachers, so that dominance behaviour need never arise. Teachers are not only adults, but they also have ascribed powers over students. This may have made a difference in times gone by, when children 'knew their place', but is of little consequence now, and each teacher must establish his own authority. One exception may be in shared teaching situations where children transfer appropriate behaviour to the weaker members of a teaching team in the presence of a stronger teacher. Unfortunately, there are many occasions when the teacher's authority is not accepted. For example, a student may refuse to comply with an instruction and it is at times such as these that dominant behaviour may be observed. This 'show of force' to assert one's status, and any submissive behaviour which results, differ markedly from the way people behave when status differences are accepted in the relationship. A superior does not have to show dominant behaviour if his status is accepted; a subordinate need not show submissive behaviour unless he is threatened.

Argyle's use of the term 'dominance relationship' is not helpful in this discussion as regular dominant and submissive displays are a feature of interactions where the status relationship is in dispute. Once this is settled, the status relationship may be maintained on the basis of the power of the superior to make the subordinate comply (see p. 53). In this sense, the term 'power relationship' might be a better description as dominant and submissive behaviour only occurs on those occasions when disputes over status arise.

Dominant behaviour is largely conveyed by postural cues, tone of voice and facial expression, and probably implies an element of threat through increased immediacy and tension, demonstrated by a lack of movement when speaking (see p. 94). Such behaviour might be judged as firm or resolute, but it can easily escalate perilously into an actual threat using a frown and a 'You'd better do as I say, or else' tone of voice. The threat need not be stated verbally, though it often is, as will be discussed later. A more animated display, such as pointing or stabbing at the addressee, shouting and speaking rapidly in a higher pitched voice, may be perceived as threatening, being associated with anger and an attempt to intimidate. However, in schools such displays can only be an alternative to physical assault, as it is illegal actually to strike children even as a formal punishment. An animated display of temper can therefore become a sign of frustration and impotence in the face of behaviour which the teacher is unable to control. In practice it is very unlikely that status differences in teacher-student relationships are maintained solely on the basis of power because, apart from the problems this may cause, teachers do not have sufficient power over students to guarantee their compliance.

The distinction between high status and dominant behaviours will become clearer in the following discussion which considers how authority is expressed in different aspects of our interactions.

Posture

Mehrabian showed that when people of different status meet and talk, the lower status person adopts a more upright posture than the higher status person. It is interesting to speculate on the practical function of this difference. In Figure 1 the boy is being questioned by the teacher about his behaviour

Figure 1 *'You completely wasted your time this lesson!'*

during the lesson. The student's relaxed, asymmetrical posture and his studied unconcern are very characteristic expressions of resistance by those who do not wish to accept their subordinate position.

As Mehrabian pointed out, we tend to assume very relaxed postures with those we dislike or do not respect. Recently, a defendant in court was fined for lounging in the dock and having his hands in his pockets, which was seen by the magistrates as disrespectful. Teachers frequently attempt to 'correct' such postures by telling students to stand up straight and remove their hands from their pockets, not because students will thereby be able to hear more clearly, but to make them show respect for the status of the teacher. The occasion is thus being defined as a formal one where such courtesies must be observed. There is little doubt that most students realise they are being disrespectful when they adopt very relaxed postures and this is evident in the deliberate, grudging way they stand up straight when told to do so. The posture they eventually reach is usually far from upright. How teachers might deal with such situations depends on a variety of factors, and these are discussed later.

There are obviously implications for teachers, particularly during their first meetings with students when relationships are in the formative stage. A vigilant, tense and aggressive attitude, apart from conveying little enthusiasm for the subject taught, suggests insecurity, as if one is actually expecting to be challenged. On the other hand, a slightly bowed posture with feet together and hands clasped in front of the body or holding on to a book, as illustrated in Figure 2, conveys a rather weak, submissive attitude. In the first meetings with students neither a 'God help the first one who steps out of line' attitude, nor a 'Hello, I'm friendly, please don't hurt me' approach will do much to communicate that the teacher is secure in his authority. A moderately relaxed posture and facial expression does not have such connotations. Ideally students should greet the new teacher in an attentive way, sitting upright and looking at him, and in some schools there is still the practice of standing when the teacher first enters the room which can be seen as a ritualised enactment of subordinate behaviour. Such an habitual act, however, may not indicate any real respect for the teacher's authority. The *way* the students rise to stand, the positions they adopt, and how attentively they behave when they resume their seats would portray the actual relationship. The fact that this practice has largely been abandoned is an expression of the increasing informality and egalitarianism between teachers and students and it is now usually reserved for occasions when the class is being noisy and inattentive and not responding to requests to be quiet. The teacher may then order the class to stand which serves to interrupt whatever they are doing (see p. 36) and requires them to act as subordinates.

It seems, then, that status difference is conveyed more by the reactions of the lower status person than by the actions of the higher status person. An

4

Figure 2 *'My name is Miss Jennings and I'm your new teacher.'*

upright posture or a deliberately exaggerated relaxed posture acknowledges the higher status of the other, in the former case complying with it, and in the latter challenging it. There is an interesting example of a ritualised form of this behaviour in the Armed Services. Officers are permitted, or perhaps expected, to assume relatively relaxed positions when returning a salute, whereas other ranks must maintain erect postures. The command 'Attention' is very revealing, as it is used to instigate an upright and tense postural position, while also requiring attention in the cognitive sense. This is quite consistent with Mehrabian's findings, as the 'attention' posture is assumed in the presence of higher ranking officers, who can then decide whether to give permission to stand 'at ease'.

Because there is an association between an erect posture and signs of respect and attention, it might follow that a high degree of relaxation could be associated not only with a lack of respect, but also with a lack of attention. Mehrabian has shown this to be the case, and there are occasions when teachers unconsciously respond to such signals from students. If a boy is lounging in his seat when the teacher addresses the class, he may be told to 'sit up' or 'pay attention' if the teacher feels he is not sufficiently alert.

I have asked teachers what their reaction would be if the Director of Education walked into the staffroom during a lunch hour. Most agreed that they would feel awkward if they were in very relaxed positions and would be inclined to adopt more upright postures, particularly if they were approached personally. Many teachers felt that it would be disrespectful not to show signs of alertness and attention in this situation, as a relaxed posture is associated with a more casual, informal attitude. It may be that the responsibility to give attention rests more with the lower status person on such occasions, while the higher status person can define the situation as he wishes, either by putting others at their ease with a remark like 'Please don't let me disturb you' or by allowing the formality of the interaction to continue. A subordinate is not expected to take such initiatives and most headteachers would be surprised if students entered their rooms and sat down without invitation. However, they themselves would probably stand if a visitor to the school came in, and they might even invite that person to be seated first, before they resumed their seats. Some headteachers I have discussed this with have argued that this is simply polite behaviour but the fact remains that *standing* is the postural action chosen to express politeness.

Orientation

In Figure 3 the teacher is explaining a piece of work to the student. If we did not know that these were the circumstances, are there any cues to suggest status difference between them? Is it significant that the teacher is holding the book whereas the student is standing passively and listening? Superiors may have to explain or give information to subordinates but the reverse is also true. One person is obviously younger than the other which makes it probable that he is of lower status, but could he in fact he a member of a royal family visiting the school? Some might argue that we naturally consider men to be of higher status than women in any occupational setting,

Figure 3 *'Put the date at the top of the page . . .'*

though such gender stereotyping is rapidly disappearing. However, if we imagine the youth in Figure 3 to be a man, would this alter our impression of any status difference?

What is probably the most salient cue to the status difference is the fact that the woman is talking to the youth *without facing him* whereas he is facing her.

7

Figure 4 *'How are we supposed to cover all this?'*

Using Mehrabian's description, he is making his behaviour more *immediate* towards her, giving a direct body orientation and attending to her. The responsibility to give attention in this positional manner rests more with subordinates than superiors and if the reader is in any doubt about this, a number of variations of the above interaction could be acted with a colleague and

Figure 5 *'Why don't you bring your books to the lesson?'*

others could be asked to judge which person appears to be of higher status. One could vary the person talking, holding the book, facing and so on as long as one avoided exaggerated postural and facial cues because these will affect interpretations. Figure 4 shows two teachers discussing a piece of work and their positioning is much more consistent with their status being equal.

It is obviously not the case that when they talk, students always face teachers and teachers never face students. What is proposed is that the positions adopted can give cues to the status relationship of the participants and to the

Figure 6 *Which person is in authority?*

formality of the occasion. The greater the status difference, or the more formal the meeting, the more likely it is that the subordinate will face the superior. He does not have the implied right to turn away when talking as readily as his superior. On some ceremonial occasions it is considered disrespectful to turn one's back to the 'leader' when leaving his presence and the subordinate is even expected to back out of the room.

In situations where students may be resisting the demands made on them, it is possible to observe them deliberately turning away in an unconcerned manner when a teacher is addressing them, as shown in Figure 5. This is often accompanied by a relaxed posture as described in the previous section. The girl appears to be looking out of the window and does not seem interested in what is being said. There may also be many other significant aspects of students' behaviour in such situations, such as giving short replies, talking in an exaggeratedly bored voice and disagreeing with whatever is being said, but the refusal to face is an important cue. This is evident when teachers attempt to assert their authority as they often demand 'Look at me when I'm talking to you!' as well as trying to get the student to stand or 'sit up straight'.

The postural cues described by Mehrabian's relaxation-tension dimension tend to be salient and override any positional cues as can be seen in Figure 6. The young girl appears to be in a position of superiority despite the conflicting cues of age, height, gender, body orientation and direction of gaze, simply because the man is standing 'to attention', and the girl is relaxed.

When teachers are reprimanding students, they may sometimes face and even lean towards them (see Figure 7). The posture is usually tense and the manner clearly has aggressive overtones. Such behaviour is not an expression of higher status but an attempt by the teacher to *dominate* the student, to 'remind' him explicitly that he should show appropriate subordinate behaviour. It is more an expression of personal power and the student can be seen looking down which is usually taken to be a submissive response to such treatment.

Use of territory and personal space

Territorial rights are 'understood' in a wide range of species, not least human beings. The way we enter a room in our own house will differ from the way we enter an unfamiliar room, particularly if we expect to find someone of higher status than ourselves in there. It follows that an observer can infer the degree of status difference acknowledged or 'understood' by a person entering a room from the way he behaves. In Figure 8 the boy is reluctant to enter fully into the room without being invited and this is quite typical of how some students enter a headteacher's room, particularly if they are new to the school. In my own school days, even to knock on the staffroom door took considerable courage and this was reinforced by the fact that very few students were ever permitted to enter. In any organisation which is hierarchically structured, subordinates probably feel similarly inhibited about entering the rooms of those in very high status positions. Having entered, they are more likely to stand and face the superior, whereas a superior might move around freely in a subordinate's room while holding a conversation.

Figure 7 *'What do you think you are playing at, Sunshine?'*

The practice of making a class wait outside the classroom before the teacher arrives and gives permission for them to enter probably has territorial implications. There are clearly more obvious reasons concerning behaviour in an unsupervised room, or safety in a laboratory, but there is also an understanding that the teacher can deny entry and that students should enter in an orderly controlled manner. If they do not, they may be ordered to leave the room and the teacher will then control their re-entry. This can be construed

Figure 8 *'Excuse me, Sir.'*

as requiring the students to acknowledge the status of the person whose room they are entering. It is not their territory, but the teacher's. The significance of this aspect of our behaviour is highlighted by the rituals controlling entry into places of worship. When entering the presence of the Almighty one's behaviour must communicate more than respect.

13

Moving freely around the classroom will help to convey that it is one's own territory, although teachers will naturally use some regions more than others. In a conventionally arranged classroom, with the students in rows facing the front, the teacher's area would be at the front of the room, and if he seldom ventured among them they would certainly notice it when he did. I remember one teacher when I was at school who would pace the gangways whenever we were working, clicking his heels as he walked. He only stopped in order to reprimand us, never to praise; so as he approached, one could feel the tension mount as heads lowered and pens scribbled. He used our 'territory' with disdain and made his presence felt. Nowadays such behaviour would probably provoke a resentful response, as teachers tend to move among students more frequently and with less hostile intentions, particularly where tables are arranged in informal groupings and where students also have freedom of movement around the room. Ideas of territory are still relevant, however, but are probably more concerned with the personal space immediately around one's body and personal territory such as one's seat or desk. In Figure 9 the teacher is casually sitting on the edge of the students' desk. Such relaxed behaviour is quite typical of teachers who prefer an informal atmosphere to prevail, but even they might feel uncomfortable if students perched on their desks while they were sitting at them. Similarly, if one student encroaches too far on another's part of the table he will probably be told to move, whether or not that space is being used. High status or 'important' people usually have a larger personal territory such as their own office rather than a shared one, and similarly their personal space is larger. This is most evident in the formal way in which members of royal families are greeted. The initiative for approach is left to them, and the other person is expected to give a submissive greeting, such as bowing or curtseying, and should not initiate conversation. There is a less dramatic example of the same phenomenon in schools where the headteacher is usually given a private room (and sometimes toilet) and is less easily approached by teachers.

There are cultural differences in how close we expect others to approach us in normal conversation. For example, Watson and Graves (1966) found that Arab students adopted closer positions than American students. We can learn to modify our notions of what constitutes our personal space and in what circumstances others might enter it. The *intention* of the other is taken into account as we tolerate actual bodily contact in very crowded situations. Argyle (1975) points out that we avoid eye contact at such times, probably to reduce the intimacy of the closeness. If another person *intentionally* enters our personal space, particularly if they are facing and looking at us, it can be very arousing or stressful, and the motives for such action are usually affectionate or aggressive. Eye contact is particularly significant at such times and will be dealt with in a later section.

The manner in which one enters a student's personal space is, therefore, very important. At onc extreme, facing and looking directly at, and if possible, down at the student is likely to induce considerable arousal and Weinraub

Figure 9 *'Don't forget to show all your working out.'*

and Putney (1978) have shown that babies as young as nine months are upset if an adult 'towers' over them. On the other hand, an indirect approach, looking at the student's work, not facing him directly and squatting down to his level, will be far less arousing and is unlikely to be perceived as directly threatening. If the student is young and unfamiliar, insecure or disturbed, such an approach would create less anxiety. Figures 22 and 23 (pp. 43 and 44) contrast these two extremes, and in Figure 22 a teacher is shown bending down to talk in a comforting way to a partially-sighted girl. Even in this example there are probably still status implications as it would seem incongruous for a child to bend down in this manner to a seated teacher, the implication being that superiority has temporarily been relinquished, to put the other at ease.

A sudden violation of personal space, particularly if unexpected, may be very stressful for the student. I observed one teacher who had warned an eleven-year-old boy on several occasions to stop talking and get on with his work. The boy was talking yet again and disturbing his neighbour, so the teacher, who was attending to someone at the back of the room, approached quietly from behind. Simultaneously she put her hand on his left shoulder and leant to within six inches of his left ear saying, 'Now take your books and work at the front'. The boy was half out of his seat before she had finished her sentence and had to be reminded to take his books. Though she had not used a threatening tone or shouted, the close proximity and surprise of her behaviour caused an immediate response. Touching the student was also an expression of status, and will be dealt with later.

Teachers frequently move nearer to students they suspect are not attending, which usually has the desired effect, and there is evidence that other aspects of their performance, such as listening comprehension, also improve. Smith (1979), in a summary of such research, concluded, '... the results are consistent with a number of other observations concerning the effects of teacher-student interpersonal distance: the closer the teacher is to the target group, the more effective he or she is according to some measure of student performance.' Any layout of furniture which restricts the teacher from moving into students' personal spaces may therefore, in some circumstances, limit the capacity to maintain their attention. In many informally arranged classrooms some students do not face the teacher and it would be interesting to discover whether there are any associated deficits in attention, though for much of the time they would probably be working independently or in small groups. Seating arrangements clearly influence the extent that teachers are able to make their presence salient for all the students and this may also have implications for their behaviour (see p. 131).

The extent that differing territorial rights are observed between teachers and students gives expression to how they regard their status relationship. It is as much the avoidance of the superior's territory by the subordinate as it is the use of the subordinate's territory and personal space by the superior, that expresses these understandings. As with posture and bodily orientation it can be seen that the subordinate is not expected to reciprocate certain actions from the superior. The implication may be that the differential rights in some way *represent* or even constitute the status differences and without them there would be *de facto* equality. Further examples of differential rights can be seen in other aspects of teacher-student interactions.

Rights to property

A teacher is reading aloud to an attentive class who are following the story from their books. She notices that one girl is writing instead of following the story and Figure 10 shows her taking the pen from the girl's hand, which she then places on the desk before closing the exercise book in which the girl had been writing. The right to interrupt others' activities and to remove their property is one which teachers frequently exercise towards students. It is so common that when I show video-taped extracts of it happening, many teachers fail to notice it or, more accurately, to realise that it enacts the status relationship between the teacher and student. A teacher told me of when he was a student in the sixth form and had arrived late one morning. The teacher came over with the dinner register and told him that he had forgotten to sign it. 'I was half asleep at the time, so I just took the pen out of his hand to sign the register, and he clipped me round the head.'

It is quite surprising for teachers to have property removed from their hands by students and the act would be considered ill-mannered and disrespectful. If one wishes to borrow something from a superior it is appropriate to ask politely and wait hopefully for the article to be handed over. Where there is a great difference in status one might be reluctant even to ask. On the other hand it would not seem unusual for a superior to ask politely to borrow something, *while in the act of reaching for it.*

There are undoubtedly differential rights in relation to property and if these rights are questioned by the subordinate, it is the authority that they express which is in question. This is evident in situations where the teacher has 'lost control' of a class; if one attempted to interrupt a student by removing her property she might object and would probably pick up the pen again and continue to write. Naturally, if the student also considered herself to be in the right this would increase her resistance to the teacher's action, but how she perceived the difference in status, or wanted the teacher to perceive it, would similarly affect her response. I saw a young student teacher hold out her hand, indicating to an eight-year-old boy that he should give her his ruler as he had just been giving an impromptu recital on it. Instead of handing it to her he hid it behind his back and there followed a short bout of all-in wrestling before the teacher emerged triumphantly holding the ruler. The student had questioned her right to take the ruler but, by winning it in a fair fight, she had behaved more like another student than a teacher. Had she remained with her hand outstretched, this would have implied that the boy did not have the option of refusing.

A measure of the extent to which students accept a teacher's authority can be seen by, at one extreme, blunt refusals to hand over what might actually be school property, to the other, where they will readily surrender money, watches or other valuable personal property for confiscation by the teacher. A close examination of video-tapes of such events will frequently show that the student actually hands over the offending object as the teacher reaches to remove it.

Figure 10 *An incidental correction.*

An attempt by a teacher to exercise differential rights in relation to property can be thought of as a *claim* to be in authority, implicitly stating that the action is legitimate. If the student complies, this will validate the claim and reinforce the teacher's authority whereas objecting will bring the authority into question. This interpretation, of course, also applies to the other expressions of status difference that have been discussed so far. Our behaviour does not *cause* others to act in accordance with our wishes. How they already perceive their relationship to us, particularly in respect of status, will affect their response.

Touching

There has been a great deal of research and observation devoted to the act of touching and though it is not possible to deal in depth with the subject here, it is important to consider how it may feature in the expression of status relationships.

There is nothing unusual in Figure 11 which shows a headteacher holding a

Figure 11 *'Are you sure Mrs Brown said you could stay in?'*

student by the upper arm as he talks to him. What would seem strange is if the student were holding the headteacher by the arm. This unilateral right to touch is an expression of the status relationship between teachers and students. There are several qualifications one would have to make regarding this observation. People differ in the extent that they normally touch others. Some teachers rarely touch students and when they do so, seem to exercise a hygienic care usually reserved for dealing with contagious materials, as shown in Figure 12 where the teacher is using a pencil to raise the head of a boy to whom he wishes to talk. Such disdainful treatment makes a claim to a considerable difference in power in the relationship, as it is difficult to imag-

Figure 12 *'What do you call that scrawl?'*

ine a situation where an adult would not feel very resentful unless it were done jokingly by a friend.

It is not unusual to observe a teacher adjusting a student's clothes during a conversation, perhaps straightening a collar or tie. In Figure 13 the boy is receiving a mild reprimand and the teacher has previously lifted his hand from his pocket. As has already been discussed in this chapter, the teacher's less immediate orientation and more relaxed posture are quite consistent with the expression of higher status and, in adjusting the boy's shirt collar without comment or permission, he shows a mixture of patronising care and correction. Such a gesture is normally only exercised by parents or carers towards young children and the teacher is therefore expressing a claim to be a superior dealing with a young child, albeit in a caring manner. In passively

Figure 13 *'But you know what will happen if I catch you fooling around again.'*

accepting this treatment, the student validates the teacher's definition of the situation.

In the examples chosen so far it has been intentional to show male teachers touching male students, as the relative sex and age of the people concerned affects the significance of the act. I have asked numerous groups of teachers whether they make any distinction between boys and girls when touching students and at the primary level it is unusual for a teacher to consider the sex of the student. However at secondary level, male teachers rarely admit to touching girls, presumably because of the possible sexual connotations. They may even have been advised not to remain alone in a room with a female student. Female secondary teachers do not usually make this distinction though some, particularly the younger ones, say they avoid touching older boys and it may be that the earlier onset of puberty in girls is a factor influencing this difference. Whether this has always been so, or whether it is the result of the present emphasis on sexual harassment by men, women are generally freer to touch men 'incidentally' than vice versa even when the men are of higher status. The act is unlikely to be construed as a sexual gesture or at least not one to which a man is expected to object and it may be that women are thus able to exercise a form of personal power in the interaction.

The 'intensity' of the touch, as well as the part of the body touched are other factors which bear upon the significance of the act. Resting a hand on another person's arm is less arousing for them than gripping their arm; touching a shoulder is less arousing than touching a leg. Primary school children are frequently touched on the head or have their hands held by teachers in caring and reassuring ways as in Figure 14 where a new boy is being introduced by the headteacher to his teacher. The comforting hand on the back of his head is repeated by the teacher when she directs him to his seat (see Figure 15). Touching the head and holding students' hands is seldom seen in secondary schools except with the youngest classes, though one might anticipate that any student with special needs or obviously in need of some comfort might receive such treatment. Among adults, normally only those on mutually intimate terms hold hands or touch each other's heads unless one is in considerable distress, as such acts would seem extremely patronising from a superior.

In any conflict or confrontation, touch is likely to be perceived as aggressive, particularly if it is intense or abrupt. Some research by Neill (1987) has shown that boys and girls greatly dislike being touched in an angry manner and teachers should be aware that they may react violently. Even the threat to use physical force, perhaps to move a student from his seat, will often escalate a situation. Teachers need considerable social skills or confidence in their status relationship with students to risk touching them during a confrontation, as it is very easy to misjudge the response.

Figure 14 *'Can you make Robert at home in your class, Mrs Wilson?'*

Differences in personal style, age, sex, manner of touch, area touched and situation all affect the significance of the act of touching, but the fact remains that when people feel they do not have the right to reciprocate, they are acknowledging their subordinate position. This is likely to be the case in any hierarchical situation, so that it would be less likely for students to touch their teachers, teachers their headteachers, nurses their matrons, privates their sergeants and so on, than vice versa. Subordinates are not expected to

23

Figure 15 *'Now you can sit over here with James.'*

touch their superiors except in strictly defined formal rituals such as hand-shaking when greeting, and if they do, it indicates a degree of informality which has transcended the status difference between them. Very young infants frequently treat the teacher like a parent and actively seek physical contact. Some children will tap a teacher on the arm to get attention but if students feel free to touch the teacher incidentally, this indicates a very informal relationship where the difference in status may be limited to specific occasions.

In Figure 16 the headteacher is 'directing' the boy as he says 'Off you go, then', an action which teachers frequently use towards students. The fact that the headteacher is not even looking at the student contributes to the implication that he will naturally follow the instruction and not object.

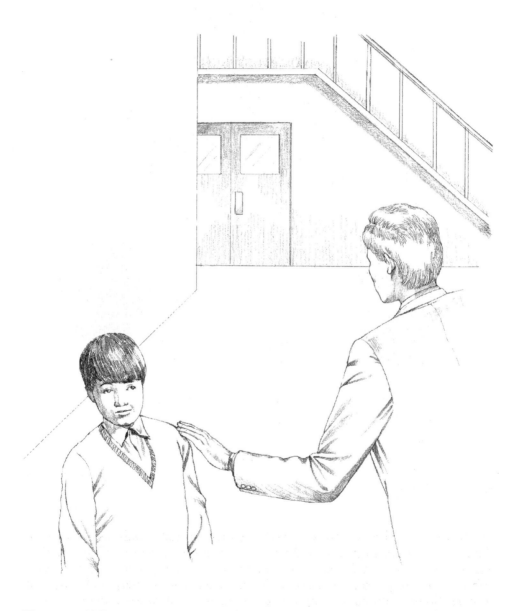

Figure 16 *'Off you go, then.'*

Should a student resist physical direction, it would not be sensible to resort to force. It is not the *act* of resistance which the teacher would be dealing with, but *what the act implied about the relationship*. If the teacher 'wins' by force or threats, this implies that the basis for the authority is physical power; students comply with teachers' demands because they can be *made to comply*. It seems more appropriate to question the student with an attitude of disbelief, to ascertain what reason could possibly have prompted him to take such a step. In so doing, one implies that students should normally *grant* such rights to teachers.

With the present emphasis on children's rights and accusations of physical abuse being levelled at some teachers, some schools' staff consider it expedient not to touch the children under any circumstances. This is unfortunate as it inhibits teachers' ability to express warm, reassuring attitudes towards students, particularly at the primary level. Even at the secondary level, teachers of the parental generation can usually use directional or appreciative touch without a hint of an ulterior motive (provided men do not touch female students) and thereby express the friendliness, caring and solidarity in the relationships. At the infant level, Wheldall et al (1986) showed that 'teacher-touch', when accompanied by praise, could also be an effective reinforcer of work and good behaviour in four classes of five- to six-year-old children from indigenous, Pakistani, and Afro-Caribbean backgrounds. It therefore must have been perceived as a positive experience to be touched by the teachers, all of whom, significantly, were women.

As unilateral touching has adult–child and superior–subordinate connotations, it follows that one way of enhancing the relative status of older students would be *not* to touch them when giving praise and hence also avoid the possibility of appearing patronising. Similarly, in any conflict, touching for whatever intended motive is extremely unwise.

The role of eye contact

Eye contact plays a very significant role in all interpersonal communication, providing those concerned with information about each other's intentions and feelings. It is particularly important in the communication of 'power and preference' (Exline, 1972) and, in this respect, it is useful for teachers to be aware of its role in their interactions with students. As with all non-verbal behaviour, but particularly so with eye contact, a reliable interpretation is only possible if given wider information about other relevant behaviour and the context in which it occurs.

When two people look at one another it usually follows that an interaction will take place. This could be in the form of a brief nod or acknowledgment, or they may begin to speak. It has already been noted that lower status is expressed by a more direct body orientation and it follows that subordinates have been observed to look more at superiors than vice versa, though they may usually be the first to look away (Strongman and Champness, 1968). Looking at the person who is speaking to you is a clear sign of attention. If eye contact is established between people and they do not speak, they usually quickly look away because to continue looking without speaking has particular significance in communication. As Exline suggests, gazing or staring at each other happens most frequently between those who are in conflict or attracted to one another. In conflict situations it usually represents an attempt to dominate the other, so it occurs where status differences have yet to be established or are in question. Boxers frequently try to gain a psycho-

Figure 17 *'**What** did you say?'*

logical advantage by 'staring-out' their opponents before the fight but not after the contest has been decided. To avert one's gaze first, particularly with a downward glance, is a submissive signal. As anyone who has engaged in a staring-out encounter will verify, it can be quite stressful and the one who looks away has probably found it necessary to relieve the tension. When very young children are introduced to a stranger they sometimes look down and cover their eyes with their hands and it may be that the downward glance of adults has its origin in this behaviour. In Figure 17 the teacher had warned the boy that he would be kept in at lunchtime and the boy had exclaimed loudly, 'You what!' The teacher reacted by looking at, and moving towards him and the boy can be seen to have lowered his head and shielded his eyes in a similar way to a young child under stress.

There is even evidence to show that such signals may operate between species, at least between humans and rhesus macaques (Exline and Yellin, 1969). In the study, it was possible to elicit threat behaviour or flight from a monkey by giving a challenging stare, whereas a deferential, downcast glance after preliminary eye contact had been established would forestall such responses. Averting the gaze in other directions does not seem to have the same significance, but the downward glance appears to be a fairly universal sign of submissive behaviour. This does not imply that teachers should be silently scanning the class, trying to stare out any student who cares to take up the challenge but should they chance to meet a student's gaze, sustaining eye contact in a relaxed way is likely to give an impression of confidence. This is particularly important when teachers first meet their classes and are likely to be the centre of attention. It is usually only a matter of seconds before students will withdraw from a chance visual encounter (though it may seem like an eternity) but should this not happen, the situation can be 'rationalised' by asking them a question, an act itself not devoid of status implications. A relaxed manner is crucial in mitigating the effects of prolonged gaze and moving closer, as any hint of bodily tension or menace in the facial expression is unambiguously threatening. One may thereby be committed to a confrontation with a determined student, without leaving the option of a graceful withdrawal. It is in such apparently trivial ways that the teacher can build up the impression of security and confidence.

If, when someone is speaking, the listener intentionally withholds or withdraws eye contact, this can have an entirely different significance. Argyle and Cook (1976) point out that if a higher status person is reprimanding a lower status person, he may exercise control over the direction of gaze. The listener might otherwise easily express a lack of interest by deliberately looking, and even facing, elsewhere, or by breaking visual contact in a non-deferential way, such as by letting the gaze slowly move upward and away from the speaker. Such signals convey that the listener's attention is wandering, and if they are carried out deliberately the behaviour is very disrespectful. Measures to control the listener's direction of gaze are aimed at preventing or curtailing such behaviour. Students can be very adept at shutting teachers off by withholding eye contact, as the following extract illustrates. A special needs teacher is talking to a fourteen-year-old girl about her work in other lessons:

Teacher: What are you going to do after you've finished the project on East Anglia?

Student: *(Looking 90° away from teacher, and scratching her back in an unconcerned manner* (see Figure 18)*)* I ain't gonna do it. It's boring.

Figure 18 *'I ain't gonna do it. It's boring.'*

> *Teacher:* Why is it boring?
> *Student:* *(Stops scratching but continues to look away)* Well I don't want to learn about that, do I?
> *Teacher:* Well, a lot of the produce of . . .
> *Student:* *(Interrupts and shifts position so that she is turned 90° away from the teacher)* When I get a job they're not gonna want to know about farming and everything like that. *(Stands and turns back to teacher, and shuffles some papers.)*
> *Teacher:* That's true.
> *Student:* Makes you sick.
> *Teacher:* *(Talking to student's back)* But it's general knowledge really, isn't it? East Anglia is . . .
> *Student:* *(Interrupts and sits back to the 90° position)* No, I don't wanna know it. *(Turns around and looks at papers again but does not stand.)*
> *Teacher:* What are the most useful subjects for you to do, Jill? What is the best one?
> *Student:* *(Still looking away)* Typing and English.
> *Teacher:* Typing?
> *Student:* Yeah, but I never learned it.
> *Teacher:* Why not?
> *Student:* Don't like the teacher, do I?
> *Teacher:* No, I know you don't. What about your other subjects, Jill? Art? English?
> *Both speak together*
> { *Student:* No, I don't like them.
> { *Teacher:* What about Child Development? . . . Do you go to that?
> *Student:* Sometimes.
> *Teacher:* Because that's a practical subject. *(Student continues to look away in a bored manner, then looks towards, but not at, the teacher for the first time in the interaction, brushes hair from face with hand and looks down.)*
> *Teacher:* *(Continues)* Are you still going out with Geoff?
> *Student:* *(Glances at teacher and smiles)* Yeah.
> *Teacher:* *(Laughs)*

Throughout the interview the girl replied in a bored tone of voice and most of her comments were negative, clearly giving the impression that she had no interest in the conversation. She also interrupted the teacher on two occasions which did not acknowledge any status difference in the teacher's favour. Although she said that English was a useful subject she denied liking it when the teacher mentioned it a few seconds later. For most of the interview not only did she withhold eye contact, but she also faced away from the teacher (see p. 29). Only when the teacher stopped discussing work and spoke about her boyfriend did she deign to glance back and smile. In contrast, the teacher looked continuously at the student and spoke in a reasonable, sympathetic manner. Exline (1972) compared 'control oriented' subjects – those who described themselves as wishing to control others – with 'low control oriented' subjects, when faced with a listener who either looked at them all the time or 'never looked at all but swept the air above their heads'. He found that the low control oriented subjects looked more if the listener withheld his gaze, whereas the high control oriented subjects looked less. The interpretation suggested was that those who like to control others may find people whose visual attentions they cannot capture more powerful than those they can. Presumably such perceived power would not be so disconcerting for someone who was less inclined to exercise control.

The teacher in the above example is clearly not behaving in the manner of Exline's 'control oriented' subjects and some may consider this entirely appropriate in the context of a fairly informal chat with a student. However, in choosing not to look and resisting the teacher's attempt to gain her attention, the student seems able to exercise some control over the communication and the teacher may subsequently have found it difficult to relate to the girl on other than her terms, as it is also the relationship which is being enacted in this discussion about school work.

Teachers often use a steady unresponsive gaze, sometimes with eyebrows raised, when alerting students that their behaviour is unsatisfactory (see Figure 19 where a teacher has entered her classroom to find a group of students fooling around.) The teacher is clearly waiting for the misbehaviour to stop before she continues and is showing disapproval with the unspoken message, 'What do you think you're doing?' or 'Have you quite finished?'. Gazing confidently with such expectations is clearly an expression of superior rank because if a student tried it with his peers they would treat him with derision, implying 'Who do you think you are?'. In a similar way, if a teacher has lost authority, the students may well resist giving way to such signals.

Eye contact, in conjunction with other aspects of our behaviour, is very significant in communicating our attitudes. The more intimate the subject being discussed or the closer that people stand, the more likely that one or both participants will look away, unless they mutually wish to increase the intimacy of their relationship. If a student is unable to look back in the face of an accusation it may appear as if he has something to hide, whereas an 'open', relaxed return of gaze gives an impression of truthfulness. In some cultures it is considered disrespectful to look a higher status person in the eyes and it has been suggested that teachers may sometimes misinterpret a downcast gaze as inattentive and disrespectful. However, we take into account other aspects of the behaviour, and if the student is also acting in a sulky, dismissive manner, one can be fairly sure about his intended meaning. In fact, it is likely that such responses can be readily modified, as new recruits in the army quickly learn to look straight ahead when being reprimanded whereas at school they were probably required to look back at teachers in similar circumstances. Gilmore (1985) observed that in America black teachers and parents dealt severely with black children who displayed bad 'attitudes' in this way but it is not surprising that white teachers would feel less confident in risking a misinterpretation of a cultural difference. Even

Figure 19 *The unspoken 'What do you think you are doing?'*

though the majority of black students are native to this country there may well be learned cultural differences as in America, and teachers are warned to make allowances for this, but the possibility then arises that one student will be admonished for what might seem the same behaviour for which another is excused, or that 'genuine' disrespectful behaviour is passed off as a cultural anomaly. It is probably wiser, therefore, to deal only with the primary reason for speaking to the student in a professional way and not to take issue with the disrespectful attitudes they may be conveying non-verbally.

Patterns of eye contact are very significant in the communication of intimacy, status and dominance and though in general teachers should learn to establish steady, focused and relaxed eye contact with students they should also be aware of the dilemma described by Exline: 'To look or not to look, that is the question.'

Activity 1 Practising the 'steady gaze'

This is a light-hearted activity to be undertaken in pairs which nevertheless involves controlling one's reactions.

One person of the pair should gaze steadily and unresponsively at the partner, who should try to make the former react in some way by joking, pulling faces or any other approach, but without touching. One should attempt to convey, 'I'm waiting for you. Settle down.' and avoid frowning and other threatening expressions.

Ten seconds or so should be sufficient as one would normally not sustain gaze for such an extended period without some further action. The receiver should then say what message he or she felt was being communicated by the steady gaze and whether the gazer had remained unresponsive.

It should become increasingly difficult to try to get a reaction if the other maintains an unresponsive gaze, in the same way that teasing requires a response from the victim.

Smiling

Smile awhile
And while you smile, another smiles.
And soon there's miles and miles of smiles
And all because you smiled.

(source unknown)

Individuals vary in the extent that they normally smile but as the verse suggests, it is a strong social signal which can elicit a reciprocal response from others though teachers are sometimes warned not to use it prematurely, as in the title of Kevin Ryan's book *Don't Smile 'til Christmas*.

Mehrabian (1972) suggests that, in awkward or formal situations, smiling is associated with a communicator's effort to release tension and placate the addressee, and so has submissive connotations. The first smiles given to a new teacher could be attempts to establish social contact and thereby reduce or avoid any potential threat: if teachers return the smiles this puts students at their ease but in some situations the teacher could appear prematurely friendly as if keen to be accepted. The more probable pitfall is that teachers will reveal their own insecurity by smiling, implying it is they who find the students threatening.

The interpretation of smiles is very complex, as Birdwhistell (1973) discovered in his research:

> '... the presence of a smile in particular contexts indicated pleasure, in another, humour, in others, ridicule and, in still others, friendliness or good manners. Smiles have been seen to indicate doubt and acceptance, equality and superordination or subordination. They occur in situations where insult is intended and in others as a denial of insult.'

This implies that there is a very wide range of smiles from sneers to warm expressions of pleasure. Lewis (1978) described five types: simple, compressed, upper, lower and broad, with the possibility of each being expressed at low, medium or high intensity, which could account for the range of interpretation found by Birdwhistell. To interpret the 'meaning' of a smile, which the giver may or may not wish to reveal, one must also take into account other non-verbal signals such as gaze, proximity and posture, particularly the angle at which the head is held.

For teachers whose aim is to appear relaxed and in control of themselves and the situation, it might seem significant whether or not they smile, *how* they smile, and whether they choose to return smiles from students, but to attempt to specify a response for every contingency would be impossible and patently unnecessary, as if a teacher *feels* relaxed, the appropriate behaviour 'happens naturally'. However, some situations clearly are stressful and it could be helpful for teachers to be aware of some of the factors which influence how smiling is perceived.

Neill and Caswell (1993) point out that teachers who smile when criticising students show they are 'actually enjoying the confrontation' and are certain of winning. Though one might want to avoid the implication of a battle, teachers who feel relaxed and confident may appear to smile 'to themselves', as if in response to their own thoughts, even when sustaining gaze with a student. The 'inner' smile does not seem intended to elicit a smile in return and for the recipient whose intention is to challenge, it can be quite unsettling as the teacher appears quietly confident and secure in the situation. For example, when a head of year was called in to reprimand a Year 10 class for their behaviour towards other members of staff she waited until she had complete silence and attention before speaking:

'As you probably realise ... *(paused for three seconds while gazing at individuals and smiling quietly to herself)* ... we're not very happy with you at the moment ... *(continued gazing but with a serious expression)* ... and from now on there are going to be some changes ...'

The initial smile conveyed that she did not feel threatened by the group and the subsequent serious expression made it clear that they should take her seriously. On the other hand, those who smile when *failing* to meet a challenge, or when 'backing down' from one, are giving a submissive signal as if wishing to placate a stronger or dangerous opponent. In such cases eye contact is likely to be avoided and the smile does not 'reach the eyes'. (In fact, if teachers 'do nothing', whether smiling or not, this is not helpful, see p. 158.)

In any conflict or potentially stressful situation, the crucial variables associated with the meaning of smiles, or the effect they have on the recipient, would therefore seem to be

- whether or not gaze is sustained or avoided;
- whether the smile is 'to oneself, i.e. unresponsive, or focused 'at' the student, i.e. interactive;
- how relaxed the person feels, as muscular tension will particularly limit the 'spread' of the smile to the eyes.

Normal relaxed warm smiles are expressions of solidarity and friendliness between teachers and students which contribute to their mutual enjoyment of the relationship and are therefore to be encouraged both after and before Christmas.

Who responds to whom?

Another finding quoted by Exline is that at the start of a conversation it is the dominant person who is the first to look away and immediately begin to speak. When differences in status are understood, those who believe themselves to be subordinates are more reluctant or inhibited about initiating an interaction than those who believe they are superior. By seizing the initiative to speak, a person may thereby be attempting to dominate the other by placing them in the position of having to respond. A *response* is not only a verbal reply but includes a wide variety of non-verbal behaviour, such as returning eye contact, showing anger, amusement or other feelings, and even a physiological reaction such as blushing, provided there is a *stimulus* of some sort. Similarly, if a stimulus interrupts a particular behaviour, the discontinuation of that behaviour would be regarded as a response to the stimulus. For example, if a student was about to talk to a friend, but was pre-empted by the teacher, the student's silence would be regarded as a response, whether or not he looked at the teacher.

Hargreaves (1972), in discussing discipline, points out that 'most experienced teachers insist that the teacher must, if he is to survive, define the situation in his own terms at once'. In the first meetings with students the status of the teacher is likely to be in question and it might be important to present oneself as one who initiates interactions rather than one who responds to the students' cues. The high status person in an interaction is able to exercise a good deal of control over the other's responses and, if status is in question, the one who exercises control will assume dominance. If a new teacher walks into a class and immediately begins to answer questions about himself in a friendly way, before he has addressed or made any impact on the whole class, it may seem unimportant, but it will certainly do nothing to establish his authority. An example of such an interaction with a group of twelve-year-olds, say, might proceed as follows:

> The teacher, on entering the room, looks at the students and returns a smile from a boy in the front. The boy continues to smile and asks a question:
>
> *1st Student:*   Are you our new teacher, Miss?
> *Teacher:*   *(Continuing to smile)* That's right. *(Another student calls out.)*
> *2nd Student:*   Are you strict like Mr Brown was, Miss? *(Teacher looks towards him, takes a breath to answer, but another boy calls out to the previous student.)*
> *3rd Student:*   He was a nut case! *(Laughter from class.)*
> *Teacher:*   *(No longer smiling, looking at new speaker)* Now ... that will do. I'd like your attention, please.

Such a sequence might last no more than fifteen seconds but would be very important. It began with one student giving a social signal, a smile, to the teacher, to which she responded appropriately. The student then asked a question which the teacher answered. This was closely followed by another question which the teacher was about to answer, but she was interrupted by another student whose remark was not addressed to her, but to the previous student. She responded by giving eye contact. There was laughter, to which she responded by giving a mild reprimand.

This example may seem harmless enough but, if this pattern of interaction were to continue, the teacher would soon find it difficult to retain any control over communication in the room as students very quickly begin to call out to one another rather than address their remarks to the teacher. Her first objective should have been to get the whole class attending as quickly as possible, but instead the students were beginning to control her behaviour.

The questions asked by the students in the above example probably had a function similar to smiling in that they were attempts to initiate social contact. Their underlying meaning was more in the nature of 'Hello, I'm friendly, are you?' or 'Look at me, I'm the clown of the class!' If the teacher answers such questions or otherwise responds appropriately, the students are again put at their ease. This may, of course, in some situations be exactly what the teacher wishes to do.

Exercising the right not to respond to students is necessary if one is to maintain control over communication, particularly in questioning sessions, as they can easily become disorganised and chaotic. To avoid this one can preface questions with the reminder, 'Now, hands up . . .' and it is then essential not to accept any answer which is called out. Older students should be expected to contribute in an orderly manner without necessarily having to raise their hands but it is important that the teacher indicates unambiguously who should be talking by looking at and perhaps naming the student, and extending an invitational hand (see Figure 20). What frequently happens is that someone else calls out and the teacher glances at them so it is unclear who should be speaking. Experienced teachers remain looking at the nominated student in such circumstances and sometimes give a further non-verbal sign of attention such as inclining the head forward while at the same time raising a hand towards the interrupter to keep him 'on hold' (see Figure 21). The right to choose when and if one responds to another person is clearly an expression of authority as one would not expect students to make teachers wait in this way while they finished their conversations with one another. When working with a small group the teacher would not need to exercise such rights as the discussion should be controlled by the usual conversational strategies.

It is interesting to consider a parallel which can be drawn between the teacher facing a new class and an interrogation with a prisoner, a situation discussed by Danziger (1976). It goes without saying, of course, that the circumstances are very different. Interrogators have much more power over their prisoners than do teachers over students, and their intentions are very different. All that may be similar is that it is in the interests of both teachers and interrogators to define the situation in their own terms. Danziger describes how manuals of interrogation techniques 'stress the need to emphasise the power of the interrogator in many small ways, telling the prisoner where he may or may not sit, making it necessary for him to ask for permission to smoke, go to the washroom, have a drink of water, use the telephone, or rest'. The prisoner is clearly being denied any rights but Danziger goes on to point out the dangers of such a hostile presentation:

> But if the interrogator limited himself to displays of power he would run the
> risk of achieving exactly the opposite of what he is after with many prisoners.

Figure 20 *A non-verbal invitation.*

By these means he may merely confirm the prisoner's definition of the interrogator as the enemy who is to be defied. This is particularly likely to happen
if the prisoner is a hardened criminal, an ideologically convinced opponent or
a member of the other side in a war.

Figure 21 *Keeping student 'on hold'.*

There are clearly implications here for the use of reprimands and punishments but in making any demands on students there is always the danger of provoking a belligerent response. Even in the harmless act of asking a student's name,

39

a hint of hostility will confirm to him that the teacher is 'the enemy who is to be defied' and he is just as likely to reply 'What's yours?' thereby throwing the responsibility to respond back on the teacher. The reader who has never been at the mercy of a group of unruly children who pay no heed to demands or pleas, may feel that too much attention is being given to the first minutes of an interaction. Nevertheless, a great deal of research and observation has shown them to be very significant in the teacher's attempt to establish authority and they will be further considered later, as it is the outcomes of these interactions which will influence subsequent meetings. One hears of footballers being told to win the first tackle decisively, as this gives a psychological advantage over the opponent, and the teacher should also try to ensure that a potentially diffi-cult class do not define the situation in their own terms at the outset. The experienced teacher will avoid bullying, shouting, sarcasm and other such methods, as these really only reveal one's own insecurity.

While supervising a student teacher on a teaching practice, I once found myself involved in a potential confrontation with a student. The school was an urban comprehensive where the vast majority of the boys spent the winter days dressed in jeans and coats. This gives a rather temporary atmosphere to the whole place, as if they won't take their coats off because they're not stop-ping. As I came down a flight of stairs during the break, I noticed that I had become the focus of attention for a group of fourteen-year-old boys lounging on a railing on the landing in front of me. I neither returned their stares nor avoided chance eye contact, but as I reached the landing one of them called out, 'Hiya, sir'. What he was really saying was something like, 'Hello, fat face', which was clearly conveyed by his sneering manner. Had I replied, 'Good morning', or even ignored the remark, he would have demonstrated to his friends his ability to be rude to adults and get away with it. Perhaps a liberal approach would have been to acknowledge his greeting and put any implied ridicule down to his immaturity, but I'm not sure whether that would have done either of us any good. Anyway, for some reason I wasn't in the mood to be an innocent victim, so I walked over to within a foot of him, looked him squarely in the face, and said in a relaxed way, 'I beg your pardon?'

Making one's behaviour very immediate for the addressee, but using a non-threatening tone and expression, makes one's feelings and intentions very ambiguous, and the boy would have been unsure how to interpret my action. He must have found my prompt non-verbal move quite unsettling, because he looked down, avoiding my gaze, and said, 'Nuffin'. There was a noticeable change in his tone, so I felt able to press on: 'Did you speak to me?' He looked up briefly, perhaps to check that my expression was not threatening, and replied quietly, 'Yeah'.

'What did you say?' I asked. He looked a little sheepish but found the courage to establish eye contact once again: 'I said, Hello.' I left a brief pause and replied, 'Good morning', then turned and walked away. Dominance in the interaction was achieved by avoiding a predictable response to the initial greeting, and then forcing the student to do all the responding. Had we met again he would probably have been more wary. It might, however, have been more sensible to have confirmed my friendliness, perhaps by asking him to direct me to my destination, rather than to score a point over him.

By attention to such details from the very start of an interaction one can quickly establish control over communication. The extent and duration of this initial 'detached' approach will depend upon the willingness of the students to respond appropriately, but it will only be effective if the teacher can convey, by relaxed non-verbal behaviour, that he is confident and at ease.

Activity 2 Having the last word

This activity, designed to be undertaken in pairs, tries to simulate a typical interaction with an unco-operative student.

Select a typical occasion when a teacher would intervene in a student's behaviour. For example, the student could be

- *off task*
- *chewing*
- *late for lesson*
- *out of seat*
- *calling out*
- *disturbing another student*

The 'teacher' should begin with a question, direction or statement to the student, concerning the behaviour.

The student should argue by denying, excusing himself, asking a question or objecting in some way.

The object of the activity is to have the last word, provided it is not a compliant agreement such as 'Yes', or 'OK'. A pause of three seconds or more, or a bizarre, unrelated answer loses the contest.

Consider

- *which sort of questions offer less opportunities for students to 'answer back';*
- *are any strategies helpful? (e.g. accepting the student's comment but repeating your direction, a technique described as 'broken record'.);*
- *what manner should teachers adopt in such circumstances?*

In practice, such arguments are fruitless and should be avoided (see page 201).

Activity 3 Who responds to Whom?

'Why do you always answer a question with a question?'
'Why not?'

This is a light-hearted activity to be acted in pairs to illustrate how responding to questions can be an expression of a subordinate position.

The status difference being claimed by the questioner is disputed if the respondent does not accept the role and replies inappropriately, and one way of doing this is to ask a question in return. For example, if a teacher asked, 'Why are you late?' and the student replied, 'What's the time?' or 'Have you started the lesson already?', the onus would then be on the teacher to respond. In the unlikely circumstance of a student actually replying in this way, the teacher would probably persist with the original question, asserting the right to have an answer: 'Never mind whether I've started the lesson or not, I'm asking you why are you late?'. In this activity the roles are not defined so the original questioner must then reply with a further question and attempt to get a reply, and so on. In this way each person tries to establish a superordinate position in the interaction.

Here are a few opening questions:

- *What's your name?*
- *How old are you?*
- *Is that all you've managed to do in half an hour?*
- *Who gave you permission to use this room?*
- *What does origin mean?*
- *Why aren't you wearing a jacket?*
- *What are you doing?*

Form of address

In Figure 22 a seven-year-old partially-sighted girl has arrived late, as the taxi bringing her got lost. It is her second day at the school, having spent her infant years in a special unit for the visually handicapped, so the teacher is being particularly attentive and caring towards her. This is evident from the hand placed round her shoulder and the way the teacher stoops down to talk to her: 'Have you got a reading book, Darling?'

The form of address chosen is in keeping with the caring attitude and is in stark contrast with the way the teacher speaks to another girl only a few seconds later, whom she discovers looking in a cupboard (see Figure 23) – 'And

Figure 22 *'Have you got a reading book, Darling?'*

what are *you* doing here, Young Lady?' On this occasion the teacher remains standing and looks down on the child (see p. 15). The forms of address chosen by the teacher in each case clearly express very different definitions of

Figure 23 *'And what do you think you are doing in there, Young Lady?'*

the situation. One child is in a caring relationship with a parent figure, the other in a formal subordinate relationship with an authority figure. The form of address we choose can, therefore, express how we wish the other person to understand the circumstances. These may only be temporary how-ever (as in the example above) because when the partially-sighted girl has settled in and the incident of the cupboard has passed, the teacher would return to using first names. In other special circumstances, such as commit-tee meetings or debating societies, we may be expected to use more formal forms of address which are adopted only on those occasions. Teachers may address one another formally in front of students but revert to first names in the staffroom.

Other factors influence the form of address we choose, such as the degree of intimacy shared, that is how well we know one another, whether we are related in kinship and whether we are roughly of the same generation. It is also clear that status differences will be reflected in our choice, a fact sum-marised by Danziger (1976):

> Where there is a choice between a polite and a familiar form of the pronoun of address the inferior person generally uses the polite form to his superior and in turn receives the familiar form. In medieval Europe the master used the familiar form to the servant as did the nobility to commoners and parents to children; in return they expected to receive the polite form. But equals would use the same form to each other, and this might be either the polite or the familiar form. Thus the asymmetrical use of pronouns of address would be used to present the existence of a status differential in the relationship.

Familiar forms of pronouns of address, as *'tu'* in French or Italian, have largely fallen out of use in England, though in some parts of the North 'thee' and 'thou' can still be heard and children would not be expected to use this form towards adults and particularly teachers. There is evidence that this principle may be widespread in human societies, as Howell (1981) found that among the Chewong, a small aboriginal group in the rain forest of Peninsula Malaysia, it was disrespectful to address 'certain categories of affines' with the familiar form 'thou' or to behave in other intimate ways.

Teachers may address students by first names or even nicknames if they so choose, but students are not expected to reciprocate. In schools where they are permitted to, it expresses a more informal and equal relationship. In the earlier example, the use of 'darling' is quite consistent with this principle, as the girl would be considered cheeky if she addressed the teacher thus but the use of 'young lady' is interesting. Teachers frequently use a variety of less 'familiar' forms such as 'gentlemen' or the surname on its own, and it may be that the higher status person can also exercise more choice than subordi-nates in the form used and hence take the initiative in defining the situation. When I was a student on teaching practice I called the register of my new fourth year class using only their surnames, as this is what I had been used to as a student. All seemed to go smoothly until I checked whether one girl who had not answered was absent. The class assured me that she was, in fact, present and pointed her out to me. When I asked why she had not answered her name she replied, 'I've got a handle to my name' which, in my innocence, I had to get translated. I had unwittingly expressed my relationship to her in a way which did not coincide with her understanding, and as I was only a student teacher she felt able to tell me. Had I been the headteacher she might have accepted this definition or at least felt more inhibited about challenging it.

Forms of address, then, are not fixed. The changes which occur may reflect temporary circumstances, attempts to convey particular impressions, or developments in the relationships between people. Where there are status differences, these are reflected in the differences in rights to use a familiar, or sometimes other, chosen form.

Gestural messages

It is not unusual for a teacher who wishes to speak to students to beckon them to come over (see Figure 24). The context, such as whether the students are working or misbehaving, and the teacher's facial expression, will convey the nature of the teacher's instruction. However, whether the teacher's intention is to correct the students' behaviour or simply to speak privately to them, the action of beckoning them over is clearly a claim to be in a superordinate position. Students do not summon teachers in this non-verbal fashion and would be more likely either to wait with raised hand or to approach them if they wish to speak privately. In a similar way, the teacher in Figure 24 would be unlikely as a subordinate to be signalling in this way to her headteacher to come over.

Gesturing towards the addressee is usually associated with giving particular emphasis to parts of one's message and is a very instructional and persuasive mode of communication frequently used by teachers. Students are less likely to gesture towards teachers (Galloway, 1979) perhaps because they are not often in the position of being able to explain something to them that they do not already know. When there is any conflict or disagreement between people, pointing at the addressee with a stabbing, palm down movement (see Figure 7, p. 12) has threatening overtones and is clearly an attempt to dominate the interaction, whereas pointing with the palm up offers the view in a more reasonable way. Gesturing towards the addressee with an *open hand*, palm down expresses a firm statement (see Figure 25) and is far less confrontational and intimidating. The message is given a firm, 'This is how it is' quality when intervening directly in students' behaviour and is characteristic of a resolute professional manner. In contrast, open hand palm up gestures are invitational and used when offering a point of view or inviting the views of others (see Figure 20). If they are used when intervening in students' behaviour they express a weak 'be reasonable' attitude and emphasise the teacher's empty-handed powerless plea to the student (see Figure 26). It is much more common to see students using this gesture to profess their innocence when challenged by teachers.

Figure 24 *An unspoken command.*

In Figure 27 the girl is feeling very indignant about being questioned by the headteacher about the suitability of her clothes as she believes he has previously approved of them. The fact that she is pointing her finger at him not only expresses her indignation at being treated unfairly but also indicates a relatively informal relationship between them. With a more distant authority figure she would be less inclined to point, and most teachers would feel very uncomfortable if students normally behaved in such ways towards them.

Figure 25 *A firm statement.*

Figure 26 *'If you don't do the work, how are you ever going to learn anything?'*

Figure 27 *'But you said I could wear them!'*

This chapter has looked at some of the ways in which status differences are expressed and, in the light of the examples discussed so far, it is possible to consider the nature of authority in the wider context of teacher-student relationships.

2 The Nature of Authority

The definition of the situation

In considering the nature of authority, the concept of 'the definition of the situation' (Thomas, 1931) is particularly relevant, as it is concerned with the understandings people hold in any interaction and the expectations they have, based on these understandings. Some situations are already well 'defined', as in a court of law, but in classrooms there is a good deal of scope for individual interpretations as is evident from the wide range of practices and conduct which can be observed. In such situations Goffman (1959) suggested that people usually try to influence the type of understandings which will prevail:

> Regardless of the particular objective which the individual has in mind and of his motive for having this objective, it will be in his interests to control the conduct of others, especially their responsive treatment of him. This control is achieved by influencing the definition of the situation which the others come to formulate, and he can influence this definition by expressing himself in such a way as to give them the kind of impression that will lead them to act voluntarily in accordance with his own plan.

When students behave as subordinates, they presumably act in accordance with the teacher's definition of the situation, which is one in which he is permitted to exercise control. What influences them to accept the teacher's authority may vary in different situations, as will the extent of that authority, and some of the factors will be discussed later in this chapter. However, the definition which is formed is concerned with the nature of the relationship between the teacher and students and, in particular, the status difference between them. Once there is an agreement between the participants about the nature of their relationship, this will influence the details of their interactions but the converse is also true: in situations which are initially 'loosely' defined, the details of the interaction will influence the form of relationship reached.

Relationships are not simply beliefs that people have about the way they should interact with other people, they are expressed and negotiated in the actions themselves and in the manner in which those actions are performed. Relationships exist *through* our interactions, where our total behaviour, both verbal and non-verbal, can be seen from two points of view. First, it is to some extent determined by the understanding which the participants already have of the existing relationship and in this sense it is an expression of that understanding. Second, it can be seen as an attempt by the participants either to restate or to modify that understanding. This view is quite consistent with that proposed by Stubbs (1976) and Torode (1976) who placed an emphasis on verbal communication in this process, but there has also been an attempt here to highlight the significant aspects of non-verbal behaviour which express and influence the status relationship as the interaction proceeds. When the teacher chose to address one child as 'darling' and another as 'young lady' (p. 42), she was, at a surface level, simply comforting one and admonishing the other. At a deeper level, she was exercising a right to behave in such ways towards those children, as had she treated the head-teacher or even another adult in those ways they would certainly have considered it impertinent. In exercising unilateral rights, such as using the other's personal space and property, or touching them, the teacher makes a claim to have the degree of authority implied. There is no guarantee that students will accept such treatment and it is only in their reactions that the relationship is continually validated or redefined. When I first began teaching I was supervising Year 11 boys who were changing after a games period. They were taking a long time and I could hear them discussing the game they had just played, so I put my head round the door of the changing room and made what would now be considered a sexist gibe: 'Come along *girls*, stop the nattering and get changed'. The reply from one boy was immediate: 'All right Miss, we won't be long'. The original presentation of the relationship I had claimed had not been accepted, at least by one of the boys, and he had expressed his understanding by claiming similar rights. He was prepared to grant me some authority but not to the extent that I had implied. Some students are far less skilful in their attempts to modify their relationships with teachers, and bitter confrontations can follow.

On the students' part, for example, when they warily enter teachers' territories, assume upright postures and face teachers, they are presenting themselves as subordinates and thereby *investing* authority in the teacher. Of course, such behaviours might be thought of simply as polite, which they are, but we convey subordination in additional ways, such as in our bodily tension, facial expression and tone of voice. 'Politeness' may be according mock respect without these additional cues but what would clearly claim a status difference in the relationship would be the failure of the other to return such courtesies by remaining relaxed in posture, not facing and using the territory freely. By the processes of claims which are legitimised or challenged by students, and investments which are accepted or refused by teachers, relationships are continually restated or modified.

There are obviously degrees of authority in a relationship; at one extreme where, say, a religious leader is treated with reverence in any context by his followers and at the other extreme, anyone with relevant specialised knowledge in an emergency is granted limited authority, only as long as the emergency lasts. Teachers are often accorded a degree of authority in out-of-school contexts by their students, beyond that which would be given to other familiar adults. It is interesting to speculate whether the extent of the authority which exists in a relationship might be observed from the range of different contexts in which the differential rights occur and also in the extent of those rights. Mehrabian's dimension of relaxation-tension seems particularly relevant here in assessing the degree of subordination in the behaviour. Subordinate behaviours may be highly exaggerated, such as in the tense 'attention' posture in the Armed Services, and it may be that the degree of status difference is observable in the extent of the exaggeration.

Authority, power and persuasion

The question of whether subordinate behaviour is voluntary or involuntary is an important consideration which reflects upon the distinction between authority and power. Do students behave as subordinates because they respect teachers or because they fear them? In a discussion of Weber's (1958) analysis of power, persuasion and authority, Spady (1973) considered their relevance for teachers. Power is the probability of carrying out one's will in a social situation, despite resistance from others. One can observe the same behaviours in power relationships as those that occur in status relationships, as described earlier in this chapter but the important difference is that the subordinate is *compelled* to act in such ways and accept such treatment. A teacher's power, then, is the capacity to make students do what they do not wish to do by controlling the consequences which follow their actions, and many would argue that this capacity is becoming increasingly limited. Even when they do comply unwillingly to avoid unpleasant consequences the situation is far from satisfactory, as Spady points out:

> Given that such compliance is essentially involuntary, the resulting condition is usually an uneasy, short-term truce the subordinate party accepts with resentment and hostility, making stable and co-operative social arrangements between parties highly unlikely.

The power to coerce or reward to ensure compliance, and the associated dangers, should not be confused with the exercise of institutional power within an authority agreement. If one compares an army camp with a wartime concentration camp there will be many similarities in the behaviour of subordinate with superior ranks, to that of the prisoners with guards. The guards only needed to use their power when the prisoners failed to comply and the same would be true of the army camp. The essential difference is that in the army the power of the superiors is accepted as part of the relationship, whereas in the concentration camp, compliance was forced *because of the power*, which was very much in evidence in the barbed wire and firearms. Once this power had gone there was no compliance, whereas in the army authority relationships are frequently sustained in circumstances where the superior no longer has any real power over the subordinate. In an authority agreement, therefore, the superior may also have a range of powers over the subordinate and the right to use them fairly would be accepted. However, the relationship is not maintained by those powers but by the respect granted by the subordinates and earned by the superiors.

In some schools there may be very formal relationships where expressions of power, such as the right to use imperatives in control instructions, are accepted by the students. In others, teachers will go to great lengths to avoid expressions of status difference. In either case the particular relationships must be understood, agreed and maintained on the basis of effective and sympathetic teaching as it is not ethical or feasible to attempt to maintain them by the use of powers to punish or reward.

Hinde (1979) has pointed out that 'Power is rarely absolute, and must be seen as a property of the relationship rather than of one or other partner' and in respect of teachers and students the difference is insufficient to ensure that the teachers' wishes will always prevail. It is possible for either the teacher or the student to define an interaction as one where force will determine the outcome, rather than co-operation. The teacher who intervenes with an unambiguous expression of power, implying 'Do it, or else', thereby denies the student any opportunity to present his compliance as a voluntary act. For example, the long and insulting harangue delivered by Mr Baker in response to a student apparently chewing (p. 157) immediately defines any compliance as capitulation. ('I can enforce it and I will.') On the other hand, the following example of the build-up of a confrontation, reported by the teacher, shows the student forcing the issue of power:

> I noticed that he was sitting next to Tony again. Last week I'd separated them – they seemed to distract each other so much. I decided I couldn't let it pass, but neither did I particularly want to make an issue of it. So, as I handed out some worksheets, I quietly reminded him that he wasn't to sit next to Tony until further notice. Would he please move? A few stragglers came in and I'd to sort out a few kids who'd forgotten their exercise books. I kept thinking 'why on earth doesn't he just move – quietly and without a fuss'. I didn't want an incident. By now the class was settled and expectant. He was still sitting, head down, next to Tony. I'd have to try again.
>
> 'Move over here, please,' I said, pointing to an empty desk at the far side of the class.
>
> 'Why should I? Why don't you move him instead of me?'
>
> 'I'm not asking him. I'm *telling* you,' I said with as much authority as I could muster. 'Move now!'
>
> The class had gone very quiet. Some eyes were on him. Most were fixed on me. There was a gathering sense of excitement.
>
> 'Make me,' he said.

If the teacher is giving an accurate description of his behaviour, the first two instructions were tactful (see p. 147) but the boy chose not to comply voluntarily. The third attempt carried strong overtones of force, so that had he then moved it could only have been construed as a result of the teacher's power rather than the authority agreement. In this case the teacher clearly felt obliged to threaten force in response to the student's lack of co-operation but he should also have stated the consequences which would follow further disobedience.

Once dominant behaviour (as opposed to relaxed, high status behaviour) is used by the teacher it is difficult for the student not to either dispute or validate the claim to power. Similarly, if the student rejects the authority agreement it is difficult for the teacher not to concede or resort to power. One alternative for both is to try persuasion and in the previous example the student's suggestion that someone else should move might have been a very crude attempt. Persuasion or reasoning with students may eventually ensure voluntary compliance, though this is by no means assured. In accepting the necessity for, or the desirability of, persuasion the teacher greatly reduces the status difference presented between himself and the students. At an extreme, if students exercise the same rights in relation to teachers as teachers do towards them, then, in effect, authority does not exist in the relationship. Some teachers would consider this desirable and there is much to be said for students being able to share in the decision-making processes in the school, particularly as they get older. However, there are dangers in relying on persuasion as the teacher may be forced to negotiate and justify every activity which takes place and this can be very time consuming. There is an essential place for reasoning with students if only to ensure a clear understanding of the rationale underlying the rules of conduct, but the terms under which it is conducted must be established. If a teacher relinquishes the legitimate powers to control consequences and tries to use persuasion as a means to gain compliance, it is easy for a few irresponsible or 'unreasonable' students to disrupt the lesson.

The essential feature of an authority relationship is that the subordinate acts voluntarily with the superior's wishes because it is an agreement between them and not because he fears the consequences of disobedience or is persuaded on each occasion that it is in his interests to do so. Authority relationships do not have the dangers of generating hostility in students as in power relationships, or of frequent time-consuming negotiations at the students' behest if one relies on persuasion.

Role and rank

When lecturing to college students there is an unstated understanding that a degree of authority will be required by the lecturer to enable the lecture to be delivered. The students 'agree' to allow the lecturer to exercise certain 'rights' which they will forgo during the lecture, namely:

- To speak publicly and control communication. When students wish to speak publicly the lecturer is permitted to decide when this is appropriate and may ask the student to wait. If they need to speak personally to a neighbour, they do so quietly.
- To expect attention from students.
- To move around the room freely. Students are not expected to move without good reason.
- To control the agenda and timing. Students are not expected to determine the content of the lecture or the time assigned to the various issues.
- To control the resources and setting (seating arrangements, lighting, audio-visual equipment).
- To give task-related instructions and expect them to be followed, for example in relation to working in groups or reading background material.
- To ask task-related questions and expect students to consider them. Students may also ask questions of the lecturer but there is an understanding that lecturers will already know the answers to the questions they pose to students.

If students do not forgo these rights during a lecture it will to some extent be disrupted. In other contexts in which lecturers and students meet, these differential rights do not apply as they are associated only with the act of lecturing. Similarly, in teaching, *these are the minimum rights which must be granted to teachers in order for them to perform their roles.* If students talk when they want to and do not attend, move around the room when they wish, try to dictate the agenda by expressing their own particular concerns, use the resources as and when they wish and refuse to follow task-related instructions and consider task-related questions, then the teacher will be unable to teach. Students must themselves assume the role of learners.

Some of the unilateral rights discussed in the previous chapter clearly relate to the nature of teacher and student roles, such as the use of territory and responding selectively. However, such rights may be denied to students in contexts other than the classroom teaching situation, for example in restricting students freedom of access to certain rooms in the school that are open to the staff. These differences are then associated with the *rank* of adult (to child) and teacher (to student), as are other unilateral rights concerned, for example, with touching and forms of address. Such 'rights of rank' are becoming increasingly difficult to impose in the context of a society in which status differences are decreasing, and students will now question, for example, why teachers alone should be permitted to dress as they wish, wear jewellery or bring food and drink into the classroom. On what grounds other than rank should we expect a student to 'Stand up straight and take your hands out of your pockets' or 'Look at me when I'm talking to you' and not to answer back when being reprimanded? As a general rule, if teachers are tempted to say or simply feel 'Who do you think you are talking to?' they are probably concerned with their own rank being respected rather than their role.

Many would argue that rather than acknowledge a change in social relationships in the wider society where respect for social position *per se* is less evident, teachers should set standards which will eventually be reflected in the society. Be this as it may, the trend towards greater equality in relationships is well established and teachers will probably find it increasingly difficult to insist on the rights associated solely with their rank.

In contrast to the more questionable rights associated with rank, it is essential that teachers claim the rights necessary to perform the role. However, these rights are not unconditional. If we consider again a lecture delivered to students, there are clearly responsibilities which the lecturer must fulfil in order to 'legitimise' the claims. Students, in turn, have the right to expect that:

- the aims and objectives of the lecture will be clear and appropriate;
- the lecture will be prepared;
- the information will be explained coherently and pitched at an appropriate intellectual level;
- the lecture will be delivered in a committed and enthusiastic manner and not be 'boring';
- the presentation will, if possible, be varied to promote interest;
- they will be treated respectfully and their views and opinions will be invited and considered seriously.

In the same way, the responsibility rests with teachers to earn the rights being claimed by demonstrating that it is in the students' interest to allow them to be the 'leaders'.

All teachers have the same institutional authority and the same legal powers in relation to students. For the most part, they can all call on the same sanctions, though the higher status teachers usually control the administration of the more serious sanctions, such as suspension from school. The considerable differences in authority granted to teachers in the same school, regardless of age, sex and seniority, must therefore be derived from the different personal qualities they demonstrate, rather than from the positions they hold. As Tattum (1982) pointed out:

> Respect for the teacher *qua* teacher can no longer be assumed as a social fact. No longer is the office held in awe and teachers who draw heavily upon unquestioned authority as an endowed right leave themselves open to mimicry and ridicule.

Tattum and Spady express the view shared here, that the basis for this personal authority rests largely on the effectiveness of one's teaching and all that this entails, together with the concern shown for one's students, in particular for their educational welfare. In short, if one does not teach effectively, if one is boring, unprepared and disinterested in the students' efforts, one cannot expect to be granted authority. However, it would be naive to believe that effective teaching alone will always result in respect from students and subsequent chapters will not only explore aspects of effective teaching such as self-presentation and group management, but will also consider those occasions when they still fail to accept the teacher's authority in the relationship.

Teacher-student relationships

When we observe two people together it is possible to make various inferences about their relationship. We have already seen how their relative status and roles will affect the way they treat one another, but we may also observe whether they are acting co-operatively or in opposition and whether they appear to know one another or are strangers. Danziger (1976) termed these three dimensions *influence*, *integration* and *intimacy* and proposed that they are fundamental aspects of all relationships and are expressed in the way people treat each other.

> These three dimensions of interaction express the fact that individuals must simultaneously relate to one another as sources of power and influence, as sources of resources that need to be shared, and as sources of personal satisfaction.

Any act, and the manner in which it is performed, may express one or more of these features at any given time and as the relationship changes the three dimensions may vary to some extent independently. In the developing teacher-student relationship one might expect expressions of intimacy, in the forms of address used, the subjects discussed (personal as opposed to professional), the humour shared and so on, to increase as they get to know one another. Teachers who initially present themselves in too friendly a manner assume a mutual agreement which has not yet been reached. Those who solicit friendship run the risk of appearing to be in need of acceptance, which some students may exploit. On the other hand, experienced teachers initially try to consolidate their ascribed authority, particularly in establishing the rights associated with their role, but if their relationships with students develop co-operatively, expressions of status difference become less evident. Once authority has been established, teachers give students responsibilities and encourage them to take initiatives and exercise authority themselves. However, when authority is not established, some students may take control and in effect determine when any teaching can take place.

In relation to integration or solidarity teachers and students are encouraged to identify with various groups such as the class, year, house, or school and it is therefore important that teachers always promote the co-operative nature of their relationships, particularly when students fail to acknowledge common goals and loyalties. We may sometimes need to dissociate ourselves from the acts that students commit but should always express solidarity with them as people and members of the same groups.

The particular relationship which develops between teacher and student will also be influenced by various factors beyond the teacher's control.

- *The general ethos of the school*, encouraging either formal or informal relationships. Students will have expectations regarding what is acceptable and appropriate treatment from teachers and changing these will not be easy.
- *The age of the teacher*, particularly at the secondary stage where older students will not perceive younger teachers as having 'adult' rank in relation to themselves but may therefore be more likely to emulate or identify with them as role models.
- *The sex of the teacher and student*. This is particularly significant at the secondary stage where male teachers must show caution in their contacts with female students.
- *The personality and appearance of the teacher*. Some of our personal characteristics, such as physical appearance, temperament and sense of humour, can be relatively permanent and the subjective impression that a student forms will influence the type of relationship that he or she seeks with us.

Students are not passive in this process and will seek to define the relationship in ways which best suit their purposes. It is probable that one reason why students and newly qualified teachers frequently experience problems of discipline is because they are not clear about the form of relationship, and all that this entails, which they can expect to have with their students. As one PGCE student observed, before the Teaching Practice, 'I think I'd just be a mass of nerves. I don't really know how I'll react in a class situation, but . . . deep breath, plunge straight in'. (Wragg and Wood, 1984a)

Teachers should be clear in their own minds how much authority they expect to be granted, what will constitute over-familiar behaviour in the new relationship and what common goals and loyalties they share with their students. The process of establishing and maintaining the relationship one deems appropriate involves confidently expressing that relationship in one's behaviour, teaching effectively so that one's claims are seen as legitimate and dealing effectively with those who still offer challenge. Authority is an essential feature of the early relationship and any student who persists in disrupting a well-prepared and appropriately pitched and delivered lesson and who does not respond to reminders from the teacher to comply, presents a serious challenge. It will then be necessary to resort to an official policy using the powers available (see p. 182), in order to assert the rights necessary to perform the role. On the other hand, boring and disinterested teachers must expect to be continually challenged as they have not established the major basis for the authority they claim.

In the illustration shown earlier (Figure 1, p. 3) the student has been asked to remain behind because of persistent talking during the lesson. The relaxed posture, leaning against the wall with hands in pockets, clearly expresses his resentment and will be perceived by most teachers as disrespectful. The student is refusing to adopt a polite, if not subordinate, attentive posture which would be appropriate in such formal circumstances but there are no hard and fast rules which can govern the teacher's response. How one reacts will be influenced by what treatment one feels the student needs and will also accept. Is it really necessary to make him stand up straight so that he accepts his subordinate position? Neill and Caswell (1993) construct a similar incident in which two boys arrive late and in a dishevelled state for their lesson with Mrs Powerhouse. She had been 'concerned for some time with their behaviour and attitude, and in particular the effect they had been having on the remainder of her class'. Having taken them outside the classroom and separated them she spoke to one.

'Look at me, Ian. Take your hands out of your pockets, do up your tie and stand up straight. Are you chewing? Well take it out and hold it; you can put it in the bin later.'

The authors describe this action as the teacher carrying out 'a series of status reducing exercises, ... an excellent way of showing that you hold the status to do these things and, in the process, strip the pupil of his assumed power.'

When we receive disrespectful treatment from students the temptation is to 'put them in their place' in the way Neill and Caswell describe. Such treatment certainly defines the interaction as formal, where rank must be acknowledged, but it will only reduce the students' status if they are compliant with the teacher's demands. An experienced teacher would take into account the age and attitude of the student before taking such risky action. Given that the boy's attitude and behaviour had been causing concern, is such treatment likely to bring about any lasting improvement? It could do just the opposite by further polarising the relationship.

Rogers (1990) suggests that we should address the primary behaviour, presumably lateness and untidy dress, and not the secondary disrespectful behaviour introduced by the student. The teacher would therefore choose to 'tactically ignore' his posture and manner, but deal with the lateness and dress, incidentally reminding him to put the chewing gum in the bin as an opening or closing remark. If seats were available, another approach would be to invite the student to sit down, defining the interaction as informal and treating him respectfully before dealing with the conduct. There would be no attempt to humble, intimidate or embarrass the student but any sign of tension or uncertainty on the teacher's part would convey that she is weak and fearful of a confrontation with a stronger opponent. If we are secure in our authority we can remain relaxed in the face of challenging behaviour and thereby not define it as a serious threat to our position. We will also be better able to maintain solidarity with students when dealing respectfully with them, and in this way might improve their attitudes towards us or at least not worsen them.

To take another less-challenging example, a student might perch on the edge of a teacher's desk while listening to an explanation. Should the teacher 'correct' this action and, if so, how, or should it be accepted as a positive sign of growing equality and friendliness in the relationship? These are questions which only the teacher can answer as one needs to take account of factors such as the context, the ages of the student and teacher, the existing relationship, how the teacher construes the intention behind the action and how the teacher wishes the relationship to develop. However, if a teacher accepts a particular treatment or remark from a student they are, in effect validating the relationship implied. Consider a young teacher entering her Year 8 class and being greeted by a girl assertively calling out,

'Miss, I reckon we ought to do revision this lesson.'

'Yeah, so do I,' chimes in her companion.

'Yes, well we will be doing revision this lesson, but first I want to give you the exam timetable,' replies the teacher.

What is significant in this brief interaction is that the student felt able to assert her view rather than ask the question, 'Could we do revision this lesson?'. In a sense she is trying to dictate the agenda, which should be the teacher's right (p. 56) and therefore is claiming the right so to do. By replying, the teacher confirms that it is acceptable for the student to talk to the teacher in that way.

In this example it may not be obvious that a particular relationship is being claimed and validated in the interaction, and the student's remark might seem quite innocuous, but had she said, for example,

'Oi, Fat face! We want to do revision this lesson,' and the teacher had simply replied,

'Yes, well we will be doing revision this lesson but first . . .', it would be obvious that a particular relationship was being enacted. In the former example, a teacher who was attempting to establish her authority might therefore be advised to ignore the remark and call the class to attend, thereby bringing into question the nature of the relationship being claimed by the student. In the latter example, a more direct approach would be called for from the teacher, implying, if not stating explicitly, 'Who do you think you are talking to?'

It is evident then that there can be no simple advice to offer teachers in the way they should respond to students other than to exercise caution before validating any actions which in effect undermine or reduce the status difference in their relationship. This relationship cannot be specified nor is it fixed but it would seem sensible for teachers to establish clearly at the outset their claims to authority regarding the rights relating to their role, to allow more personal or intimate aspects to develop naturally over time, and constantly to foster a sense of solidarity with their students.

Activity 4 Words and meaning

The production and understanding of language always has a social setting. Both must take into account the nature of the relationship between speaker and receiver, as well as the wider context in which the exchange takes place. What the sentence means and what the speaker means when saying it, may be very different (Austin, 1962).

1. *What might be assumed about the relationship between two people if one says to the other, 'You're looking very smart today, Adrian.'?*

2. *Consider one person saying to another, 'I don't think you should go out.' How would the delivery and the intended meaning be affected in the following contexts?*
   (i) *An armed terrorist speaking to a hostage who has made a move towards the door.*
   (ii) *A mother talking to her adolescent son who has been unwell but intends to go out to meet his friends.*
   (iii) *A friend supporting another in her refusal to leave the room as the teacher has instructed.*
   (iv) *A teacher addressing a student who is about to leave the room because of a heated confrontation with the teacher.*
   (v) *A teacher counselling a student who says he will not have time to do the homework set.*

DISCUSSION

1. *The relationship might be between two adult colleagues, one who has turned up dressed more smartly than usual, or between a teacher and a student or*

a parent and a child. The use of the first name and the comment on physical appearance would make it extremely unlikely that it was being addressed to someone of superior rank, or to a stranger of equal rank.

2. (i)   The terrorist could say the sentence in a measured way, without the need to use a threatening tone because of the power imparted by the weapon. The meaning of the utterance would clearly be 'You're not going anywhere'.

   (ii) The delivery would probably express the mother's concern for her son. As an adolescent he might normally expect a degree of independence, so the mother might be reluctant to try to force him to stay in. Her meaning would probably be a concerned plea to his good sense, 'You know you really shouldn't go out'.

   (iii) A friend supporting another in a conflict with a teacher would probably make such an assertion in a challenging, indignant manner, reflecting the mood of her friend. The remark would be meant equally for the teacher and would mean, 'I support you against the teacher'.

   (iv) A teacher would be trying to stop the student leaving the room and would want to sound resolute. However, he or she would not have the obvious power to stop them as the terrorist would in (i) so might be tempted to try to sound more personally threatening. The intended meaning would impart this vague threat, 'You had better not leave this room or else . . .'.

   (v)   In the role of counsellor the teacher would advise but not instruct the student, with his best interests at heart. In a similar way to the mother in (ii) the tone would express concern, but in a more formal, less pleading, manner. The intended meaning would be, 'My advice is that it is in your best interests not to go out'.

3 Establishing Authority in First Meetings

Discipline in schools is desirable not simply in order to create conditions in which students can learn but also so that they learn to behave in socially responsible ways. The implication of the 'educative' function of discipline is that as students mature they must increasingly share in the responsibility for maintaining an orderly atmosphere in the classroom and school (Tanner, 1978). In the most successful classes the students choose to act co-operatively with the teacher and accept responsibility for their own learning so that expressions of authority, particularly in relation to rank, are inappropriate. However, in order to share authority with students one must first establish that it exists and many teachers and educational researchers have stressed the importance of the initial meetings in consolidating this understanding. Hargreaves (1972) in his earlier writing reflected the views of many teachers when he described them as battles which the teacher must win.

> Whatever the causes, the phenomenon itself remains. If the teacher does not establish his own dominance, the children are likely to turn the classroom into a circus without a ringmaster and the teacher will become rapidly exhausted and demoralised.

Wadd (1973) makes a similar point:

> In establishing the order he has decided upon, the teacher must be fully aware that what happens in the first few encounters with the pupils is likely to establish the relationships which he will have to live with for the rest of his contact with that particular class.

Ball (1980) gives several examples of what some students and teachers described as the 'honeymoon' of the first lesson, when students are passive and essentially 'weighing-up' the teacher. The second stage was, as one student described it, when 'the boys muck about to see if they can get away with being stupid'. Ball suggested that this 'information gathering' and 'testing out' may be considered conceptually as having two major purposes for students. The first is 'to discover what parameters of control the teacher is seeking to establish over their behaviour' and the second, 'to explore in practice whether or not the teacher has the tactical and managerial skills to defend the parameters he or she is seeking to establish'. This analysis, however, does not bring into consideration the teaching skills which essentially form the basis for any claims the teacher makes to establish certain 'parameters of control' over their behaviour. Students will also be influenced by how confident the teacher appears, how interesting they find the lesson and what work demands are made on them, as well as the teacher's ability to enforce any rules of conduct imposed.

In 1976, Ralph Exline carried out a detailed analysis of the American Presidential debate to test whether there was any evidence to support the view that the first impressions we form can strongly influence our judgements of people's competence. National polls showed viewers had judged Gerald Ford to have 'won' the first debate with Jimmy Carter, but Exline's analysis of the two hours of the debate revealed little difference between the two in the quality of the arguments and on average measures of 'tension leakage', that is, signs of nervousness and uncertainty that might well influence impressions formed of the speakers[1]. There was, however, a striking contrast in the *pattern* of differences that occurred in the opening minutes as compared with the closing portion of the debate. In the opening minutes, Carter showed much more tension leakage than Ford, a finding consistent with the view that Ford had 'won', but in the closing minutes the reverse was the case; Ford looked more nervous.

Subsequent studies were carried out comparing observers' ratings of the first ten minutes and last nine minutes of the debate, which produced the following results:

1. Those who saw the first segment rated Ford as the more competent. Those who saw the second rated Carter more competent.
2. The quality of the arguments from both candidates did not account for this difference.
3. Signs of nervousness and uncertainty were judged as reflecting negatively on the perceived competence of the speaker, whereas a steady gaze at the audience and the use of head nods to accompany emphasised words enhanced perceptions of competence.

This set the stage for the final part of the study. Would observers who viewed both segments in one sequence be influenced in their judgements of overall perceived competence by the order in which the segments were presented? This is indeed what Exline found. When observers saw the sequence in the original order, good Ford, poor Carter first, Ford was given the higher competence ratings as in the full debate. However, when the order was reversed, showing good Carter, poor Ford first, *Carter was given the higher competence rating overall* (Exline, 1985).

This series of studies clearly supports what Exline describes as the *primacy effect*, which is that our first impressions can have a disproportionate effect on our judgements of others' competence.

Experienced teachers understand the importance of their first meetings with

---

[1]Speech non-fluencies, gaze shifting, moistening lips, eye blink rate and body sway.

students. Wragg and Wood found that, at the start of the school year, they made a 'massive combined effort ... to establish a working climate for the whole year'. Most of them 'sought to establish some kind of dominant presence ... to temper any initial harshness with humour and convey to their class that they were firmly in charge, using their eyes, movement and gesture to enhance what they were trying to do'. They seemed clear in their minds before the year began about how they would conduct themselves in the first meetings in contrast to the student teachers in the study who were less certain about their roles and aspirations before the teaching practice and were self conscious about being looked at.

> 'I'd be a bit apprehensive, what they'll be like. Will they be noisy? Will I be able to control them? Will they give me a hard time? I'll wonder if they'll compare me with their usual teacher. I wonder how they'll measure me up. I'll wonder how they'll react as I go through the door, will they all be making a great noise whooping around, or will they be sitting down waiting?' (Male PGCE student, Wragg and Wood, 1984a)

In contrast, a teacher of several years' experience reflects on her first meetings.

> 'When you first walk into the classroom you're conscious of you. You're conscious of failing, you're conscious of being shown up, you're conscious of getting everything wrong. Well, I don't, I'm not conscious of any of these things any more. When I go in I'm far more conscious of them, aware of what they should be doing, aware of what standards they should be reaching. I'm quite assured that if we have a confrontation I'm really not going to be losing out.' ('The Lions Den', BBC TV, 1992)

Student teachers rarely have the opportunity of observing an experienced teacher meeting a class for the first time, yet the initial contact may be crucial in determining the later relationships with the students. By the time the student teacher observes a class the pattern of the interaction has been established, and the teacher is either comfortably sustaining a satisfactory situation or desperately trying to retrieve an unsatisfactory one. Quite understandably a headteacher does not usually allow students to observe the latter, because of sympathy for the teacher or perhaps guilt that such a state of affairs should exist in the school. This is unfortunate, as there is much to be learned from those who are doing the wrong things, as well as from those who are apparently successful. The temptation for student teachers is to model their own behaviour on the first warm and responsive person they observe or on a teacher they remember from their own schooldays. This can be a big mistake as it is very unlikely that the successful, friendly relationships which are established later bear much resemblance to the relationships in the first meetings.

If students learn that they need not attend to the teacher and can, to a large extent, control his behaviour, some of them will not surrender this power easily and it only takes a few to disrupt a lesson. Once any relationship is established it is difficult for one partner to alter it in ways which the other considers disadvantageous and persuasion may not be sufficient. A teacher who has established a controlled but not repressive working atmosphere will find that students will tolerate the occasional lapse in the standard of teaching whereas a class which has developed into 'a circus without a ringmaster' may still not attend even when the lesson is well planned, interesting and relevant.

Whenever students are asked what characteristics they value in teachers they invariably include the ability to keep control in the class (for example, White and Brocking, 1983; Wragg and Wood, 1984a). In practice it might seem that they do all they can to prevent this happening but the paradox could be explained by the fact that usually only a small proportion are persistently disruptive. Teachers who set out to gain control will probably have the support of the majority of students, provided they are also seen as fair and not 'boring'. Those who are authoritarian and confrontational will be disliked and resented as Wragg and Wood concluded after observing a teacher who was universally disliked by his students:

> Those who wish to make a firm start and establish control should recognise that, whilst pupils can see the need for and even expect such a beginning, if they are over-bossy or fail to temper their authority with humanity, they may never secure a positive working relationship with their class.

Confidence and firmness

Imagine a situation where you are driving towards a junction and the traffic lights begin to change as you approach. You decide it is too late to stop and manage to cross without any problems arising. Very shortly afterwards a car overtakes you and the driver indicates that you should stop. You do so, pulling up behind his car. He gets out and walks unhurriedly towards you, looking at your number plate as he approaches. Reaching your window, he looks down at you and says 'Good afternoon, Sir. Are you the owner of this vehicle?' Most students and teachers agree that their first assumption would be that the driver had some authority to stop you, probably because he was an off-duty policeman. The measured, confident approach, the characteristic language and your own expectations, having just committed a minor traffic offence, would all influence this assumption. What is less obvious, but probably more important, is that only the Police would be expected to stop a member of the public in such circumstances. Anyone carrying out such an action is therefore likely to be taken for a policeman. In a similar way, any adult in a school who exercises rights towards students which normally only teachers exercise, is likely, initially, to be taken for a teacher. However, just as one would want to see some identification from the driver to prove that he had the authority he was claiming, so students would have to be convinced that the adult's claim to have authority was legitimate. As suggested earlier, this would rest more on the capacity of the adult being able to demonstrate that he could teach effectively, than simply on having the institutional status of teacher, though this would initially be an advantage. Ideally one's teaching should always be stimulating, pitched at the right level for each individual and carried out with warmth and concern for the students. Unfortunately, it is not always possible to achieve this standard but it is never more important to try than in one's first meetings with students as this is the essential basis for one's claim to be granted the authority to perform the role.

In the example above, the confident, unhurried manner in which the driver approached and his use of characteristic language also contributed to the perceived legitimacy of the action. They gave the impression of his being experienced in such matters and of being secure in the right to take such actions. If the posture had been tense and the vocal and facial expressions had shown doubt or anxiety then you would immediately begin to question the authority claimed in stopping you and asking questions. The nature of our claim is expressed in the actions we carry out but our security in making that claim, our belief that we have a legitimate right to behave as we do, is expressed in the *manner* in which the actions are performed. One factor, therefore, which influences whether students accept a teacher's treatment of them is the degree of confidence and certainty with which the teacher behaves. Experienced teachers often advise students to behave confidently when facing a class as this helps in establishing good classroom control. If we feel confident or self-assured there is an implication that we expect others to respond appropriately and that even if they did not, we would be able to manage the situation without difficulty. If we lack confidence, it implies that we feel uncertain about our ability to gain students' attention and deal effectively with any problems. Like all good self-fulfilling prophesies this is usually just what happens. If the teacher feels confident, the students are noticeably more responsive and this in turn reinforces his own assurance; if the teacher lacks confidence, the process can begin in reverse, and he can quickly become thoroughly demoralised.

It follows then that such feelings must have very obvious effects on our behaviour as it is through behaviour that feelings are communicated. Mehrabian's relaxation-tension dimension again seems very relevant in this respect, as relaxed behaviour is consistent with high status and also implies that one does not feel threatened. It is easy to say that one should appear relaxed but it is very difficult to control feelings of anxiety and these can usually be detected from the tone of voice and other non-verbal behaviour. Only the brilliant actors will be able to hide such signs and the best that most of us can do is to reduce any possible reasons for feeling anxious by being thoroughly prepared and regarding the students as friendly rather than hostile. The discussion in the next chapter on non-verbal communication of feelings may also be helpful.

It is also sometimes recommended that a new teacher should be firm at first and ease off later as it is much more difficult to be firm after one has been lax at the outset. This traditional advice may be quite sound but unfortunately fails to describe what being 'firm' entails. Some interpret firmness as coming down like a hammer on the first child who does the slightest thing wrong, but they then often find themselves in a confrontation. Kounin (1970) attempted to identify features of firmness, so that observers could rate teachers for this behaviour. He suggested that it meant the degree to which the teacher conveyed, 'I – mean – it' and 'now!' in a *desist* order. This is open to question as there seems to be a strong suggestion of threat in Kounin's description, which implies that the student might choose not to follow the instruction. The threat is a warning not to make such a choice. Kounin goes on to say that the message of an instruction should have *clarity* – it should stand out from whatever the teacher was previously doing, and provide a sharp contrast. High message clarity would be conveyed by the teacher making a clean break from a previous location in the room, stopping his previous activity, giving a warning signal and using a tone of voice that stands out. The other aspect of firmness Kounin mentions is the *follow through*, which entails moving closer to the deviant, looking firmly at him during and for a while after the instruction, using a *physical assist* (e.g. leading by the arm), and using a *repeat urge*. That is *not* a repeat in response to failure.

This description clearly shows aspects of aggressive threat on the teacher's part, which is again a debatable aspect of firmness. Also, the 'physical assist' would surely be an unwise act, unless the teacher is a great deal stronger than the child and is sure of no resistance. 'Mr Howie' (in Torode, 1976) found this out to his cost:

> John Cannon was slow in entering the class one day, when Mr Howie was directly behind him. The teacher said, 'Get in, Cannon', and pushed him. Cannon held his ground and engaged in struggle. He laughed, and appeared to find it a great joke, for he said 'What a weakling!' as the teacher had to concede defeat.

As discussed earlier, the use of any physical force whatsoever towards a student is extremely unwise and could leave the teacher open to accusations of physical abuse. Students are also increasingly likely to retaliate and an otherwise trivial matter could quickly escalate into a serious confrontation. However, physical direction, if carried out in an *incidental* fashion so that the teacher is not looking at the student and apparently attending elsewhere, can be a very effective reminder to the student to comply, and a clear, warm expression of the teacher's adult rank. It should never involve the slightest force, nor should it be accompanied by the other non-verbal threats described as aspects of 'follow-through', and looking away from the student may serve to mitigate any aggressive connotations.

A student who is talking as he enters the room with his classmates might be quietly guided to one side, or a teacher might remove a pen from the hand of a student who is writing at the wrong moment, without the teacher inter-rupting what he is saying to the rest of the class. It is the ability to do this, or to give an instruction with a degree of certainty, which implies one expects co-operation, which conveys an impression of firmness, though one would also have to deal effectively with any objections from students, to reinforce this understanding.

To be firm one must be confident and this can only arise from a belief or certainty in one's legitimate right to behave as one does. If we consider the example of taking a student aside because he is talking as he enters the room, the manner in which this act is performed is likely to reflect the strength of the teacher's belief that the student should not be talking at that time, and that he has the right to stop him. Firmness should have no over-tones of force as this can provoke a confrontation and it is noticeable that experienced teachers frequently carry out such actions incidentally, while apparently attending to other matters (see p. 151). Confidence and firmness, then, arise from being certain in one's own mind that the actions one is tak-ing are necessary and that one has a legitimate right to take them.

In their interactions with students, teachers present claims to particular rela-tionships (in actions), express degrees of confidence in those claims (in man-ner) and present 'credentials' (in teaching skills) on which the claims are based. The students, for their part, may be doing similar things and hence the definition of the situation is negotiated. This process goes on all the time but is particularly relevant during first meetings.

Addressing the class

When I lecture to a group of postgraduate students who have recently arrived at college or experienced teachers on courses, I am sometimes able to start by giving a clear instruction after clapping my hands sharply, 'Right, stop the noise and pay attention'. The teachers usually laugh because they know I have to be joking no matter how convincing I have tried to appear. The students usually stop talking but look at me in disbelief as being new to the college they are far less certain of their own status. Although the instruc-tion is quite functional, using the imperative form claims a degree of power which few people would accept. For adults to comply unquestioningly with such commands they would have to be subordinates in organisations such as the Armed Forces or inmates of a prison, where their superiors would also have considerable powers over them. In a Court of Law the injunction 'Silence in Court' is not questioned and it would express a very different relationship if the usher asked, 'Do you think we could have a little quiet please?' Such a form is more appropriate when giving a lecture as it conveys a more equal relationship with the audience. The lecturer cannot claim the same power as a court usher or even a teacher, and the authority granted is largely on the basis of the students requiring the knowledge one is communicating. Teachers often use the more 'polite' forms not necessarily because they do not have the power implied by the use of commands but because they wish to characterise the relationship as co-operative (see p. 147).

Teachers frequently need to gain silence and attention from students and it is evident that the particular contact signals they use express their understanding of the situation and of the relationships. The functional attribute of contact signals is that they should be loud enough to be heard or noticeably visible. In a room where students are working silently it would be sufficient to say quietly, 'Could you just stop what you're doing and pay attention please?', but if there is any noise a louder signal would be called for.

It is desirable to have silence and attention when anyone, teacher or student, is addressing the class but as this entails everyone stopping whatever is being done, the message must be important enough to warrant the interruption. If students are busily working, frequent interventions will only upset their concentration. It might be possible to leave the message until later, or perhaps it concerns only a few who could be approached individually. Even highly co-operative groups need time to switch their attention away from whatever they are doing and on to the teacher, and allowing time for this, using positive reminders or 'coaxing', is time well spent. A Year 9 class are working quietly, copying some work from the board, when the teacher decides to introduce some further information. Walking from the back of the room where he has been helping a student, he announces,

'Some of you haven't got as far as finishing this and you haven't done the labels but I want you to put your pens down now because I want to talk about it . . . and . . . I'm going to really . . . anticipate some of the work that we'll be doing . . . later this week and next week, so *(raises voice slightly and gestures with both hands towards the class)* so all of you, . . . put your pens down and give me your full . . . concentration . . . *(stands facing the class)* . . . consecration *(smiles, looking directly at class for four seconds. Gestures with both hands towards the class)* Resist the temptation . . . pens down. *(Leans to one side to smile directly at one boy who still holds his pen. The boy returns the smile and puts the pen down and the teacher acknowledges with raised eyebrows and a 'thumbs up' sign* (see Figure 32, p. 177). *He then turns to the side of the class.)* OK? *(Turns back to face the class and gestures towards the board.)* All eyes on a very simple diagram *(Turns to board and begins explanation)* Most of this is self explanatory.'

This episode took forty seconds and had the class been less co-operative or involved in discussions it would no doubt have taken longer.

A common habit with some teachers is to shout out a request for the class to stop talking or pay attention, and then quickly continue with the message in a raised voice before the noise has subsided. The expectation is that the students will hear the teacher talking and attend, but this can take a considerable time during which some of the message may be missed. The class are also learning that they need not respond to requests for silence, and on future occasions the talking may persist for increasing periods of time. The teacher, in turn, has to raise his voice in an attempt almost to smother their talking with his own noise, so that they are unable to communicate with each other. This generally briefly interrupts most other communication in the room and the noise lessens but, surprisingly, many teachers will often begin to talk again before there is complete silence, and the noise slowly builds up once more. From the outset it should be established that the class has to attend when told to as it is important not to teach them to ignore one's signals. Negotiating a voice level policy can be helpful (see p. 195).

As suggested, the form of contact one chooses can express a definition of the situation and it may therefore vary from occasions where it prefaces information about a task, to interventions where it presages a reprimand. An unconventional example is quoted by Stubbs (1976):

> At the start of one English class which I observed, the teacher, after talking quietly to some pupils at the front of the room, turned and said to the whole class: 'Right! Fags out, please!' No pupils were smoking so the teacher did not mean his words to be taken literally. I interpret his remark as having a primary function of attracting the pupils' attention, of warning them of messages still to come – in short, of opening the communication channels. The remark had a 'contact' function of putting the teacher *in touch* with the pupils.

The humorous and esoteric nature of this message expresses a close and informal relationship and it would be unlikely if the teacher had then followed with any serious critical remarks. Humorous instructions are probably not appropriate when first meeting a class because the relationship between the teacher and students has not developed sufficiently to allow them, and they might be seen as attempts to ingratiate oneself.

The form of speech used, the humour, and the non-verbal behaviour all not only contribute to and develop a relationship, but are expressions of that relationship so far. This interdependence of communication and context is pointed out by Stubbs:

> Speech is therefore not just something that happens *in* situations – a sort of epiphenomenon. It is part *of* situations. To say, therefore, ... that certain situations 'determine' certain kinds of language-use is to over simplify. It is, rather, a two way process ... the characteristic 'contact' language of teachers creates, and is created by, a specific social situation in the classroom.

In the same way, when Mrs Newman asked Carol where she had been and was told, 'Shut your mouth' (Furlong, 1976), or when Alan Jones was told to leave the room by Mr Howie and replied, 'Get stuffed' (Torode, 1976), this language not only affects subsequent events but is an expression of the type of relationship which exists between the teachers and students. It is characteristic of the control exercised by the students that, in both these instances, they do not respond appropriately to the teachers but 'turn the tables' so that the teacher must react in some way. In so doing they are challenging the teacher's definition of the status relationship, and expressing their own. Such situations rarely develop immediately. They are usually the product of previous meetings during which the students have gained in confidence and learned that they can speak to those teachers in that way.

With a new group the form of teacher–student relationship has yet to be established. It has not been determined whether there will be a friendly co-operative atmosphere, or one in which students are either repressed or can tell the teacher to 'get stuffed'. Informal language from either side could be premature, and the teacher would risk sacrificing some authority. It would therefore be safer to rely on conventional ways of gaining attention, such as banging a board rubber, clapping, or saying in a raised voice, 'Pay attention everyone' but whatever one does it must be clearly established that when attention is called for it is an instruction and not a request. Absolute silence must be achieved before the message is given and the class must learn at the outset to be quiet when anyone, including one of their own members, is addressing them.

It is often preferable at the start of a lesson to establish contact without having to say anything, as at this time one should *expect* attention. The novelty of a new teacher entering the room will usually gain attention and silence, particularly if he stands confidently and prominently in front of the group. As a general rule, the less one has to say to gain attention, the better. If it were possible to quell a rowdy mob simply by entering the room this would, by inference, reflect the considerable authority or power of the person entering. It follows that if one has to go to great lengths to get attention from a group who are simply talking, one lacks authority in the relationship. If the teacher considers that the class is not paying sufficient heed, then the form of instruction chosen is important as it expresses one's definition of the situation.

When complete silence is achieved it is possible to talk in a normal voice, or even a little quieter than usual, which emphasises the students' responsibility to listen. If one wishes to make any point forcibly then either lowering or raising one's voice, when there is absolute silence and attention, will have a dramatic effect provided it is not done too frequently. It is never advisable to compete with noise in a room by shouting above it, other than to give a signal for attention. This can become a habit, so that teachers always talk loudly over the noise in the room, and this gives the voice a boring quality as the vocal variations are reduced in the effort to make oneself heard.

There is no need to deliver a lengthy lecture on behaviour when students have been slow to attend, though some teachers might want to discuss the need for certain rules at this stage. What is essential is for the teacher to establish his requirements by what he does. Having gained silence and begun to talk it is vital to be aware of the first student who shows any intention of talking or who is clearly not attending. The teacher need only stop talking in mid-sentence to interrupt him, as the resultant silence will be immediately noticeable. Obviously, this tactic will have little effect if there is so much noise that many students are hardly aware that the teacher is talking, and so do not notice if he stops. They can also learn that a particular teacher will not do much if they don't attend or, regrettably, may have little worth attending to. For the best effect, when the teacher breaks off in mid-sentence this should leave near silence in the room and it can therefore only be used to gain attention from an individual when the great majority of the class are already attending. Later, when a teacher can reliably gain attention and a personal relationship begins to develop, he can express his own personality, whether it be with a 'Fags out, please' or something a little more formal.

In the initial meeting with a class, experienced teachers probably unconsciously assess their demeanour, taking into account a range of impressions and information such as their age and dress, how orderly they appear, how they react to one's presence, the time taken to respond to the first contact signal and their previous reputation. This will influence and be influenced by how secure the teachers feel in the situation and what action they think is required to establish their authority. My favourite anecdote concerns gaining the attention of the class and was told to me by a deputy headteacher about his first day in the school. It was the registration period on the first morning of the new school year and as a newly appointed member of staff he had not been introduced to the students. As he walked down the corridor he heard a rumpus coming from a Year 10 group so he decided to make an early impression by settling them down.

> 'I walked into the classroom and looked directly at those making the most noise and waited. It took some considerable time before they began to notice me but slowly the elbow prods went round and the noise subsided as they attended to the stranger in front of them. Eventually I had complete silence and attention so I savoured the moment briefly while scanning the expectant faces before speaking.
>
> "At last . . . I was beginning to think I was invisible."
>
> With an air of feigned surprise a boy in the front immediately retorted,
>
> "Who said that?" '

Understandably, the class roared with laughter so I asked him how he responded. When I ask student teachers how they would react they frequently feel it would be necessary to regain the lost initiative either by delivering a stern reprimand to show they 'won't stand any nonsense' or by trying to 'top' the remark with another rejoinder. In contrast, most experienced teachers say they would laugh, which is exactly what he did, acknowledging the student's wit. He could do this because he was confident that he could subsequently quieten the class, introduce himself and then remind them to wait quietly for their teacher.

> 'OK, now . . . Settle down . . . Now my name is Mr Jones . . . and I'm the new deputy headteacher . . . and when I come past this room in future I don't expect to hear a racket like that . . . *(aside to one student)* Who are you waiting for?'

Those who appear flustered and embarrassed or angry and aggressive in such situations reveal their own insecurity in their position.

In summary, it has been argued that authority exists in a relationship and is to a large extent granted by the students. It is in everyone's interest that there should be a context in which teaching and learning can take place and teachers must be granted the authority required to perform this role. For their part, they will have to earn this authority by the quality of their teaching, but it is also helpful from the outset to behave as if they already have it, in a more formal manner consistent with their rank.

When a person behaves in a confident and efficient manner we are inclined to believe that such behaviour reflects knowledge and experience. In the school situation the reality is that teachers *are* in positions of authority in relation to students, but their behaviour must be consistent with this and hence imply knowledge and experience; thus the teacher can claim authority in his first meetings with students, but it can easily be eroded. First, he may lack the knowledge and expertise he needs. His lessons could be poorly prepared or badly presented so that the students become bored. He might fail to deal quickly and effectively with any problems which arise. Second, his characterisation of the situation could be inadequate – his behaviour might be inconsistent with that of a person in authority. He could be too responsive or show signs of anxiety or submission. Third, some students might openly challenge his definition of the situation as one in which he is in authority, by lack of co-operation or disruptive behaviour. In this event, the teacher might need the support of senior staff or reliable procedures in the school, which would confirm and reinforce his status. If this support does not exist, then the reality of his authority is in question and there is then the possibility of the students beginning to impose their own definition of the situation, in spite of the ascribed status of the teacher.

In the first meetings with new classes, the task for the teacher is mainly one of reinforcing his initial authority. If the students successfully manage to challenge or disregard that authority, then subsequent meetings will express their definition of the situation and the teacher will then be faced with attempting to modify or redefine that definition. Though not impossible, this requires much more effort than merely consolidating or reinforcing an initial definition which is in the teacher's favour, and Goffman's words can be seen as having particular relevance for teachers here:

> It would seem that an individual can more easily make a choice as to what line of treatment to demand from and extend to others present at the beginning of an encounter than he can alter the line of treatment that is being pursued once the interaction is under way.

Though it is vital for a teacher to convey from the outset that he is in authority, the basis of his long-term authority rests in his superior knowledge and ability to communicate effectively. Students who regard lessons as uninteresting and pointless are more likely to challenge the teacher, and the next chapter will explore the ways in which a speaker can convey enthusiasm for his subject and influence the emotional climate in the classroom.

Activity 5 First impressions

1. Make a list of the things you would say for a couple of minutes to introduce yourself to:
    (a) a group of fellow students on a course;
    (b) a class of Year 8 students you are going to teach for the year.

    *   Compare the lists and consider the reasons which might explain any similarities and differences.
    *   Would you feel it appropriate to ask questions when giving either introduction?
    *   What impressions would you hope to give in each situation?

    A small group of colleagues is required for the following activities.

2. Two colleagues should each introduce themselves as new members of a university discussion group, and two others as new teachers to a class of Year 8 students. The other group members should observe:

    *   the type of information chosen by each speaker;
    *   the speaker's non-verbal behaviour, for example, facial expressions (smiling?), eye contact, posture, tone of voice;
    *   whether questioning or any other interaction with the group took place.

    Each group member should rate each speaker on the following dimensions, giving reasons if possible why these impressions were formed. (Any previous knowledge of the speakers should be discounted.)

WARM REASONS	*1*	*2*	*3*	*4*	*5*	COLD
CONFIDENT REASONS	*1*	*2*	*3*	*4*	*5*	ANXIOUS
INFORMAL REASONS	*1*	*2*	*3*	*4*	*5*	FORMAL
HUMOROUS REASONS	*1*	*2*	*3*	*4*	*5*	SERIOUS
INVOLVED REASONS	*1*	*2*	*3*	*4*	*5*	DETACHED

After each introduction the ratings should be collated. A quick way of doing this is to have the above dimensions displayed on a board or a flip chart and for each member of the group to have five small sticky labels which they can affix at the appropriate points on each dimension. It is then easy to count the labels and display the totals.

- *Is there much consensus in the impressions formed?*
- *What behaviours mentioned in the 'reasons' tend to be noticed as significant?*
- *Do the impressions of the 'students' vary from those of the 'teachers'?*
- *What might be the 'best' and 'worst' impressions to convey on the five dimensions as (a) the student? (b) the teacher?*

3. *The aim of this activity is to convey a particular attitude to the group by the way in which one presents oneself.*

   Those trying this activity should first write down some details as listed in 1(b) above which will take two or three minutes to present, for example:

- *your name;*
- *the subject you will be teaching;*
- *learning their names;*
- *rules you expect them to observe;*
- *a few opening questions to introduce the subject for your session.*

   The 'teachers' should each imagine they are introducing themselves to a Year 8 group but should try to communicate one or more of the following attitudes:

(a) Intimidating	*Make them wary of you*	
(b) Anxious	*You are wary of them*	

(c)	Ingratiating	You want them to like you
(d)	Bored	You are not interested in the subject
(e)	Self-assured	You feel confident about speaking to them
(f)	Flirtatious	You fancy yourself
(g)	Disdainful	You think they are stupid and not worth your time
(h)	Parental	You will take good care of them
(i)	Organised	You are businesslike. Time is important
(j)	Indecisive	You are disorganised
(k)	Friendly	You are approachable
(l)	Patronising	You think they are rather young and need encouraging

After each presentation the group members should discuss the impressions they have formed and why, and what attitudes or reactions they have towards the 'teacher'.

● What expectations has the 'teacher' created?
● Are these expectations likely to be helpful or unhelpful in the developing teacher–student relationship?

4. Only those with some dramatic flair (or who have had a few drinks) will want to attempt this activity. It is meant to be lighthearted but it will probably be necessary to take time to prepare the performance beforehand.

You are not a teacher but have been invited to speak to the Year 8 group on a topic of your choice. Introduce yourself and your topic, without revealing your occupation (your topic should not obviously reveal your occupation). Use whatever language or behaviour you think appropriate and try to convey to the group that your occupation is one of the following (or another of your choice):

(a)	A trade union official	(g)	A waiter in a restaurant
(b)	An army officer	(h)	A psychotherapist
(c)	A vicar	(i)	A street trader
(d)	A policeman	(j)	A TV game show presenter
(e)	An airport announcer	(k)	A punk rock star
(f)	A spaghetti western hero	(l)	A used car salesman

The group should try to guess what your 'real' occupation is, by raising their hands in the normal way during your presentation.

It should be clearly understood that this activity is a light-hearted look at occupational stereotypes and not meant to denigrate any particular group in any way.

N.B. For Activities 5.2, 5.3 and 5.4 the 'student audience' is not meant to be disruptive but should attend to and co-operate with the speaker.

Activity 6 Who do you think you are?

A newly appointed teacher walks into his (or her) classroom on the first morning of the new school year. His Year 8 class have not previously met him and are re-establishing friendships after the summer break, chatting about what they have been doing, so they do not immediately notice their new teacher. He walks over to his desk, put his books and materials down, looks around the room and approaches a student sitting at the front. Bending down to speak personally to the student, he asks,

'What's your name?'

'Adam,' replies the student.

'Adam, could you open a few windows, please?' As Adam gets up, the teacher addresses the class.

'Right, I'd like everyone's attention now, please.'

In this brief interaction, list the ways in which the teacher is claiming to have authority. When you have done this, read the following discussion to compare your views.

DISCUSSION

We can best recognise the aspects of the teacher's behaviour which claim authority by considering how he would behave in a context in which he is not in authority. Imagine it is his first day in the new school but this time, having arrived early, he enters the staffroom, puts his books down, approaches a seated teacher, bends down and says 'What's your name?' It should be immediately obvious that:

- *if one wishes to speak to an adult stranger of equal status one would first greet them (e.g. 'Good morning') and then introduce oneself;*
- *one does not bend down to an adult stranger of equal or superior rank but would remain standing to introduce oneself;*
- *one does not give instructions, however politely, to an equal;*
- *even if the staffroom were stuffy, it would be presumptuous not to ask if anyone minded before opening a window, until one was 'established' as a member of staff. Similarly one would exercise care in where one put down books, and which seat and mug one used;*
- *one could not call for everyone's attention unless there was an emergency or for some other very good reason.*

Perhaps less obviously, the superior in an interaction can choose when and if to start an interaction (see Who responds to whom? p. 35) and when to finish it. Teachers can frequently be heard saying to the class when the bell has rung for the end of the session, 'Just a minute . . . I haven't said go yet. (see Figure 28) or to an individual 'Come back . . . I haven't finished yet.' On the other hand, one would be unlikely to hear a student saying to a teacher. 'Just a minute . . . come back . . . you haven't explained it properly yet.' Nor would teachers being interviewed for a new post take the initiative to draw the interview to a close, as in that situation they would be subordinates.

In the brief interaction, therefore, the teacher claims to be in authority by:

- *initiating the interaction with the student and bending down to speak to him;*
- *asking the student's name without introducing himself or giving a greeting;*
- *giving an instruction;*
- *implying it is his room by having the windows opened;*
- *giving the class an instruction to attend.*

It must be stressed that this approach is not necessarily being recommended, as older or more challenging students might well take issue with the teacher's initial question (for example, 'What do you want to know for?').

Figure 28 *'I haven't said go yet.'*

4 Effective Teaching

Good classroom control does not rest solely on the ability to act as if one is in authority: teachers must demonstrate at the outset that they are keen to communicate their subjects in a committed and organised manner, or it will quickly become evident that their authority has no legitimate basis. It is in such skills as organising, presenting, communicating and monitoring that teachers' actual authority rests. Without them they will fail to capture the interest of their students or to gain their respect, and attempts to retain control by wielding power will be resented. The skills of communicating effectively are easy to recognise but difficult to describe, and this may be one reason why they have been neglected in comparison with other aspects of successful teaching. It is essential to communicate in a lively and compelling way and in this chapter there will be an attempt to draw attention to the characteristic and subtle ways in which enthusiasm is conveyed.

Sustaining students' attention

People watching an interesting television programme are not easily distracted, and they may even be reluctant to switch the set off when an unexpected visitor calls. Teachers rarely exercise such magnetic power over students in their classes, who often attend only out of a sense of duty or fear. Any alternative to a teacher who drones on and on is readily sought or created. Though it is not possible for every lesson to be exciting, the moral is clear: students who are interested and involved in the lesson will attend more, misbehave less and consequently be more likely to learn something. Evidence to support this was presented by Rosenshine (1970), who summarised the results of studies into 'enthusiastic teaching' and concluded that if students rated teachers as 'stimulating', 'energetic', 'mobile', 'enthusiastic' and 'animated', this was related to increased achievement scores on tests given at the end of the lesson.

Enthusiastic teaching could be regarded as something of a performance by the teacher. Ross (1978) makes just this point in relation to lecturing:

> One writes 'performance' because this is what a good lecture often is. The language of the theatre does not come amiss here; the tyro is directed not to turn his or her back on the audience, to articulate clearly, to project, to maintain eye contact, to practise timing, to use gestures appropriately, to relate to his audience, etc., etc.

This does not mean that teachers are always performers and can never relate to children in genuine ways, or that they must never reveal their 'true' personalities and feelings. What it does mean is that certain aspects of teaching call for special skills; skills such as sustaining attention, establishing control, organising and selecting materials and monitoring students' work. If teachers are competent in these skills, then this can only enhance their capacity to make genuine relationships with students. On the other hand, the incompetent teacher will always be preoccupied with his own survival.

As Rosenshine's survey suggested, enthusiasm is considered important in sustaining a listener's attention by displaying a strong interest in a subject, almost in a persuasive way. Of course, it is possible to show enthusiasm without necessarily capturing other people's interest, and most of us have been bored by a fanatic who insists on going into minute detail about his personal passion. Rosenshine nevertheless demonstrated that successful teachers were judged as being enthusiastic in their performance, so it seems that enthusiastic teaching must involve not only a strong interest in the subject, but also a need and ability to communicate that interest to others. Here the boring fanatic fails: he is insensitive to the feelings of his listeners. Any communicator, be he teacher, salesman, politician or actor, must always be searching for the listeners' reactions and modifying his performance accordingly.

But what constitutes an enthusiastic performance? It seems to be stating the obvious to draw attention to non-verbal behaviours such as movement, gesture, variation in voice and eye contact. In fact, we usually fail to notice such things if they are relevant and appropriate, because they serve to emphasise the meaning of the communication rather than the act. They give the listener additional information, or convey how the speaker feels about the ideas he is expressing. As Argyle (1975) put it, they provide 'the message about the message'. It is only when non-verbal behaviour is inconsistent with the verbal message that we may begin to notice it. If a speaker is fidgeting with a pencil or using exaggerated or repetitive movements, our attention may be drawn to the act of communication and away from the meaning.

Gestures and speech

If we see a group of people talking together, or a discussion between two people on television, it is easy to identify which person is talking even if we can't hear the sound. Most of the listeners will be looking at that person as, even in a conversation between two people, the listener looks much more at the speaker than vice versa (Kendon, 1967). It will be particularly noticeable that the speaker is moving more than the others, and when he stops talking his body becomes still, as he takes on the role of a listener. The other people in the group will move from time to time, sometimes to give a nod of approval, a smile or some other feedback, perhaps to indicate that they intend to speak. In contrast, the speaker will keep up a fairly continuous stream of nods, and perhaps arm and hand movements, and will change his facial expression from time to time. Any doubt about the extent of these movements is easily dispelled by turning off the sound when a speaker is expressing a forceful point of view on the television. The effect can be quite bizarre, as one is suddenly aware of the vast amount of activity taking place. The more the speaker is emotionally involved in communicating his ideas, the broader and more staccato become the movements. Mehrabian (1972) found that speakers who were trying to be persuasive looked more at their listeners, used more gestures and nods, more facial activity and spoke faster and with less hesitation. If we take the extreme case of two people arguing angrily, we see them directing highly animated behaviour at one another.

Clearly such behaviour serves to sustain the listener's attention, but how does it enhance the meaning of the message? If we look again at an enthusiastic speaker this will become evident. It is important not to choose someone who is attempting to give an objective, unbiased presentation, such as a newsreader, as this affects the bodily behaviour. Someone trying to put over a point of view in a discussion would be ideal. Just as a singer's movements reflect the rhythm of the music and the meaning of the lyrics, so an enthusiastic speaker has a similar relationship with his message. Though he has no music, the words he is using provide their own rhythm. This is determined by the stressed syllables. If we take the word 'rhythm' the stress falls on the first syllable *rhy*thm, whereas in the word 'determined' the stress is on the second syllable, de*ter*mined. We can accentuate some of these stressed syllables more than others by vocal changes in volume, timing and pitch, and this affects the meaning of the message as well as producing a different rhythmic pattern. To illustrate this point, compare two ways of saying the same sentence:

'When we speak ... we can ac*cen*tuate some of the stressed syllables.' If we alter the vocal stress we make a subtle change in the meaning and affect the rhythm:

'When we speak ... we can accentuate *some* of the stressed syllables.' The first presentation draws our attention to the capacity to accentuate while speaking, whereas the second implies that only some syllables may be accentuated.

The rhythm which exists in speech is, therefore, determined partly by the normal stresses occurring in words but also by the intended meaning of the communication. The phenomenon seldom noticed by the listener is that bodily movements occur in relation to that rhythm, provided the speaker is relaxed and involved in what he is saying. If we now listen to our speaker on television and attend only to the rhythm, and not to what he is actually saying, the impression we have is that the body is dancing to the rhythm of the speech. This synchronisation of bodily movements with speech rhythms has been observed by many researchers. For example, Kendon (1972) in a careful analysis of a speaker's behaviour noted:

> When such a flow chart of the body movement is matched against a chart showing how the flow of speech sounds changes from frame to frame of the film it is found that these 'configurations of change' occur synchronously with the articulation of the sounds. In other words, the body moves synchronously, and synchronously too, with the changes in the geometry of the oral-pharyngeal regions that occur with speech. thus as the subject speaks so he moves, the whole organism behaving as an integrated whole.

It should not, of course, seem strange that speech and body movements are frequently synchronised. When a dog barks it does not move its head before or after the bark, but *as* it barks, and to a much finer degree the same relationship occurs in human beings.

Kendon (1983) suggested that children's capacity to make use of gesture expands in close association with growth in their capacity for spoken language. Gestures are not an unwanted distraction for the listener, as some would have us believe, but an integral part of the communication. They serve to enhance and clarify the message but, unless they are inappropriate, are seldom noticed by the listener. Some students, when giving video-taped talks, decide to sit on their hands to avoid 'waving them about' but as they relax and become involved, it is quite comical to see their trapped arms flapping like a young bird attempting to fly.

This self-synchrony does not occur all the time. If a person is anxious he may remain quite still when talking apart from fidgeting nervously. The stillness is probably due to muscular tension and the fidgeting can be regarded as a lack of synchrony between speech and movement, which is distracting for the listener. The speaker is concerned with his own anxiety rather than what he is saying. It seems reasonable to suppose, therefore, that the extent to which self-synchrony occurs is an indication of the involvement of the speaker with communicating his ideas. It is also claimed that one can observe the level of a listener's involvement from the extent that he moves in close harmony with the speaker, a phenomenon described as 'interactional synchrony' (Condon, 1976).

Not all movements are rhythmical or emphatic. Sometimes the gesture gives a visual representation of the idea being communicated, particularly of size, shape and position. One instance of this would occur if we asked someone to describe a spiral staircase, but less dramatic examples regularly accompany speech. Some gestures convey specific meaning and can be used in place of words, such as screwing one's finger into the temple to indicate madness. There are relatively few of these and they are obviously learned, as different cultures use different signs for the same concept, just as each has a different verbal language.

Another instance of the clear relationship between gesture and meaning occurs when the movement precedes the word to which it refers, perhaps to suggest an element of uncertainty or choice in the information being conveyed, so that the word is offered as an approximation or as one of several alternatives. The gesture occurring before the word, in a brief pause, takes the emphasis away from it. For example, if in the sentence 'It took me (gesture) an hour to get here' the speaker paused briefly before 'an hour', raised his lower lip, looked away and gave an outward movement of the arm or hand, this would indicate that it took approximately an hour. Had the gesture and vocal emphasis fallen on the word 'hour' and been directed towards the listener, we would assume that the journey took exactly or at least an hour and perhaps that the speaker was not very happy about it: 'It took me an *hour* to get here.'

Facial expressions also enhance meaning by showing how the speaker feels about the message. An enthusiastic speaker will be producing a stream of facial expressions which convey his excitement, disbelief, surprise or amusement about his message. Some expressions are extremely brief, lasting about one fifth of a second, and may highlight a particular word, whereas others last much longer, perhaps accompanying the verbal expression of an idea. The overall effect is to provide a running commentary for the listener on how the speaker feels about the ideas expressed. In contrast, a speaker who is not involved in his subject shows little variation in facial expression. The impression conveyed is that the ideas are brought out automatically and are failing even to capture the attention of the speaker. This lack of involvement is also communicated by the voice, which sounds regular and monotonous, making it very difficult for a listener to attend for any length of time.

As Kendon (1972) noted from his analysis, the relationship between verbal and non-verbal behaviours can be so precise that one may conclude that whatever mental processes generate the speech also generate the bodily movements:

> It seems that the speech-accompanying movement is produced along with the speech, as if the speech production process is manifested in two forms of activity simultaneously: in the vocal organs and also in bodily movement, particularly in movements of the hands and arms.

Sometimes a speaker will pause for a second or two and look away from the listener, as if gazing into space. At such times most bodily movements also cease, and the impression is that he is thinking what to say next. Such an instance occurred during a lecture on epilepsy, given by a student:

> The child will simply go vacant for up to, probably about twenty seconds, probably no more than that, and several of these could happen during the day

(speaker paused, looked upward and froze all movements for about 1½ seconds except for blinking twice) ... There will be no falling down, no convulsions, just simply the eyes just go vacant. The major convulsion is of a much more serious nature.

The streams of both verbal and non-verbal behaviour are interrupted when a speaker is searching for, or organising, the next idea. This lack of movement contrasts strongly with the experience of having the idea but not being able to find the right words to express it. This is described as having the word 'on the tip of the tongue' and during such pauses the speaker might trace out fairly small rapid circles with one hand in an impatient way, as well as showing a rather pained or frustrated facial expression.

Bodily movements, therefore, are generated by involvement with the ideas being communicated and are not consciously 'added on'. In order to convey enthusiasm for a subject we must therefore become involved with the ideas and with the need to tell others about them. It would be fatal to concentrate on the movements we are making, as this would inevitably look like 'ham' acting. If we concentrate on communicating the ideas, the movements will take care of themselves, provided we are relaxed and free to move.

To summarise: gestures, bodily movements and facial expressions may be performing a variety of functions in an enthusiastic communication. They may highlight the rhythm of the speech, add emphasis to particular words and phrases, provide visual information about shape, size and position, and sometimes convey specific meaning in place of words. The degree to which this behaviour is related to the rhythm and meaning of the speech provides the listener with an index of the extent to which the speaker is involved with communicating his ideas.

Vocal behaviour and meaning

One need only consider the numerous ways the word 'yes' can be said to recognise how vocal variations play an essential part in conveying meaning (Brazil, 1976). Without variations in timing, pitch and volume, meaning would not only often be ambiguous, but speech would also seem very dull, as if produced by a computer or a very young child when first reading aloud. The word 'monotonous' itself suggests that speech which does not vary in pitch is boring to listen to. Vocal variations are obviously not introduced at random but play a vital role in clarifying and extending the meaning of a communication, as the following brief extract from the lecture on epilepsy illustrates:

> ... and the most important thing that you must remember here is never, ever, put anything between the teeth. If you put something between their teeth you can break their jaw, or as a policeman did to a girl in the British Epilepsy Association who had a fit down Tottenham Court Road, he put his whistle between her teeth and broke three front teeth.
>
> (Robertson, 1978)

Argyle (1975) points out that a slower speed of delivery and pauses of more than one fifth of a second give emphasis, and in the passage above the words 'never, ever' are spoken at the rate of two syllables per second, with a clear pause before and after the word 'ever'. The listener is thereby primed to attend to the important information which follows. In contrast, the phrase 'in the British Epilepsy Association who had a fit down Tottenham Court Road' was spoken at a rate of approximately ten syllables per second. Argyle notes that such a rapid rate is used when conveying less important information, such as one might put in brackets when writing, and this is quite consistent with the nature of the information in the phrase above, which serves only to set the scene for the illustrative anecdote. The phrase is also spoken without much variation in pitch, and the impression given is that the speaker is dealing with an irrelevant detail to which the listener need not give much attention. Variations in volume are also evident in the passage, ranging from the emphatic 'never, ever' to a much quieter delivery for the less relevant details.

Vocal variations, therefore, give the listener extra information beyond that conveyed by the words alone. A rise in pitch at the end of an utterance can change a statement into a question; a whining intonation tells us how hard done by the speaker feels; a softer tone may signal that the speaker is attracted to the listener. Of course, a speaker may also need to produce appropriate gestures and facial expression if he is to sound convincing, although the listener may interpret the meaning of the vocal variations correctly from the voice alone.

Eye contact and speech

Kendon (1967) has demonstrated that in normal conversation a listener looks more at a speaker than vice versa. When a speaker looks away his speech becomes less fluent, and Kendon suggested that this may be because he is concentrating on organising what he is about to say; when he looks at the listener, his speech tends to be more fluent. The listener is expected to look more continuously and provide appropriate feedback. If either participant deviates from this expected behaviour particular impressions are conveyed such as anxiety or perhaps threat.

When a teacher is addressing a group of students it is important that he behaves as if he were speaking to each one, and this is achieved mainly by establishing appropriate eye contact. It may not be possible to remember to look at every student in the room, though Marland (1975) suggests that this can be achieved if one imagines the room divided into sectors and attends to a different student in each. It is important not to let one's eyes wander from person to person in a way which is unrelated to what one is saying. Worse still is the habit which some teachers acquire of looking at the back wall or out of the window when they speak (although it can sometimes be appropriate to do this as it contributes to an impression of 'thinking aloud'). If one delivers discrete sentences or phrases to individuals in the group, not only does one give the impression of speaking to them personally, but it is also possible to see whether they are understanding or concentrating on what is being said. This feedback from individuals will, in turn, affect the manner in which the teacher proceeds, just as in a dialogue each must take account of the reactions of the other. Each student should feel an active participant in a communication process, rather than merely a passive listener. It is useful to remember that you don't talk to a space as you do to a face, though presumably television presenters are trained to do just this.

A phenomenon associated with eye contact is that when a speaker is involved in communicating his ideas, even his eyeblinks are affected. Blinks tend to occur at times when they interfere least with the information being communicated, such as during pauses or between ideas, rather than at random during the speech. The previous extracts quoted from the lecture on epilepsy have demonstrated how the speaker's non-verbal behaviour was involved in the communication, and this extended to her blinking. Each blink is indicated by a vertical line.

> | and the most important thing you must remember here is never, ever, put anything between the teeth. | If you put some | thing between the teeth | you can break their jaw | or as a policeman did to a girl in the British Epilepsy Association who had a fit down Tottenham Court Road | he put his whistle between her teeth and broke th|ree front teeth. . . . | so nev|er put anything between the teeth. The other reason is that if | you don't break their jaw | you might, you just might kill them | because there'll be no air coming through | and oxygen to the brain is one of the most important things.

It would also be interesting to measure the speed of the blinks, as they seem to be very rapid during fluent speech, when eye contact is established with the listener, but slower when the speaker has paused briefly.

If a speaker is nervous or for some reason not involved with the ideas he is expressing, blinks may become more frequent and the relationship between speech and blinking no longer takes place. There is evidence to show that blink rate is associated with anxiety (Harris *et al.*, 1966) and increases may be part of the overall difficulty in looking at the listener when one is nervous. The following brief extract taken from a speaker who gave the impression of being rather tense and anxious illustrates this well. The student is describing what she intends to teach to a small group of children on her next school visit:

> Three em | girls who are between nine and te|n and they're above average in mathe|matics a|nd | about average in E|nglish so it was a bit difficult. I don'|t know quite what they're doi|ng in Maths at the moment s|o that I've decided to do | first I'm going to do some|thing on | the topic of fear | because I thought this would be interesting | to them all | and I thought if I went in | to

> sort | of some of the superstitions an|d about witchcraft and things like that
> and then they could, you know, give | a break fo|r the children abou|t um
> half|way through the morn|ing.

Not only does the speech lack fluency, but the unrelated and frequent blinking increases the disjointed effect of the communication and contributes to
the impression of the speaker being nervous.

People vary considerably in the rates at which they blink, but there is a tendency for the pattern of blinking to be affected by their attempt to establish
communication with a listener. It is easy to observe this close relationship
between speech and blinking in those who are experienced in television
appearances or acting. As with other non-verbal behaviours, it is not a conscious process but occurs naturally as the speaker becomes intent on communicating his ideas clearly.

Aspects of non-verbal self presentation communicate one's feelings and it is
this 'charismatic' quality which, to a large extent, enables a teacher almost to
conduct a class through a range of emotional states from happy or excited to
sad or serious. It is this capacity to capture students' attention in this way
which is a major basis for the teacher's authority.

Implications for teaching

This chapter has so far been concerned with the ways in which enthusiasm
and other emotions are conveyed. Communicating knowledge and skills is
important, but teaching is not simply a process of passing on information.
This could be done in a variety of other ways, but an essential role for the
teacher is to create the right attitudes in students to gain their interest and
involvement. Teaching is an affective process as well as a cognitive one and
it is essential therefore that one conveys positive attitudes not only towards
one's subject but also towards the students.

Revealing negative attitudes towards students

Regular offenders frequently complain that teachers 'pick on them' unfairly
(p. 214) and though this may be untrue in the great majority of cases, some
revealing research by Babad *et al.* (1989) suggests how students might gain
this impression. They showed that observers were able to discern differences
in teachers' behaviour depending on whether they were talking about one of
their 'good students of high potential' or 'a weak student of low potential'.
This might not seem particularly impressive except that these differences
were able to be spotted simply from viewing ten-second extracts of the
teacher's face when talking, without any sound.[1] Moreover, when these

---

[1] In fact, the differences were less apparent when the additional information of sound and
body movements were present.

teachers were filmed while teaching the children they had described, and brief video extracts shown to observers, clear differences in behaviour towards low and high expectancy students were again noted. When talking *about* their low expectancy students the teachers were judged to show more negative affect in facial expressions and more dogmatic behaviour in both verbal and non-verbal channels. When *teaching* these students their faces carried a dual message: energetic and active teaching on the one hand but negative affect and hostility on the other. The authors surmised, 'Maybe they wished to demonstrate that the low expectancy students were not so "bad" after all, pushed them harder, but were also disappointed with them'. (p. 291)

They go on to make the very important and cautionary inference that in the context of this experiment, where their actions were on view to the experimenters, '... teachers were trying to act "appropriately" or compensate these students. Nastiness, however, seems to have slipped out ... If judges could pick up these negative feelings from isolated ten-second clips when teachers might have been on their best behaviour, the accumulation of negative affective messages absorbed by low expectancy students over years of continuous interaction must be rather intense.' (p. 293)

As Rosenthal and Jacobson's original work (1968) and the abundance of subsequent research has pointed out, teachers may unwittingly influence students' self-concepts in unhelpful ways and hence compound any learning difficulties they may have. Babad's work suggests how such messages could be conveyed and by the same principle it is likely that teachers behave differently towards persistent offenders than towards those who are normally well behaved. Whereas the well-behaved student might be corrected in a positive way, perhaps suggesting, 'I'm surprised at you', a teacher could reveal signs of frustration or annoyance when correcting a persistent offender for a similar offence, thereby confirming and consolidating this identity. If this is also done publicly, the offender may try to show the other students that he or she is 'not bothered' by the teacher's attitude, perhaps with a show of bravado or by re-offending. Thus, the subtle non-verbal negative attitudes from teachers may contribute in no small measure to the process of 'labelling' described by sociologists (for example, Delamont, 1983).

It is probably inevitable that teachers will sometimes feel tired and frustrated in their work. Nevertheless, if one reacts with a sudden 'headache' (See Figure 29) when the student again fails to get the right answer after a painstaking explanation, or one ushers in the class with a mixture of boredom and resignation, any negative attitudes towards the subject or teacher will be reinforced. Perhaps with the exception of the initial few meetings with a class, a warm and relaxed greeting before the lesson begins will often make all concerned feel better.

91

Figure 29 *'When will you ever learn?'*

As one Year 10 student perceptively observed about some of her teachers:

> If they tried to enjoy it I think, if they tried to enjoy teaching us, um, everyone would be better for it because they, they're thinking, 'Oh Gawd not again!', you know. And if you ask them, 'Excuse me can you explain it again?', they think 'Oh Gawd we've got a right one 'ere' and er, they think 'Why should I enjoy it?' and er, 'I've got to do it. It's a job', and they don't enjoy it.

So we can't enjoy it either.

Expressing a lack of involvement

The quickest way to lose the students' attention is to show boredom with the topic being taught. This is a risk that all teachers run, as they are sometimes called upon to repeat the same material to several classes in the course of a year. When one is no longer freshly involved with the ideas being expressed, one's non-verbal behaviour does not enhance the meaning and may even detract from it. It is common to see a speaker fidgeting with an object, and so attention is drawn to that behaviour and away from what is being said. The speaker is, unfortunately, demonstrating that he is insufficiently involved with communicating his ideas, because the bodily movements he makes bear no relation to the rhythm or meaning of his speech. This lack of involvement can also be manifested by a reduction in the variety of non-verbal behaviours so that speech becomes monotonous and the body and face less animated. While the speaker appears otherwise relaxed and fluent, he is perceived as being uninterested in what he is saying, and this feeling is rapidly passed on to the listeners.

The words we choose can also unintentionally reveal unhelpful attitudes. When the teacher begins, 'Now, it's a short lesson, so . . .' (p. 130), this suggests she does not regard it as a proper lesson and what follows confirms this impression. It is never advisable to devalue what one is about to teach and introductions such as 'I had hoped to show you some beautiful slides of the festival but . . .', or 'Now I know this is very boring, but we've got to cover this topic', will do little to get the students involved. It may be that a teacher has a genuine dislike for the material, and some would argue that it is quite legitimate to express this but surely it is better to present the subject to the best of one's ability and let the students decide whether it has any intrinsic merit.

Any circumstances which cause a speaker to be tense or anxious can also create a disjunction between non-verbal behaviour and speech. One's thoughts can be preoccupied by the stressful situation, and consequently the body tends to express this, rather than further the meaning of the speech. Tension also reduces the variation in non-verbal behaviour but, in addition, may produce signs of withdrawal if the speaker is anxious. It is interesting that Mehrabian found that when a speaker was not telling the truth he looked less at the listener, used less gestural and bodily movement, talked less and smiled more. The significance of smiling in stressful situations has already been discussed (see p. 34), and these other behaviours would seem to be a product of the anxiety or unease experienced by the speaker.

A nervous speaker may avoid eye contact with his listeners, speak with more hesitation and fidget nervously. This is immediately perceived by the listeners, who may feel uneasy or embarrassed in sympathy. A more common reaction from students is to challenge the teacher's authority and thereby increase his anxiety. In order to reduce anxiety it is important to do everything possible to make the lesson run smoothly, particularly with new classes. Insufficient or inadequate preparation can induce stress, and this may distract one's attention from the subject being taught. The teacher may, for example, be worried that there will not be sufficient material for the whole period, or that gaps in his knowledge will be revealed. His body is likely to display this anxiety rather than enhance any ideas he is expressing, and the students will soon lose interest. An experienced teacher can cover up or even exploit his lack of knowledge, but it is far easier and safer if one is familiar with the information and has planned its presentation carefully.

The situation itself can be another source of stress. Meeting a new class which has a reputation for being troublesome and unruly can inhibit one's performance. Anxiety should be concealed, and the sooner one can appear relaxed and enthusiastic, the more likely it is that the group will attend. One can promote these conditions by consciously doing a number of things. Positions in the room where one cannot see or be seen by all the students should be avoided. Talking to a class while seated at a table or behind a desk inhibits and obscures one's bodily movements, so it is better to stand in such a way that one is free to move. Establishing immediate eye contact with the listeners in a relaxed way also promotes effective interpersonal communication. Avoiding eye contact, adopting tense and static postures, holding on to furniture, fidgeting and other self-effacing behaviours all indicate one's anxiety and detract from any message being conveyed. This makes a difficult situation even worse as some students will feel encouraged to challenge one's declining authority. The rest will just be bored.

When non-verbal behaviour is not reinforcing meaning, therefore, it communicates instead the speaker's lack of involvement. Rather than being the message about the message, it becomes the message about the messenger.

Creating a serious atmosphere

Two dogs about to fight adopt rigid and alert postures. Cats stare at each other, motionless except for the slow movements of their tails. This extreme alertness is characteristic of many animals in aggressive confrontations and can also be observed in human beings. The behaviour is obviously very functional, as each must be prepared for an attack and this demands mutual vigilance.

In contrast to the relaxed and synchronised movements which accompany speech in an enthusiastic communication, speaking without bodily movements while steadily maintaining eye contact with the listener has overtones of aggressive threat. If the speech is also controlled and deliberate, the tension is increased. The dangers of showing signs of aggression have already been discussed but it is sometimes necessary to create a serious atmosphere and once the class are attending this can be achieved by speaking in such a way, without bodily movements. Heavy silences in extended pauses can create quite dramatic effects which every student senses. One student recounted how she was reprimanding her class with little success as they did not appear unduly concerned. She became aware that she was rubbing her left arm with her right hand as she spoke, and was therefore probably communicating her own insecurity. Moving to a more prominent position in the room, she continued speaking in a measured way but without moving her head or body and was surprised to find the class became very attentive.

One must beware of 'going over the top' by scowling and approaching to within inches of the victim's nose, because the credibility of such behaviour depends on one's capacity to follow up with an actual physical attack in the event of a continued challenge. This would hardly be appropriate even if one were fairly certain of winning. The object is to create an air of seriousness, so that one's words are heeded, rather than to invite a confrontation. In this respect it is safer to direct such behaviour towards a large group, rather than an individual.

Reading aloud

Teachers are often called upon to read aloud to the class, perhaps from a textbook or a student's written work. This calls for special skills, because reading aloud imposes a number of limitations on one's capacity to sustain a listener's attention. First of all, it is difficult to establish visual contact with individuals without considerable practice in reading ahead, and even then one must remember to leave a finger marking the place to which one's eyes must return. The best compromise many teachers can hope for is an occasional quick glance round to check that no-one has quietly nodded off to sleep.

Another limitation is that one's movements are greatly restricted. If one hand is left free to gesture, it is not then available to mark the place on the page. Any movement of the head or hands can cause one to lose the place and interrupt the flow of the reading. Much of one's gaze is necessarily directed at the book, and one may therefore feel inhibited about displaying appropriate facial expressions for fear of looking bizarre: it is very difficult to sound convincingly happy, surprised or angry without producing the corresponding facial expression.

The major limitation imposed on the reader, however, is that he is not generating the thoughts and ideas he is expressing, but is merely reproducing words from a page. Any vocal variations must therefore be added as a conscious act, in order to clarify and extend the meaning. They are not spontaneously generated, so that one must read ahead to decide the author's intentions and how best to convey these to the listener. The major burden of clarifying meaning rests with vocal variations because gestures, facial expressions and eye contact are greatly reduced. Considerable practice is required to sustain the listener's attention, particularly if the text is uninspiring. When reading from a book it is often advisable to put a difficult story or explanation into one's own words either in place of, or in addition to, the text. This not only simplifies the language but also allows one to enhance the meaning with spontaneous non-verbal behaviour.

Children are themselves called upon to read aloud to the class and may do so in a 'flat' and uninteresting way, or give a repetitive and inappropriate variation on every sentence. Apart from giving them practice, and checking that they are able to read the words, reading aloud would seem to be better left to the teacher.

It is, of course, easier to supervise the class if a student is reading but, if the reading is dull and uninteresting, supervision will be all the more necessary.

Responsiveness and persuasion

Establishing eye contact with the listeners in a relaxed way not only contributes to an impression of being confident but also allows one to search for the reactions to one's teaching. Mehrabian found that there was an association between the apparent responsiveness of a speaker and the extent that he was seen as being persuasive: 'During persuasion, increased responsiveness to the listener is only natural since he is the primary focus of one's attention; however, it is interesting, too, that increased responsiveness also contributed to the perceived persuasive quality of a message.'

Enthusiastic teaching must use persuasion, and Mehrabian's work implies that if a teacher is searching for students' reactions, not only will he appear more responsive but the enthusiastic quality of the delivery is likely to be enhanced. It is notable that this readiness to respond to students' relevant and appropriate reactions contrasts with the apparent lack of responsiveness needed to create conditions in which that teaching can proceed (see p. 36).

Associated with the notion of responsiveness is the teacher's sensitivity to the involvement of the group. Prior to the recording or broadcasting of a television show there is often an attempt to 'warm up' the studio audience so that they become more responsive, which in turn allows the performers to be more informal. A similar phenomenon occurs at parties where it may take some time (and alcohol) before people can relate to one another in a relaxed manner. It may also take time for a group to empathise with the mood of a speaker. Highly animated behaviour may enhance communication between two friends who are sharing the same mood or involvement with a subject, but it would seem totally incongruous from a person one had just met. In the same way a teacher who attempted to be very enthusiastic in the first moments of a lesson with new students would run the risk of drawing attention to his own behaviour, rather than to the information being conveyed. If one's involvement develops naturally in the course of introducing a topic it is more likely to be shared by the group.

Providing examples

Wherever possible one should provide relevant first-hand experiences as there is little point in, say, extolling the qualities of a piece of music without letting the students hear it. When I have the opportunity to teach the topic of 'Sustaining Attention', video-taped illustrations are essential if the group is to appreciate fully the points being made. Telling people about non-verbal behaviour is not enough, because when they later see an interesting speaker the great majority still fail to notice the way bodily movements relate to speech rhythms and meaning. It is necessary to take particular phrases and draw attention to the accompanying non-verbal behaviour in order to ensure that everyone understands. There is always an air of surprise as people first notice the relationship, even though they have already been told about it. Until they have the experience there is no real understanding. Only if this chapter has been read together with an attempt to observe the behaviours described will the reader be likely to appreciate the full significance of non-verbal behaviour in interpersonal communication.

Activity 7 Expressive Teaching

1. *This is an exercise in communicating information and instructions without the use of language, using only vocal variation and other non-verbal behaviour such as gesture and facial expressions. It is particularly relevant for teachers of modern languages who are encouraged to teach and even correct behaviour in the target language, which means that the students may not understand what is being said.*

    The task is to teach the group the numbers 1 to 6 (you can devise more if you wish) in a new language. The numbers are:

1.	'VELO'	4.	'FODOR'
2.	'TUN'	5.	'VANIS'
3.	'FET'	6.	'REX'

    You must teach these numbers to the group without saying anything but the words 'Bread and Butter' or any other similar phrase, such as 'Fish and Chips'. You may say only one of the words, for example, 'Bread' or 'Butter' if you wish, or the complete phrase, but in the course of your teaching:

    - *get individuals and sometimes the whole group to repeat a number or sequence of numbers;*
    - *ask individuals to stand to give answers;*
    - *if individuals or the group respond quietly, get them to repeat it louder (for example, holding a hand to one's ear would indicate 'Can't hear you');*
    - *praise individuals or the group for their efforts, showing surprise and pleasure;*
    - *correct any behaviour you think is inappropriate, such as inattention, talking or writing, showing an appropriate serious mood.*

    The group is free to speak in their native language and ask you questions. They do not speak 'Bread and Butter'.

    You may use the blackboard or cards to show the number and its name if you wish.

2. *Using only all or part of the phrase 'Fish and Chips' as many times as you wish, try to convey the following emotional meanings to your partner. Give*

them the number of your message and ask them to write down what they
have understood for each one. If they wish you to repeat the message, do so.
When you have completed all four, compare your partner's received
messages with the meaning you intended to convey.

(i)   ADMIRING/APPRECIATING. (This is an excellent piece of work. It's far
      better than I could do! I wish I could have done it!)

(ii) DETACHED/DISINTERESTED. (You have to do this exercise. I know it's
      boring but it's got to be done.)

(iii) SERIOUS/CONCERNED. (You must realise this is very serious. What
      you are doing could affect your whole future.)

(iv) EXCITED/ENTHUSIASTIC. (This is really important! I want you to listen
      to this. I find it really exciting and I know you will.)

Effective questioning

A great deal of teaching involves asking students questions and the ability to
do this effectively with groups and sometimes whole classes will have beneficial effects on both their behaviour and learning. The ability to ask appropriate challenging questions is a function of the teacher's knowledge of the
subject and it is not surprising that there are moves towards more specialist
teaching in primary schools in key subjects such as mathematics and science
lessons (Richards, 1994).

It is generally agreed that the main functions of questioning are:

● to express the teacher's status;
● to create interest, motivation and improve understanding;
● to keep students alert and accountable;
● to provide diagnostic information for both teacher and student.

Questioning and status

It is immediately evident that teaching differs from other occupational and
social contexts as teachers almost invariably already know the answers to
the questions they ask, and consequently this is an expression of the status
associated with their role (see p. 56). When students do not attempt to
answer appropriately they challenge that claim: when they do, they validate
it. The way questions are asked and answers are responded to can reveal the
motive behind asking the question and therefore has implications on the
nature of the relationship being claimed. For example, if we take the question 'How do we know that cream is lighter than milk?', the underlying
intention of the question could be revealed in the intonation and facial
expressions of the questioner. It could be a test, for example, 'You ought to
know', or a check on learning, 'Do you know?', both of which would imply

that the answer is already known, or it could be that the questioner really is seeking the information from someone who knows, i.e. 'Please tell me', which suggests a student's question to a teacher or child to a parent. However, where the problem is apparently *shared*, that is both are seeking the answer, the intonation would convey, '*How* do we know?', which therefore implies a more equal relationship.

We can also discern these differences in the way the response is given to the answer, so if the reply had been 'Because cream always floats on the surface of the milk', the responses, 'Quite right' or 'Well done' would express higher status, whereas a thoughtful, 'Oh yes, I understand' would be consistent with a subordinate reply. If the relationship were more equal, the reply would probably express *agreement* as if the questioner had considered the answer, implying, 'Yes, I see what you mean'. It follows that if teachers wish to elevate the status of their students, to improve their self-esteem, and make them feel they are making a useful contribution, they should ask questions and respond to answers in a manner that suggests mutual enquiry rather than testing and checking, even though they already know the answers.

Questioning and motivation

Before you sow the seed, prepare the ground

When we ask questions as if they are tests, the motivation which arises in the student is to get the *right* answer and there is likely to be some stress induced if this is not known. However, if it is asked in a way which suggests we are genuinely interested in the answer itself, or *whether* the student knows it, they are more likely to become involved and feel that their answer will be given consideration. A pitfall for the teacher who has become over-familiar with a particular subject is to treat students' answers in an automatic, matter-of-fact manner. The reply may be predictable and expected by the teacher but for the student it may be a new discovery or the result of some effort to attend. It is therefore important to show pleasure or surprise, or at least to nod approval so that the student's contribution is seen to be valued. Even if the answer is incorrect it is better not simply to dismiss it but to find some aspect which is of interest or to suggest why such an error might easily be made.

When students give speculative answers it may be preferable not to reveal whether they are right or wrong. Once the right answer is established, the class are no longer motivated to find out for themselves, and if incorrect answers are ruled out they can use the strategy of guessing to get the right answer by the process of elimination, but without any real understanding. I once heard a Year 9 boy in a small special needs group describing a car racing round a corner and he gestured with his hand to describe its movement. I could have taken this opportunity to give a short lecture on the physics of motion but instead I asked each of them what happened to the wheels when a car raced round a corner. They all agreed that two wheels would lift off but disagreed about which two these would be. They looked expectantly at me to provide the right answer but instead I acted as devil's advocate. This can encourage students to reflect on their understanding and become more involved in the problem. To those who thought the wheels nearer the kerb would lift I asked whether they had seen a motorcycle going round a corner. Everyone knew that it inclined towards the bend so surely a car ought to behave in a similar way with the off-side wheels lifting? This delighted those who had chosen that possibility so I asked them to imagine themselves as passengers in a car which suddenly swerved round a bend and to think which way they would be thrown. After some discussion they agreed they would be thrown away from the bend so why did this not also happen to the car and hence the near-side wheels lift? This prompted considerable argument, each side trying to account for these anomalies. Having publicly committed themselves to a particular view, they either had to change their minds or defend their positions and hence examine the problem in greater detail. In Piaget's terms, the incongruities had produced a state of disequilibrium which they needed to resolve. At the point where the teacher provides the answer the motivation ceases, and it is far more satisfying if one can find the answer for oneself, as this group did by the next session. In case some readers are unsure of the solution I shall leave it open in the hope that they experience some of the frustration which prompted the students to find out!

With a larger group it would have been much more difficult to get such a discussion underway and to keep everyone involved. Techniques such as redirecting a student's question by asking if anyone else can give an answer or checking whether everyone is following by calling on those who are not volunteering their views can be helpful but, nevertheless, the problems of quiet, reluctant or lengthy replies can still arise and the pace of the lesson will be lost.

Different subjects impose different constraints on the type of questions which can be asked (Barnes, 1969). For example, in subjects such as the sciences or English one can often ask for analysis or speculation from students whereas other subjects, such as modern languages, have a very strong factual content and do not easily lend themselves to this form of question (Brown and Edmondson, 1984).

Questions which require thought and extended contributions from students are very valuable in promoting conceptual development and motivation but are perhaps better left to small group discussions or well-disciplined classes.

Keeping the group alert and accountable

Thought provoking, or 'open' questions, as opposed to 'closed' questions which require specific answers, can increase students' involvement and hence can be a positive feature of good classroom management. However, it may first be necessary to have co-operative and responsive attitudes before such questioning can take place. It is frequently assumed that open questions promote more responsiveness from students and many studies have shown such a correlation. However, Hargreaves (1984) in a series of careful observations of two classes taught by the same teacher, showed that it was the greater responsiveness of one class, in particular a small group of students, which probably *allowed* the teacher to ask more open questions than in the other class. It is not simply that open questions *cause* greater responsiveness, it may first be necessary to have conditions in which open questions may be asked.

Hargreaves went on to speculate on the risks involved in asking open questions.

> My own ethnographic observations suggest that open questions can pose management problems for the teacher, since they authorize pupils to indulge in long and sometimes irrelevant answers, which leaves the teacher with the unpleasant task of cutting off the speaker in mid-flight as well as the task of restoring relevance. Moreover, the long answer is not always audible to, or comprehensible by, other pupils, and this then requires the teacher to repeat or explain a pupil's contribution. Long pupil answers sometimes lead the rest of the class to become bored or distracted and the teacher has to develop strategies to cope with such routine troubles.

To avoid such problems it might be preferable to split up large groups for discussions though the teacher then has the problem of seeing that each group keeps to the task set. Closed questions which require short factual answers, if handled well and distributed widely among the students, can help maintain the momentum of a lesson. Such questions can rapidly test them on what they know and are therefore an incentive for them to attend to the teacher. Experienced teachers frequently use a 'Guess what I'm thinking' approach as this next extract of some very successful class teaching illustrates.

Teacher: All that falls as *precipitation* ... Good word that ... (1) Why do I use it instead of rainfall? *(Teacher waits for two seconds but as a reply is not immediately forthcoming he goes on to explain)* I'm covering myself really because, although it's rainfall now, if I was talking to you ... in the middle of January it might well be (2) *(nods with brow raised towards student)* ...

Student: Snowfall.

Teacher: Snowfall, and then we would have to say rainfall or snowfall. Precipitation. All that falls will eventually get into the rivers, therefore, all that falls will eventually (3) *(rising intonation and pointing to a diagram on the board. Points to one student with other hand and uses brow raise)*

Student: Reach the sea

Teacher: Reach the sea ... *(Smiling)* Nearly all of it ... because sometimes, we use up some of it … The plants use up some of it …

And a few minutes later

> *Teacher:* … If you grease the wheels and make it run, what are you overcoming? … What is the thing that's holding you … slowing you all the time even though you're going to get there? (4) *(Student has put his hand up while the teacher is speaking. Teacher with brow raise, points to him)*
> *Student:* Friction
> *Teacher:* Friction!

and later

> *Teacher:* … and when the river is flowing over the surface of the land *(gestures one hand moving over the other)* … in the river's bed, there is *friction* … And what is the river *doing* because of that friction? It is (5) *(rising intonation, brow raise and pointing towards student)*
> *Student:* Getting bigger.
> *Teacher:* Pardon?
> *Student:* Getting bigger.
> *Teacher:* Well, the river's getting bigger because there's more and more rain coming into it, but as it **runs, through, its, bed,** *(emphasised with one hand running over the other)*, what's it doing to the bed? (6) because the bed is holding it back, there's friction *(one boy has his hand up and the teacher points excitedly towards him, again with brow raise)* **Go on!**
> *Student:* It's wearing it out.
> *Teacher:* It's *wearing* it … That's why … *(slowly)* a river is capable of work and it is capable of making a mark on the land's surface … and when you go to find a river it's always flowing in a (7) *(rising intonation, gesturing a 'V' shape with both hands and looking at student expectantly)*
> *Student:* Valley.
> *Teacher:* A valley …

On some occasions the question is only implied by the teacher's intonation and brow raise, inviting particular students to 'fill in' the next word (2) (3) (7). This invites participation, keeping the students alert, and checks whether they are closely following the teacher's line of reasoning in exactly the same way as a written cloze procedure tests the students' understanding. When the correct reply is given the teacher repeats it and continues with the explanation. On one occasion (5) the teacher frames the question and begins the sentence but the answer 'Getting bigger' is not what he requires. He does not dismiss this but realises that his question needs to specify the river bed to reveal his train of thought, (6).

In a similar way, when the answer is not immediately forthcoming, (1), the teacher uses a 'train of thought' question to clarify the concept of 'precipitation'.

A direct factual question is asked (4) and it is one which the teacher probably anticipates will be easily answered so that the explanation can continue. Though there was no verbal praise from the teacher, the repetition of the correct answer and the teacher's obvious satisfaction and sometimes excitement must have been very rewarding for the students.

Short closed questions can therefore keep students alert and accountable, and if used skilfully may also help students to follow closely a teacher's train of thought, serving to check if they are still on the same track. However if one's train of thought is obscure and one's questions are poorly phrased it is extremely difficult for students to supply the required 'linking' answers. This can lead to teachers not accepting some correct answers or in continual rephrasing of the question in an attempt to elicit a specific answer as in the following extract from a revision lesson on triangles with a Year 7 class.

Teacher: Triangles all have straight sides. Yes, now um ... can you define them or tell me what they are in full? What sort of shapes are they? ... What's the full description? ... What sort of shapes? ... Now, we've established so far that they have three straight sides, but what are they really? ... What are they? ... What's the real description?

Student: Polygons.

Teacher: Yes they are polygons but I don't want to go into that for a moment. They're special polygons and we can use a special name for them can't we, because they are ... particular sort of polygons ... Now I don't want to tell you what they are ... Remember when we went ... when ... when we did it before ... um ... I pointed out to you the difference between a certain part of the triangles, and the triangle itself. ... Well now, I'll just give you a tiny bit of help. These are triangles. Right? *(Points to five cut-out triangles on the board.)* They are bounded or surrounded by three straight sides. That's important. ... They are straight sides. Not any old sides. But what are they really? John?

Student: Quadrilaterals.

Teacher: Oh steady now, steady ...

The students in that lesson were surprisingly well behaved and eventually provided the required answer, which you may not have guessed was 'plane areas'. If this teacher had been faced with a difficult class, however, such repeated re-phrasing and rigid attitude towards answers would have had a disastrous effect on their attention, dramatically slowing down the momentum of the lesson.

Questioning to provide diagnostic information

Just as a doctor will use particular instruments to examine more closely the integrity of a patient's organs and physiological systems, so questions can be used by teachers to probe the integrity of the concepts which are beginning to form in students' minds. We can observe what they do and say, but what do they think they are doing and what do they understand by what they say?

A bizarre question can reveal how certain a student is of concepts they are apparently using with understanding. One Year 6 girl had carefully drawn a number of different rectangular shapes on graph paper, all with the same area, covering 16 squares. Under each, she had written the area, '16 square cm.' and then the perimeter of the shape, for example, '20 cm'. One might deduce from this that the girl was clear in her mind about the distinction between the linear units and the square units but previous experience warned me that students often write in 'square' centimetres without under-standing that it is a very different, though related, measurement than cen-timetres alone. When I asked her, using her 8 cm $\times$ 2 cm rectangle, 'Is the perimeter (20 cm) bigger than the area or is the area bigger than the perime-ter?', she thought the perimeter was bigger, still being uncertain that they could not be compared. I therefore asked her height and weight and then whether she was heavier than she was tall, or taller than she was heavy, which she knew was a silly question. Had she been equally clear about length and area she would not have tried to answer the question.

Straightforward questions can also be used to check that students under-stand what they are doing. I observed a group of eight-to-nine-year-olds mul-tiply with the aid of apparatus. The problem was to multiply 34 by 6 and each child had correctly set out the problem and calculated the right answer thus:

$$34 \times$$
$$\underline{6}$$
$$24 \ (6 \text{ sets of } 4)$$
$$\underline{180} \ (6 \text{ sets of } 30)$$
$$\underline{204}$$

It therefore appeared as if they understood the process as they had meticu-lously used their blocks on a card divided into units, tens and hundreds. However, constructing six piles of four blocks, counting them, converting them to 'ten' blocks and so on is a lengthy process during which one can lose sight of the problem. Everyone could show me the answer but when I asked what were six sets of thirty four, or even six times thirty-four, nobody could tell me. It was evident that the apparatus had been used just as mechanically and mindlessly as algorithms sometimes are. Children fre-quently operate mechanically with little thought for the processes which underlie their actions and appropriate questions can reveal this lack of understanding.

In summary, the use of questions which require thought and extended con-tributions from students are helpful in promoting motivation and conceptual development but may give rise to management problems in large groups. In these contexts short, closed questions can be useful to check understanding and, if handled with pace and widely directed, can help to keep the group alert and accountable. Students should always be made to feel that their con-tributions are acceptable and, if appropriate, valuable.

5 Understanding Unwanted Behaviour

If we can understand the reasons why students misbehave we will be better able to create conditions in which there is less need or fewer opportunities for such behaviour. In the main, the reasons for unwanted behaviour are very straightforward. The child is not disturbed or showing symptoms of adverse home circumstances, nor is there some ulterior motive, conscious or unconscious, underlying his behaviour. He talks because he has something he wants to tell a friend at that moment; he runs in the corridor because he is in a hurry; he does something silly because it seems a good idea at the time and may relieve the boredom of a long day confined in the classroom. In such cases, if the teacher happens to notice the child and takes some decisive action to stop the behaviour, the child responds favourably. This compliance, though delayed, reflects and restates the authority relationship. However, there are some children who receive frequent reprimands and sanctions yet still persist in unwanted behaviour and thereby bring the authority of the teacher into question.

With more persistent unwanted behaviour it can be helpful, though time consuming, to record disruptive incidents in some detail. If one particular student is the subject of a number of incidents with various teachers, then a much clearer picture can be built up of his behaviour during the day. Is he tending to avoid work, disrupt others or disobey teachers? Yes, will come the cynical reply from hardened campaigners, but a closer look at a student's behaviour may reveal some underlying pattern. Pik (1981) suggested a number of questions which might help in this respect.

- Does the pupil tend to have more confrontations with male or female staff?
- Are there more confrontations with junior staff and, if so, does the pupil's timetable show a large number of lessons with junior staff?
- Do there appear to be more confrontations during the more formal lessons or during the more 'free ranging' lessons such as art, PE and home economics, in which movement around the room, gym or kitchen is essential?
- Does the class size appear to be a significant factor?
- Is there a small group of his peers who might be providing a suitably provocative audience for the pupil in several of the classes during which confrontations take place?
- Is there a pattern of failure or difficulty with certain subjects which might be a contributing factor to confrontations during these lessons? (Often signified by the days of the week on which the pupil poses difficulties or is absent from school.)

- With which teacher(s) does the pupil get on particularly well in and out of the classroom? (This person, even if he or she doesn't actually teach the child could be useful in a counselling role.)

It can be revealing to find out if unwanted behaviour is more likely to occur at particular times or places or with particular teachers. Badger (1992) found that in one comprehensive school Monday was the day most prone to disruption and the last period in the afternoon was sixty per cent more likely to produce disruptive behaviour than the first three morning periods. Only five students in a population of 1,200 accounted for eleven per cent of the referrals to the 'quiet room' and five staff made thirty per cent of all referrals. Clearly, the more information one has on the nature and frequency of unwanted behaviour, the more efficiently one can target one's attempt to lessen it.

This chapter will look at three approaches to understanding why students misbehave and what action might therefore be appropriate to deal with it.

Misbehaviour can be explained in terms of

- the *cause* of the behaviour, i.e. why do particular students choose to misbehave?
- the *motive* or *goal* of the behaviour, i.e. what might students be trying to achieve by misbehaving?
- the *contexts* which offer opportunities for misbehaviour.

Causes of unwanted behaviour

The association between inadequate or distorted early care of children and subsequent behaviour problems was highlighted by Bowlby's work in the mid-1950s on maternal deprivation. This prompted a great deal of research into the effects of separation and loss in a child's early experience, and the emphasis has now shifted away from the mother to the importance of a continuous and warm relationship with a mother figure. The effects of grossly distorted care, such as for children brought up in some institutions, were very pronounced and sometimes irreversible, and these children frequently had difficulty in establishing and sustaining relationships and suffered from lowered general ability. It now seems that these effects were due not only to the absence of warm continuous care with a mother figure, but also to insufficient sensory and intellectual stimulation. Today, children seldom suffer such extremes of privation, but there is little doubt that many are subject to distorted or inadequate care throughout childhood, due to a variety of family and economic difficulties. For example, one report (DES, 1978) noted that, in a first-year intake of one inner-city secondary school, the head of the family was unemployed in forty-four per cent of the cases, and thirty-four per cent had a mother or father suffering from chronic illness. Rutter *et al.*

(1979), summarising the comparative study of children in an inner London borough and children on the Isle of Wight, concluded:

> Family discord and disharmony, parental mental disorder, criminality in the parents, large family size and overcrowding in the home, admission of the child into care of the local authority and low occupational status were all associated with emotional or behavioural disturbance and/or reading retardation. As with previous studies there was ample evidence of the immense importance of family circumstances and family relationships in shaping children's development.

Adverse social and economic factors have long been associated with educational disadvantage and there is no reason to believe that matters have improved since that report.

The importance of environmental factors has, to a large extent, overshadowed the possibility that some children might be predisposed, genetically or congenitally, to experience learning and behaviour problems. Low general ability is, of course, a major factor in school failure, but specific learning difficulties may also affect a child's progress. The influence of inherent factors on certain types of reading problems has long been recognised and it may be that other subjects such as mathematics require specific abilities.

School failure and behaviour problems are strongly associated, but there is also evidence to suggest that some children may be more liable to develop behaviour problems due to temperamental factors. Thomas Chess and Birch (1968) showed that the clinical cases in their longitudinal study were, as a group, 'characterised by an excessive frequency of either high or low activity, irregularity, withdrawal responses to novel stimuli, non-adaptability, high intensity, persistence and distractability'. They stressed the interaction of these traits with each other, and with environmental factors, as being crucial to the development of behaviour disorders.

Similarly, Mednick *et al.* (1987) found that the criminal records of adopted children showed a greater association with the records of their biological parents than the records of their adoptive parents, implying an inherited factor in the susceptibility to commit crime. However, it is not possible to *predict* with certainty whether any particular child will develop behaviour problems, let alone the nature of those problems. Perhaps the unknown factor of inherited qualities determines how each child will interact with his environment, and the extent to which he can tolerate extremes of experience.

One of the comments I received from a teacher drew attention to a cycle of deprivation in which many children seem trapped:

> The boy has a number of problems in the home known to many staff. Attendance is infrequent and motivation is poor. Consequently his achievements are low and this does little to improve his motivation. His misbehaviour

is an attempt to seek attention from the teacher and other pupils, to break the tedium.

It is obviously crucial to bear these circumstances in mind when consideration is being given to offering special educational help, removing a child into care or suggesting residential schooling, but knowledge of them gives little practical guidance to the teacher on how to cope with the behaviour in the most effective way.

It is not within most teachers' power to compensate for very adverse home circumstances, even if they are eager to help. In primary schools, where there is prolonged contact with the same group of children, it is difficult to attend to one child for any length of time in a large class. In secondary schools, teachers have limited contact with whole classes, let alone individual students. Even when parents are apparently contributing to their child's problems, they are sometimes incapable of changing the situation because of emotional and economic problems. I saw one eight-year-old boy who had been referred for persistent stealing in school and at home. He could not be left for a minute in reach of anyone's property, and had even entered a neighbour's house and stolen jewellery. Hoarding food and stealing in young children can sometimes be a symptom of early lack of affection, and it seemed likely that this might be a significant feature in the boy's behaviour. His mother said that she had never been able to show her son any physical affection, because she could not bear to be touched by anyone. She did not even feel able to put her arm around him. At such a late stage, some children find great difficulty anyway in accepting affection, so whether or not this would have helped was by then probably purely academic.

What, then, can teachers do when faced with students who suffer from adverse home circumstances? Clearly they will try to help by giving as much time and personal attention as possible. It is unlikely, though, that one will be able to bring about a lasting change in attitude in a deviant student by concerning oneself with his problems at the expense of actually teaching him. We may be aware that the father is in prison and the mother has no time for the child, and our hope is that, by understanding his problems and developing a relationship with him, he may feel less inclined to misbehave and will improve his attitude to work. But if we fail to teach him anything, he will have yet another problem. If we are to earn a child's respect or thanks, or if a relationship is to develop, it will probably be more as a result of our having taught him something. In this respect teaching is caring.

Children, like some adults, sometimes take advantage of their disabilities. I remember one boy who was short-sighted and who certainly did have a problem which could affect his progress, but the teacher suggested he used this as an excuse for doing very little work. I came across a similar instance when supervising a student on teaching practice. The Year 7 class had been set to work on a piece of creative writing, but one boy was spending most of his time looking out of the window at a nearby football match. I picked up his exercise book and pointed out that he had written twenty words in as many minutes, and that eight of those were incorrectly spelt. 'Ah yes, sir,' he announced, 'That's my problem.' Someone had probably mentioned that he had a spelling problem and, as far as he was concerned, this was his passport to educational immunity. What he did not realise, or chose to ignore, was that *greater* effort is called for from those who suffer the disadvantages of a disability.

In many cases a child obviously suffers from an educational or social disadvantage, but there is a danger that he will regard his problems as inevitable and insurmountable. Teachers must always encourage children to take responsibility for their own development, rather than regard themselves as passive victims of circumstance. We have, perhaps, been encouraged to regard a child's psychological integrity as far more fragile than it really is.

A causal approach should, therefore, take into account factors like previous experience, intelligence, personality characteristics and physical condition in attempting to explain why certain children persistently misbehave. This information can enable teachers to provide appropriate work and remedial help, which could have an indirect effect on the child's conduct.

More immediate experience can also affect children's behaviour. A bout of untypical misbehaviour, or a decline in the standard of work, might well be symptoms of some temporary trauma or set-back in the home or with friends. A child obviously needs support and understanding at a time of crisis, and teachers should be sensitive to sudden changes of work and behaviour as these might be the only indications that something is wrong.

Disagreements also arise between students in school which necessitate the teacher's intervention but these are rather different from the unwanted behaviour discussed so far. They occur fairly frequently and can sometimes impose a great deal of stress, particularly for those students who are the objects of bullying. It is probably better that students as well as teachers should take responsibility for keeping the peace, as arguments and fights usually take place well out of sight of the staff.

To summarise, therefore, a knowledge of relevant factors in a child's background can contribute to an understanding of the problems faced by the child. Such knowledge, however, does not necessarily leave one any wiser about treatment. In fact a sympathetic teacher may unwittingly confirm to a child his inadequacies by too readily accepting lower standards of work and behaviour so that his problems are compounded. Similarly an unsympathetic and coercive regime may further alienate the student. The question that must be addressed is 'In what ways can schools help to overcome the various disadvantages suffered by some children?' As Galloway *et al.* (1982) noted:

> We are not saying that disadvantaged homes and delinquent neighbourhoods have no effect on pupils' behaviour at school. That would be absurd. We *are* saying that our own research confirms the evidence of other research teams in emphasising the school's own influence over its pupils' behaviour.

It might be more fruitful, in terms of suggesting measures which teachers might take to help children, to examine the possible ways in which unwanted behaviour may unwittingly be reinforced in schools.

The motives behind unwanted behaviour

If we can find out why students engage in unwanted behaviour we may be able to avoid responding in ways which satisfy their motives and consequently reinforce the behaviour. Solomon (1964) pointed out that punishment can be very effective in helping children control impulses provided they have an alternative way of getting what they want. In the same way that a rat which receives an electric shock when choosing one pathway to food will readily travel a safer route if it is available, so children will behave in more acceptable ways if they can secure the same goal by so doing. If they continue on the 'unsafe' route, experiencing the consequences of their actions, it suggests that our reaction, instead of acting as a deterrent, may be encouraging their behaviour.

Dreikurs *et al.* (1982) offered teachers some excellent advice on how to recognise what they suggest are the more common motives underlying young children's difficult behaviour and how to respond appropriately to it. The authors are guided by the model of human behaviour developed by the psychologist Alfred Adler who believed that all our actions are purposive, that is they are directed towards particular goals. Human beings, he believed, are social animals with the overriding goal of belonging or finding a place in society and much of what we do is aimed at creating and maintaining our own particular social identity. However, children may develop what Dreikurs describes as 'mistaken goals'.

> The child who misbehaves has lost his belief that he can find the belonging and recognition that he desires and erroneously believes he will find acceptance through provocative behaviour by pursuing the mistaken goals of behaviour.

Whether or not one accepts this explanation for children's misbehaviour, the four goals themselves will be familiar to teachers as they are:

- to gain undue attention;
- to seek power;
- to seek revenge or get even;
- to display inadequacy (real or assumed).

Though these goals are particularly evident in children under eleven years of age they may also explain much of older students' anti-social behaviour but the problem for teachers is to identify correctly what they are consciously or unconsciously trying to achieve by their actions. This is not straightforward because they may be misbehaving in various ways to achieve the same goal, or particular behaviour may be aimed at achieving two or more goals. For instance, if we consider the incident with Mark (see p. 160), standing up and playing with the orange was probably attention seeking, 'notice me' behaviour, but his refusal then to sit down was seeking power.

If teachers can correctly discern what students are trying to achieve it may be possible to help them understand why they behave as they do as they may be unaware themselves of their mistaken goal (see p. 204). Teachers can also avoid unwittingly encouraging the behaviour and provide opportunities for them to achieve the same goals in acceptable ways.

The two most reliable indicators for recognising the goal to which the behaviour is directed are:

- the teacher's immediate reaction to the child's provocation, that is the feelings experienced when confronted with the behaviour;
- the manner in which the child responds when the teacher intervenes to correct the behaviour.

Seeking attention

Dreikurs suggests that the child's faulty belief underlying this behaviour is that he is acceptable to others only if being noticed or served. He may achieve this by active means such as 'showing off' or passively by being over-dependent or shy. If a teacher's immediate reaction to the misbehaviour is irritation and annoyance, thinking 'Oh no, not again!' then the behaviour is likely to be attention seeking. Our second clue is the children's reaction when the teacher intervenes: if they stop what they are doing and comply with the instruction but very quickly misbehave again, not necessarily doing the same thing, this confirms the goal of the behaviour.

The most common 'faulty' reaction from teachers is to intervene publicly, expressing their irritation and admonishing them for misbehaving, or trying to coax and cajole them into complying. However, reminding, warning and punishing will reinforce the attention-seeking goal and if possible the teacher should try to ignore the misbehaviour but give attention for acceptable behaviour when the child is not making a bid for it. This may sound obvious, but it is very common for teachers to regard such moments as an oasis of calm when they do not have to attend to the child.

Should one have to intervene because the behaviour is too disruptive or dangerous to ignore, it is essential not to reveal the annoyance and irritation that one is experiencing but to take calm, firm and decisive action. This will be made easier if one has planned for such eventualities (see p. 174), particularly in organising a time-out area or room where children can be sent so that they receive no attention from the teacher or peer group for five minutes or so.

Other students will provide the attention which is being sought by laughing or younger children will sometimes tell the teacher who is trying to ignore a child's misbehaviour that 'Michael is out of his seat again'. In such cases one should remind the informants to continue with their own work, to discourage their attention. Various researchers, particularly in the field of behaviour modification, have attempted to manipulate peer group approval by rewarding the whole class for the good behaviour of one member. For instance, the class might be allowed extra games if a certain child avoids getting into trouble for a specified time. In this way the class are discouraged from approving his bad behaviour as they will suffer as a result, and the child has the opportunity to earn group approval by acceptable behaviour. Some schools and units for children with behaviour disorders run token economy schemes whereby, when a boy behaves in an unacceptable way, every member of his group or house forfeits tokens which could otherwise be exchanged for goods or privileges. Group reprisals against one unfortunate member are discouraged by the same pressure in that they would all lose further tokens. Such approaches have also been used successfully in normal day school settings, though the class teacher is usually given support and advice (Coulby and Harper, 1985).

When a group of friends are evidently performing for one another and disrupting the work of the class it is clearly helpful to separate them if the school organisation permits, and a more extreme measure is to transfer a key disrupter to another school. This is a drastic measure to be taken only as a last resort, but it does give the student an opportunity to make a fresh start as he does not have to maintain the identity he has created with the previous group of friends. Unfortunately they may well be sought out by similar groups in the new school and try to establish themselves in the same old ways. If they can be prepared to expect such pressures and shown how to resist them they may avoid making the same mistakes.

Seeking power

Dreikurs suggests that the faulty belief underlying this goal is that the children feel they are acceptable only when they are the 'the boss' or in control and they therefore have to prove that they can get their own way and no-one can make them do anything. Such attitudes obviously promote power struggles, as when the teacher intervenes to correct the behaviour the child will refuse to comply.

112

If previous incidents have resulted in long drawn out battles or escalating confrontations in which children have stood their ground, then the teacher is likely to feel threatened and apprehensive when the behaviour occurs subsequently. On the other hand the teacher may have learned to 'win' these battles by reacting aggressively to intimidate the children into compliance. Dreikurs would therefore reason that if the teacher experiences either apprehension or anger, the child has been making a bid for power and control, though one could equally argue that because these are the teacher's typical reactions to misbehaviour the incident is turned into a personal battle which results in some children either refusing to comply or doing so with grudging hostility.

Battles for power and control may therefore be instigated by students or teachers, but teachers have the major responsibility in trying to avoid them. Faulty responses would therefore be to reveal apprehension and impotence by trying to placate the children, giving in to their demands or doing nothing about their behaviour, or to react with a show of anger directed at the child. It is far better to cut short any potential power struggle with a student and see them later to discuss the matter calmly.

Some students seem intent on challenging the teacher's authority, and it may well be that the school does not offer legitimate ways in which all students can be given responsibilities and share in the decisions which affect their lives. If they have played a part in formulating the rules which govern their behaviour they will be less likely to challenge the teacher's right to enforce those rules. Just as teachers have to exercise the powers they have in objective and professional ways, children too should be given opportunities to have positions of responsibility in the class and school and learn to exercise their legitimate powers in non-provocative and decisive ways.

Seeking revenge

Dreikurs suggests that students' faulty belief in this goal is that they belong only when they hurt others as they themselves feel hurt. Children who have suffered rejection may feel they cannot be liked and consequently mistrust those who are friendly towards them. When teachers feel hurt and let down, it is therefore argued that the children are seeking to inflict on them what they have suffered themselves, in a form of revenge.

Dreikurs advises that teachers should build up trusting relationships but it can be very frustrating to continue to place one's trust in someone who usually lets you down. If one reveals one's disappointment or hurt feelings and reacts in vindictive ways this simply confirms the identity that the child is constructing as someone who cannot be persuaded or won over by kindness. They view the teachers 'trust' only as an attempt to manipulate their behaviour and consequently thwart it. When we say to children, 'I'll let you sit there, ... use the apparatus ... play with the model ... *but don't let me down*', this implies that our relationship with them is conditional on their being trustworthy, which in reality it probably is, but by stating it we acknowledge that we are dealing with someone for whom it needs to be said. When we feel it necessary to give such warnings it is probably better to deliver them generally, 'to whom it may concern', rather than to specific individuals and then to react with surprise that 'a good lad like you should have done that' rather than hurt because 'you've really let me down'. We should also try to acknowledge the qualities that they have and build their self-esteem because if they value themselves more they will have less need to try to upset others.

Displaying inadequacy

The faulty belief underlying this goal is that the children feel they belong only by convincing others not to expect much from them. The identity they construct is of someone who does not join in with others and wants to be alone. Dreikurs suggests that they do not feel as capable as their peers and so try to avoid participating. The teacher's feeling is either despair and hopelessness expressing an 'I give up' attitude, or of worried over-concern for the child, both of which confirm the identity of a child unable to help himself. When the teacher intervenes, usually to try to engage them in the task set, they passively comply but only superficially and show no improvement.

One must be sure that such children can manage the tasks set and encourage their efforts without being over solicitous. If they appear seriously depressed they may need therapeutic help and it may be necessary for the parents to be contacted, though one must always be cautious that this could confirm the identity which they are constructing.

For teachers interested in Dreikurs' approach, particularly at the primary stage, Linda Albert (1989) has developed a disciplinary programme based on his views which offers a detailed account of students' motives and appropriate corrective action. However, there are other explanations, some less benign than Dreikurs', which have been suggested as motives for students' misbehaviour.

Causing excitement

Mills (1975) has proposed an interesting theory which offers an explanation for a wide range of unusual behaviour from children. His suggestion is that in order to cope with the various problems and stresses of life, the arousal level of the brain is increased so that it functions more efficiently. If the stresses are within normal limits for the individual, the arousal level of the brain drops during sleep, but if there are difficult problems to cope with, the brain becomes highly aroused during the day and does not recover its normal resting level during sleep. The person therefore wakes in the early hours of the morning and worries over the problems of the day to come, usually to little effect. Although he is too aroused to sleep, he is not sufficiently aroused to cope with making difficult decisions, and this can cause him to feel very depressed because he can see no way out of the problems which are depriving him of his rest.

Mills cites research showing that, with prolonged periods of stress or excitement, there is a build-up of an underlying depression which is manifested only when the arousal of the brain lowers. The person therefore seeks excitement to ward off the feelings of depression. Mills suggests there are alternative ways of increasing the arousal level of the brain, such as by not eating, and offers this theory to account for the illness anorexia nervosa.

The main concern for Mills is with those people who are depressed because they are unable to cope with the problems in their lives, but he also suggests that many children are subject to considerable stress in their homes. Perhaps the parents quarrel frequently and the children may have no opportunity for quiet and privacy. The mother may be tired and often hit out or scream at them. Perhaps when they watch television, which they tend to do for long periods of time, they choose the exciting programmes and so maintain high levels of arousal. When such a child is at school his lessons probably seem very 'flat' by comparison, because he is geared up or conditioned to a high degree of stimulation. Mills suggests that the child therefore actually tries to create excitement, which usually involves behaving illicitly. The risk of being caught and punished, which normally acts as a deterrent, would only encourage such a child. In fact without that risk his action would be pointless:

> Nowadays a number of children and young people have found that mild depression may be overcome by doing something exciting. This may be going to a pop concert with music at pain-producing intensity: it may be challenging authority at home or at school or it may involve stealing or other law breaking activities. The more depressed they are, the more exciting the challenge has to be to mask their depression. Many of these young people have described the progressive increase in devilment that is necessary to stop feeling depressed. Producing an intense disturbance in class, in which the other children soon become involved, is a favourite and effective mechanism.

We all seek some excitement in our lives, though most of us learn to achieve it in socially acceptable ways. Some choose sports which are either competitive or have an element of danger, others find their business provides sufficient risks or competition. Most people now enjoy excitement vicariously, from television and films, without any actual risk involved, but Mills' theory suggests that all this need not remain a static or balanced process, with different people requiring different levels of excitement in their lives. It is a dynamic process, such that an increasing diet of excitement can, up to a point, feed one's need for further stimulation to the extent that one tries to create more. A child, through no fault of his own necessarily, could be continually subjected to a highly stimulating environment in the home and so become over-aroused. This would develop a compulsion for dangerous and forbidden behaviour, so that school life becomes as exciting as life at home.

There is now a great deal of evidence from physiological studies to show that people differ considerably in the extent that the brain is aroused by incoming stimuli, and that these differences are present in young children (summarised in Moir and Jessel, 1995). An alternative to Mills' theory is therefore that some children create excitement simply because their brains are more easily bored than their normal counterparts. They are unable to maintain concentration for an extended period as they quickly become bored and seek new experiences. The level of stimulation they create would be too stressful for those with normally aroused brains but such children find the dangers exciting. Stimulant drugs such as amphetamines, which induce greater activity in the normal person, actually have a calming effect on such individuals due to the increased arousal in the brain making them more sensitive to, and satisfied by, the normal levels of stimulation. Rather than being the victims of an over-stimulating environment, as Mills suggests, they could be instrumental in creating such conditions.

However, whether they are the victims of their environment or their own brain chemistry, it is clear that some children find greater problems in sustaining attention to everyday tasks and are more likely to disrupt the concentration of those around them. When a teacher reacts emotionally to unwanted behaviour he may believe that the experience will be unpleasant for the child, but in fact he could be taking a leading role in the drama which the child is trying to create. Instead it would be better to attempt to appear relaxed and unruffled, neither smug nor insecure in whatever action he takes. Advocates of behaviour modification would suggest trying to ignore the misbehaviour, but, as mentioned earlier, it is difficult to stop other children attending. The idea of 'time-out' periods when the behaviour is too disruptive or dangerous to ignore, however, is quite useful.

'Time-out' entails removing the child from the class in a quiet, unemotional way, to a room where he has nothing to do at all. He must be supervised, though not spoken to, and this may present problems of staffing in some schools. In primary schools the headteacher's room will suffice, provided no-one takes any notice of the child. After about ten minutes or so the child should be returned to the classroom without comment, and the teacher should speak to him on the first occasion he does something right, not mentioning the events leading to his removal.

The crucial factor in the effectiveness of this approach is probably the calm attitude which the teacher conveys. Children are more usually removed from the room as a last resort after warnings and reprimands, and so it is often an emotional and exciting affair. In contrast, if the child is removed quietly before he has created any excitement to a place which he finds even more boring than the classroom, he will learn that unwanted behaviour is not always effective in enlivening the situation. When he is returned to the classroom he is likely to find it relatively stimulating compared with the time-out period and may therefore behave better. Some secondary schools set aside a classroom where students from any group can be sent to work under the supervision of a teacher for an extended period of time, and this would seem to have a similar effect.

The difficulty arises for some teachers in getting the child to leave the class-room without actually throwing him out. Hamblin *et al.* (1971) describe one difficult boy whom they had to restrain from leaving the time-out room, and then found that this treatment did not improve his behaviour. (This exciting experience could be its own reward according to Mills' theory.) They there-fore allowed him to leave the room and wander around the school, but not to return to his class until he had willingly served his ten minutes back in the time-out room. They found this much more effective, but one wonders what there was to prevent the boy from damaging school property, wandering back into his room or leaving the school premises entirely. There is less like-lihood of resistance if the child is removed in an unthreatening manner by another teacher before an emotional confrontation and battle of wills has arisen.

The theory associating high arousal with deviant behaviour is attractive, though it does not explain why some children find legitimate means of creat-ing excitement and others behave antisocially. It does, however, reinforce the points which were made earlier about the need to present an interesting and varied lesson and to develop the skills of enthusiastic teaching. If teach-ers can make school life more stimulating, the difficult child will not only have less need to make his own excitement, but will also find it harder to involve others in his schemes.

Malicious teasing

Alison, a thirteen-year-old, tells of an incident with her teacher, Mr Baker: 'I once threw something on to his desk. He wasn't sure who had thrown it. He didn't do anything. He just glared at me. I like getting him stewed up. I don't know why. It's fun, but sometimes he frightens me too.' (Wragg and Wood, 1984b)

It may come as no surprise to some that children should actually enjoy annoying teachers, and this idea, as put forward by Hamblin *et al.* (1971), seems to offer a plausible explanation for some instances of misbehaviour. They suggest that a great deal of children's unhelpful or annoying behaviour can be regarded as a form of malicious teasing whereby they engage in a game of 'Let's get the teacher'. They describe a group of five extraordinarily aggressive four-year-old boys referred to their laboratory by local psychiatrists and social workers. All had been diagnosed as hyperactive and none had responded to amphetamine therapy. Hamblin provided the group with a trained teacher and, after the eighth day, was recording an average of 150 sequences of aggression per day, which included such extreme behaviour as knocking over the record player and throwing chairs at the teacher. Hamblin comments on the way the situation developed:

> What she [the teacher] did not realise is that she had inadvertently structured an exchange where she consistently reinforced aggression. First, as noted, whenever she fought with them she always lost. Second, more subtly, she reinforced their aggressive pattern by giving it serious attention – by looking, talking, scolding, cajoling, becoming angry, even striking back. These boys were playing a teasing game called 'Get the Teacher'. The more she showed that she was bothered by their behaviour, the better they seemed to like it and the further they went.

Clearly, although the teacher was dispensing what might be considered fairly aversive treatment for most four-year-olds, she was the real victim in the exchanges.

The objective of malicious teasing, therefore, is to annoy and upset another individual by mental rather than physical cruelty. It is often a shared 'sport' among children so that a number of them will 'gang up' on one individual. The victim need not be weaker or smaller than others; indeed, there is probably an added pleasure in seeing someone stronger than you under your power, albeit a shared power.

If teachers are not careful in their first meetings with children, they can soon find themselves the victims of malicious teasing. It may start in the form of apparently innocent questions and comments which delay the progress of the lesson, but can develop into deliberate disobedience calculated to enrage the teacher. When I first taught at a comprehensive school the headteacher asked the staff to be more vigilant about students' conduct around the school, particularly concerning the amount of litter on the premises. As I walked across the playground a group of 'anti-school' fifteen-year-old boys were standing nearby and one threw some paper on the ground. I walked over and, in what I thought was a reasonable manner, asked him to pick it up and put it in the bin. I felt the tension from the group immediately, as they waited to see what he would do: 'I didn't drop it . . . , sir', the last word being slipped in to pay lip-service to my position, at the same time as showing contempt for it. He was immediately supported by his friend apparently providing an impregnable alibi. 'That's right, sir, he never dropped it. We've been wiv 'im all the time, and he never dropped nuffin'. Did you see him drop anyfin', Steve?' Steve immediately complied: 'No, we was just standing 'ere talking'. Someone else must 'ave dropped it before we come 'ere.' They had all immediately sensed the game. It wasn't anything to do with waste paper being picked up or not, it was a battle between them and teachers. They were telling me, within the rules of teacher-student relationships, to go jump in the river. At that stage in my teaching career, challenges were never to be refused. I ignored the others and looked straight at the first boy. 'I saw you drop the paper, but it's not important whether you did or not, I'm telling you to pick it up now.' After a brief contemptuous pause he reluctantly bent down and picked up the paper. I held my hand out for him to pass it to me, but in a sudden moment of defiance he passed it to his friend. Before I realised what I was doing, I had clipped him across the side of the head with my outstretched hand. He and his friend who had the paper were outraged and erupted into threats of 'going to the courts' and swore to get me 'slung out', as they had witnessed my assault. I immediately took the two main offenders to the headteacher, where they made their accusations, but he caned both of them.

No more was heard of the matter, but in many ways I was lucky. I didn't hit him harder, they didn't hit me back, the headteacher backed me up, and their parents presumably didn't back them up. I should not have hit a student, as the matter could so easily have leaped out of control. Although I had demonstrated my power they would probably have been confirmed in their anti-school attitudes. I say probably because after that event the main culprit always gave me a cheery 'mornin', sir', which never ceased to amaze me and I still can't see why.

Here was an example of a typical confrontation forced by the students, where the only motive seemed to be to challenge the authority of the teacher in a form of malicious teasing, not because he was unfair or wrong, but because he was in authority. Corporal punishment is now illegal in schools and we are compelled to think of better ways of handling such incidents. Picking up the paper was such an insignificant act but I believed that my authority rested on the boy's compliance so I immediately resorted to a show of power.

Challenging authority is a common motive for misbehaviour, particularly among anti-school adolescents, and one can suggest many reasons why such attitudes may have developed. Perhaps the students are frustrated by failure and are hitting back at the system which they consider responsible. It might be an attempt to establish their individuality by challenging anyone in authority, and there are those who would regard it as a form of self-expression. Be that as it may, unless the teacher is very careful, he can be left frustrated by his own impotence and unable to exert any control over the culprits, which renders him ineffective as their teacher.

Malicious teasing is only successful if the victim is left annoyed, upset and frustrated. If an emotional response is not forthcoming then the teasing may escalate at first but, if this in turn fails, the offenders usually begin to feel very uncomfortable. From the teacher's point of view, the most successful outcome would be one where the students did as they were told without the satisfaction of seeing the teacher annoyed, and which maintained a good working relationship.

It follows, then, that in giving directions a teacher should not show any signs of tension, even if there is obvious reluctance or aggression from the students. The aim should be to sustain a calm atmosphere, without giving way to unreasonable pressure. If students are obviously determined to challenge the teacher from the outset, it is not helpful to react aggressively, as this implies that their challenge is realistic and therefore invites an escalation. Relaxed behaviour is certainly important in avoiding potential confrontations, as it offers no reinforcement to malicious teasing, so if one doesn't feel relaxed then at least one must try to appear so. In order to do this it is helpful to keep matters in a low key, or in the words of Gnagey (1975): 'Don't make a Federal case out of it!'

If the teacher knows what steps he intends to take if a student refuses to follow instructions, this will also help reduce the possibility of an emotional outburst. It is when one doesn't know what to do next that one either shows signs of anxiety or, perhaps to disguise this, becomes aggressive in an attempt to force the student into submission. Any plan is useful in this respect, as it provides the teacher with a clear course of action.

Avoiding work

Ideally one should always derive pleasure from work, but this does not mean that work can be pleasurable all the time. Children have a very clear idea of what work is, perhaps because their level of mastery is low, so that they have less opportunity to derive satisfaction from their efforts or possibly because they possess what Ausubel (1968) described as 'the typical human proclivity towards procrastination and aversion to sustained, regular and disciplined work'. Any parents who have tried to make their children practise a musical instrument regularly will know what he means. It is not necessarily that children lack interest in the subject, but often that the effort of mastering a difficult skill, or of ordering their thoughts to produce a piece of written work, causes them to delay beginning the task. Almost always, talking about a subject is preferable to writing about it, and it is worth remembering that nearly every day of their school lives children have to produce written work in some form or other. The topic can be fascinating, the resources provided can be stimulating, the class visit can bring first-hand experience and the discussion can enlighten them to others' views, but the crunch still comes when they have to put pen to paper. Gannaway (1976) compiled a 'popularity table' of activities, based on statements and comments from students, and suggested that writing was often synonymous with work: 'Writing is not only bottom of the table, but it is also the only activity that is always referred to as "work". A distinction is commonly drawn between writing and talking, the former being work and the latter being not work.' It is some consolation that the full onset of the affliction is delayed until adolescence, giving junior school teachers a somewhat rosy view of children's capacities or their own powers of motivation.

Buzan (1971) vividly describes what must be a fairly universal experience for students as they settle down to private study:

> Having decided to study on a certain evening the student will spend approximately five to ten minutes tidying and 'getting ready' his desk, making sure that everything is in the right place before he starts. Just as he is about to sit down, however he will 'remember' that there is an important telephone call that he has to make and that if he doesn't make it he will be ill-at-ease during the study period. He makes the call (which is seldom brief!) and returns to his desk where he again adjusts the position of the study book, perhaps opens it and then suddenly 'remembers' that there is a television programme he was particularly interested in, so he goes to the next room to check the television schedules. Sure enough it begins in fifteen minutes! As fifteen minutes is not enough time to commence studying he decides to wait until after the programme.

We no doubt differ in our capacities to overcome this inertia; or, putting it another way, some people are lazier than others.

These feelings are apparently not confined solely to the human species. An American psychologist, giving an account of the progress which had been made in the remarkable work of teaching monkeys to use sign language, described how, when it was time for a lesson on learning new signs, one monkey regularly gave the sign for 'Me tired'. We all know that feeling!

One way that teachers will be more likely to overcome work avoidance is to make the minimum requirements for the session clear to the students and remind them of the consequences of failing to meet these. Regular marking not only provides valuable feedback to the student but also enables the teacher to set realistic goals in a lesson. If a student is then required to complete work during a break or lunchtime it must not seem that it is a punishment for failing to do the work set but simply that he is being given extra time to do it properly. It is important to identify those students who fail to meet the targets set and to persist until they do, and one should not feel guilty about detaining those who may be having genuine problems tackling the work as this provides the opportunity to give individual help. Setting realistic targets discourages students from time-wasting or otherwise misbehaving but it is often very difficult, or impossible, to ensure that everyone does sufficient work in each lesson. With large classes, and methods which sometimes involve students working on different material at different rates, it is difficult enough keeping track of what each is supposed to be doing, let alone ensuring they have done a reasonable amount. Some teachers go to elaborate lengths to record the students' progress in their work, and this is time well spent because with individual learning it is too easy for them to do very little.

When in doubt, one should demand a little more from a student than he can comfortably do, as, if he never has to make a real effort, he is likely to lose interest. Teachers sometimes praise work which may have entailed little effort, in the hope that the student will feel encouraged to work harder, however, Festinger (1961) pointed out that success without effort will probably decrease interest and motivation. It is therefore wiser to be sure that there has been some effort before giving praise, for, as Festinger noted after reviewing experiments on animal and human motivation, 'Rats and people come to love the things for which they have suffered'. The task for teachers then is to persuade students to suffer willingly in the hope that they will ultimately gain satisfaction from their efforts. It should always be easier to do the work than to avoid it.

Regardless of what we might speculate are the underlying motives for misbehaviour, it is evident that it is far safer for teachers to respond in a detached professional manner than to react emotionally and run the risk of becoming part of the problem.

Activity 8 Identifying Motives

1. The following descriptions were provided by postgraduate students from their observations on teaching practice with five to seven-year-old children. What is the most probable motive for each child's behaviour and what could the teacher do to help?

    (a) We have a Year 2 boy who is basically very able but very quickly frustrated and socially inept. Displays confrontational behaviour to children and staff. Various strategies have been tried and failed (by permanent teaching staff and by the headteacher). He very quickly becomes hysterical and his behaviour disrupts the whole class. His behaviour appears wilfully disruptive even when he is not faced with work he finds difficult.
    (b) Competent child but never participates. Sits on the edge of the group and doesn't attend. Will creep off while rest of the group on task. Always on periphery of whatever is happening.
    (c) A child in my class is always being silly. His speech is rather babyish but he is quite competent, especially on the computer. He is a happy child but is always being told off as he won't settle and attempt his work. He would rather talk and be silly. The other children know his behaviour and tell him off and he gets upset sometimes and cries.

2. The Year 3 class were engaged in individual and group activities when the teacher asked them to stop and gather round her so that she could have a session on 'telling the time'. One boy appeared to take no notice but stayed at the back of the room fiddling about with some equipment. The teacher told him to leave it and come and join the others seated around her but he showed no reaction to her having spoken. After similar fruitless attempts she said that if he came quickly he could turn the hands of the clock she was using. He came immediately and spent the session happily on her lap, turning the clock hands.

    What is the most likely explanation for the child's initial refusal to join the group and was the teacher's action appropriate?

3. The following is an edited extract lasting four minutes from a session with a small group of pre-school children being taught in a special unit.

    'Mike, John and Dan are seated together playing with pieces of Playdoh. Barry, some distance from the others, is seated and also is playing with Playdoh. The children, except Barry, are talking to each other about what they are making. Time is 9.10 a.m. Miss Sally, the teacher, turns towards the children and says, "It's time for a lesson. Put your Playdoh away." Mike says, "Not me." John says, "Not me." Dan says, "Not me." Miss Sally moves towards Mike. Mike throws his Playdoh in Miss Sally's face. Miss Sally jerks back, then moves forward rapidly and snatches Playdoh from Mike. Puts Playdoh in her pocket. Mike screams for Playdoh, says he wants to play with it. Mike moves towards Miss Sally and attempts to snatch the Playdoh from her pocket. Miss Sally pushes him away. Mike kicks her on the leg, kicks her again and demands the return of his Playdoh. Kicks her again. Miss Sally pushes Mike down on the floor. Mike starts up, pulls over one chair, then another; stops a moment. Miss Sally is picking up chairs. Mike looks at her. She moves towards Mike. Mike runs away. John wants his Playdoh. Miss Sally says, "No." He joins Mike in pulling over chairs and attempts to grab Playdoh from Miss Sally's pocket; she pushes him away roughly. John is screaming that he wants to play with his Playdoh. Mike has his coat on; says he is going home. Miss Sally asks Dan to bolt the door. Dan gets to the door at the same time as Mike. Mike hits Dan in the face. Dan's nose is bleeding. Miss Sally walks over to Dan, turns to the others and says that she is taking Dan to the washroom and that while she is away, they may play with the Playdoh. Returns Playdoh from pocket to Mike and John. Time 9:14 a.m.'

    How might such behaviour be explained and what action could be taken to improve it?

Some responses to activity 8

It is clearly not possible to be certain about the children's motives and most appropriate teachers' responses and the following are therefore offered only as possibilities on the basis of the information provided.

1.   (a)   *There seem to be some indicators of attention seeking as the outbursts occur when he is faced with work he doesn't find difficult. The confrontational behaviour and resorting to his ultimate weapon of becoming hysterical suggests he is seeking power and being quite successful as the various strategies have failed. The frustration, presumably when working, even though he is able, could be an attempt to display inadequacy though at this stage he clearly wants to be noticed, or could he simply be trying to avoid doing the work? One would also need to know more about his being 'socially inept' and whether he feels isolated from the other children and is getting revenge by disrupting the lesson.*

      What does seem to be clear is that he is being successful in generating concern and attention from a number of people. He not only gets teachers to notice him but will then take them on and win. Whatever other counselling or therapeutic strategies one adopts it would seem sensible to impose a 'time-out' procedure (see p. 116) when he disrupts the lesson, particularly when he is being hysterical, but also to offer praise and possibly rewards in the form of 'helping teacher' jobs when he behaves well. What is essential is that the teachers do not reveal the frustration they clearly must experience.

  (b)   *From the few notes provided it seems that the child is displaying inadequacy and withdrawal as there is no mention of any attempts to cause disruption when on the periphery or creeping off. The teacher might therefore unobtrusively encourage greater participation by ensuring the child sits closer to her or has an active role to play, as well as building self-esteem by focusing on his or her strengths. Some form of counselling to discuss the child's behaviour and to agree a plan of action would also be appropriate.*

  (c)   *The 'silly' behaviour and babyish speech both suggest the child is attention seeking though it would be helpful to know exactly what his 'silly' behaviour was. It could be that he is unsuccessfully trying to build relationships with the other children, trying to get their attention, but doing so in a way which they also perceive as babyish. The teacher might try showing him more appropriate ways of relating to other children as well as praising or otherwise acknowledging those occasions* when he perseveres with his work or behaves more in accordance with his age.

2. The motive behind the boy's initial action in not joining the group would be unclear as there are elements of attention seeking and power in his refusal to join the group. Though the teacher was able to gain his co-operation quickly and avoided any disruption or confrontation, she did so mainly on his terms. The reward of turning the hands of the clock was not for joining the group but for initially refusing to join the group. The child has bribed the teacher by making his co-operation conditional on receiving special treatment. Parents often reward pestering and whining from their children in the same way by giving them what they want or 'distracting' them with an equally desirable alternative.

The teacher's action would therefore have reinforced the disruptive behaviour so she would have been better advised to have rewarded the first child ready to start and then to make the session as exciting as possible to entice the boy to join in. He would also need to know, or at some stage be told, the consequences which would follow from his failure to join in as instructed.

3. This extract featured the behaviour of the five 'extraordinarily aggressive' four-year-old boys described by Hamblin et al. (1971) and mentioned earlier. The motive behind their behaviour could be seen as seeking power or as creating excitement but the authors viewed the teacher as the victim of their malicious teasing. 'These were barbarous little boys who enjoyed battle. Miss Sally did her best but they were just more clever than she, and they always won. Whether she wanted to or not, they could always drag her into the fray, and just go at it harder and harder until she capitulated. She was finally driven to their level, trading a kick for a kick and a spit in the face for a spit in the face.'

The authors devised a strict programme for the teacher to follow which involved ignoring unco-operative behaviour and rewarding co-operation with tokens, and within a few weeks there were great improvements. They were also able to give the teacher immediate first-hand advice through radio contact which she alone could hear, and this may well have helped her remain calm in the face of such determined provocation.

Contexts for unwanted behaviour

In a questionnaire exercise I conducted with teachers, many of them realised their own responsibility for creating the circumstances in which unwanted behaviour would be more likely to occur: 'I feel the fault is mine – I should create more interest in the students' and 'My approach to the lesson may not have been very imaginative and stimulating – but I don't expect that every lesson can be so'. As well as taking the lesson as a whole and making an overall judgment such as 'uninteresting', one can identify circumstances during the lesson which could contribute to unwanted behaviour.

Kounin (1970) deals with what he calls *movement management*, which involves the skills of initiating an activity, directing students through it and sustaining their attention, and then successfully terminating it. Movement management concerns the pace and flow of one type of activity to another, such as from listening to the teacher to writing in books or carrying out an experiment. He distinguishes two aspects of movement management: *momentum* and *smoothness*.

Momentum

This is the liveliness and pace with which a lesson progresses. The comments made in Chapter 4 would be relevant here, but Kounin's approach is to look for what he terms *slowdowns*, which prevent or interrupt the momentum of a lesson. Slowdowns can be caused by *overdwelling* – spending a disproportionate amount of time on an inappropriate subject – or by *fragmentation* – dealing with individuals one at a time when one ought to be dealing with the whole group.

If the teacher spends too much time dealing with a minor aspect of a topic, particularly if the majority of students have already grasped the point, or if the aspect is somewhat irrelevant and uninteresting, this will cause a slowdown in momentum. Kounin calls this *actone overdwelling*. Similarly, *behaviour overdwelling* refers to excessive nagging or reprimanding of a student in the course of a lesson (see p. 157), and the reaction would be one of 'Doesn't he go on!' (In my experience, on these occasions there is also an absence of any direct constructive action, such as giving a sanction.) The teacher should always be looking for the students' reactions to what is being said or done, because signs of disinterest or other unwanted behaviour will indicate that the momentum of a lesson is being lost.

'Fragmentation' entails the teacher dealing with individual students when it would be more appropriate to deal with the whole group. The effect is to keep the rest of the class waiting unnecessarily. Teachers of drama and games are well aware of the importance of involving the majority of the children in an activity, rather than leaving them to be passive spectators for any

126

length of time. The same principle applies in class teaching when, for example, a line of children wait for their work to be marked before they proceed further. Most teachers avoid such obvious 'group fragmentation', but a similar situation can arise when one is supposedly addressing the whole class but becomes involved in lengthy talk with students close by, so that the others cannot hear clearly. Rutter *et al.* (1979) point out the dangers of such actions:

> Relatively inexperienced teachers in all schools seemed to have difficulty in maintaining contact with the class as a group, and were particularly likely to concentrate on individuals, either to give specific instructions on work or to deal with disruptive behaviour. The effect of this focus on the individual was often to lose the interest and attention of other members of the class, with adverse consequences in terms of the children's behaviour. In the schools with less satisfactory behaviour and less good examination results even the more experienced teachers tended to focus unhelpfully on the individual to the detriment of overall class management.

Kounin also drew attention to the skills of initiating and terminating an activity, and research by Partington and Hinchliffe (1979) endorses the importance of these aspects of movement management:

> Many of the observers drew attention to critical events at the beginning and end of lessons. It seemed that the successful teacher usually arrived at the classroom before his pupils, personally admitted them to the room, probably in single file, gave a friendly word here, a gentle admonition there, as his pupils passed him at the door. This was seen as establishing himself with the class, prior to a swift and compelling start to the lesson ...
> ... The ends of lessons did not attract as much attention as the beginnings. It seemed that badly managed classes 'disintegrated' when the bell went and pupils left without any reference to the teacher.

Rutter *et al.* also found that teachers in successful schools in their study began and ended their lessons on time. The teachers ensured organised endings perhaps by recapitulating on the main points of the lesson, reading out or commenting on some of the students' work or allowing silent working to continue. In each case they anticipated the end of the lesson and allowed time for packing away books and materials.

If one delays the start of a lesson to wait for latecomers to arrive, this implies that one has not planned to use the full allocated time. It is inevitable that students will sometimes arrive late, particularly if they come from different parts of the building, but if a prompt start is not made after allowing a reasonable time for them to arrive, they are liable to drift in at their leisure. One should not interrupt the lesson to deal with latecomers but they should be seen later at a suitable time to give their explanations. The following extract is a transcript of an incident from a student teacher's lesson, and may well be typical of the sort of unhelpful practice referred to by Rutter. He had been speaking for some minutes to the class of Year 10 students when a boy entered from the back of the room and sat down.

Teacher:	What time do you call this Richard?
Student:	*(Looks carefully at his watch then back at the teacher)* Two fifty-three.
Teacher:	Right, you're ten minutes late.
Student:	*(Studying his watch again and replying in a matter-of-fact manner)* Eight minutes, sir.
Teacher:	Do I get an apology?
Student:	Uh?
Teacher:	Do I get an apology?
Student:	*(Continuing in the same manner)* Yeah. Sorry about being late.
Teacher:	Do I get an explanation?
Student:	No.
Teacher:	Why?
Student:	Because I can't.
Teacher:	Why were you late?
Student:	I can't tell you.
Teacher:	What kept you when every other person got here on time?
Student:	No ... No, I ain't tellin' you. Sorry. *(Quietly)* This girl ... No, I ain't tellin' you ... Sorry. *(Again his manner is not embarrassed or even apologetic.)*
Teacher:	*(Continues to look at boy for about ten seconds but the boy shows studied unconcern. He turns to face the class and continues with the introduction.)*

The incident was not brought up again during or after the lesson.

Regardless of how inappropriately one feels the student teacher managed the incident, as the student had entered unobtrusively, he could have been seen later when the class were working rather than interrupt the momentum of the lesson. The public examination may have contributed towards the boy's cheeky reply which challenged the teacher's authority.

It is very important to start the lesson with some urgency, not only to capture students' attention but also to create an organised and efficient atmosphere. Ideally the lesson should be introduced with an air of pleasure and expectancy, as if unwrapping an unexpected gift for the students, not with a sense of duty, dispensing their daily dose of medicine.

The ways in which a teacher asks questions and deals with students' replies can also affect the momentum of a lesson as was discussed earlier (p. 100).

Smoothness

When there is a transition from one type of activity to another, it is important that this should be done smoothly. Most teachers have at some time turned away from talking to a class to play an extract from a tape, to put up a wall chart or find a passage in a book, only to find that the tape is at the wrong part, the wall chart won't stay open, or they can't find the passage in the book. The students become restless and some begin to talk. The continuity of the lesson has been broken, and unwanted behaviour is more likely while the teacher is occupied rectifying the situation.

Kounin identified circumstances which produce *jerkiness* – the lack of a smooth transition from one type of activity to another, or breaks in the continuity of one activity. There are many occasions when the flow of an activity is broken by circumstances beyond the teacher's control. A window cleaner might appear at the window, or a student might interrupt a discussion with a message from the headteacher. However, the teacher can produce 'jerkiness' by poor management. Adequate preparation beforehand would ensure that the tape is at the right place, the chart stays open, and the page in the book is marked; but there are many other ways in which teachers interrupt the smoothness of class activities.

Referring back to a previous activity, then resuming the original one, Kounin describes as a *flip flop*. I have noticed when lecturing to students that if I stop what I am dealing with to mention something that I had forgotten earlier, there are noticeable signs of annoyance as they shuffle around to find the relevant notes. Kounin uses the terms *dangles, truncations* and *stimulus boundedness* to further distinguish the nature of the break and whether the original activity is resumed, but the important feature common to them all is that the smooth flow of class activity is interrupted.

The following extract from a lesson shows how an experienced teacher can manage to introduce appropriate blackboard work without interrupting the flow of his lesson. He is discussing architectural features of buildings and is explaining what a gargoyle is to a group of thirteen-year-olds:

> *Teacher:* You've probably seen them sticking out of the sides of old buildings and churches . . . *(turns to board and begins a rough sketch of a gargoyle but continues talking to the class)*. . . . They carry the water away from the gutters . . . clear from the walls. . . . They're really ugly . . . grotesque sort of faces *(continues the sketch but looks round at one of the students)*. Hold still a minute, Larry . . . *(pretends to use him as a model. Larry tries to suppress a smile and groans; others laugh)*.

The teacher was not engaging in unnecessary talk as he drew on the board. Had he neglected to sustain contact with the group, even for that short period of time, the smoothness and progression of the lesson would have been interrupted.

Unwanted behaviour can also occur during transitions between activities which entail students moving to another location. Inexperienced teachers soon realise that one must give carefully worded instructions before letting them collect apparatus in a laboratory, say, unless they have already learned to move about in a controlled and orderly way. Here, unruly behaviour is not only dangerous but also disrupts the lesson.

The following extract is from a lesson given by an experienced teacher. It is taken from the start of the lesson and lasts only about one and a half minutes, during which the teacher attempts to introduce a discussion. The introduction must stimulate some interest in the subject, but in this case it is unsuccessful. The extract illustrates some of the features that Kounin has drawn attention to, and these go some way to explain the unwanted behaviour which occurs and the lack of interest shown by the students. The lesson begins with a class of fourteen-year-olds seated quietly and facing the teacher:

> *Teacher:* Now, it's a short lesson so we're going to take ... what in fact some of you wrote about yesterday ... quite well. Something that's been in the news a great deal lately and this is that hijacking business *(turns and writes on the board as she continues talking)* that's going on *(turns to face class).*

With a difficult class it would be unwise to turn away from them at such an early stage, before one had fully gained their attention and involvement. It certainly wasn't vital to write anything on the board yet, and on this occasion it provides the opportunity for one boy to start fiddling with an elastic band. The use of the word 'business' also suggests that the teacher is detached from the subject (see p. 93).

> *Teacher:* I looked up the meaning of the word 'hijack' ... Put it away ... put it away *(turns to write 'origin' on board)* and it says in the dictionary 'obscure origin' *(raising voice)* What does *(turns to class)* origin mean? ... Origin?
> *Student:* *(While the teacher is still speaking)* Where it comes from, Miss.

She has turned away again and one or two students begin to make audible comments. She hears this and raises her voice in response. A boy at the back rapidly calls out the answer, as the teacher immediately repeats her question. The teacher ignores this.

> *Student:* Where it comes from. *(General noise as others call out answers.)*
> *Teacher:* No, no ... no ... can't hear you ... can't hear you ... Jennifer *(looks towards girl)* ... Origin?
> *Student:* Origin means where it's come from.
> *Teacher:* *(Looking at boy who has called out)* Origin means where it's come from.

General noise reduces but continues, and as Jennifer fails to answer promptly, a boy at the back clearly calls out above the noise and the teacher accepts his answer. Another student then answers but before the teacher has time to respond there follows a great deal of calling out from the rest of the class.

Noise continues in the room and is clearly unrelated to what the teacher is saying.

> *Teacher:* Now ... What I ... John *(loudly)*, I'm glad you know so much about this subject because you obviously know more than I do, more than the papers do, more than the Italian government does or the Chief of Police, more than the hijackers themselves it seems! *(As she turns away, John huffs on his nails as if to say 'Aren't I clever!').*

As well as handling the question and answer session badly – refusing to accept calling out, naming a student to respond, then accepting calling out – she has engaged in 'actone overdwelling'. The meaning of the word 'origin' is not important and detracts from the main theme getting underway. It would have been far more appropriate to read out some extracts of what the students had written previously 'quite well' (damning with faint praise) and hence re-focus their attention on the subject. She has also introduced a 'truncation' because she was about to define 'hijack' but went back to the word 'origin', and we hear no more about 'hijack'. She engaged in 'behaviour overdwelling' by nagging John. There had been talking in the room for some time, so she also failed to act promptly and decisively in response to unwanted behaviour. In Kounin's terms, she had failed to show 'withitness' (see p. 141).

> *Teacher:*   *(Leaning forward on desk so that she is speaking from a little above the height of the students' heads and in a rather tired voice. The expression on her face says 'It's going to be another one of those days!')* Now in order to make sure we discuss the subject *(pauses for three seconds as the noise continues)* and not what we're going to do on Saturday morning and Friday night, we'll have a secretary as we've had before *(raises her eyes and brows and looks to the back of room for five seconds, without standing up however, in a vain attempt to check the noise)* ... secretary we've had before *(gets quieter as she continues)* in order to get some sort of points ... at the end of the discussion. *(Raises voice.)* Should we in fact, ... should governments give in to the hijackers' demands?

Her own behaviour shows lack of interest in the subject, and the attempt she made to check the noise had no clarity – it did not stand out clearly as few people noticed she had stopped talking. She stopped briefly before and continued, so one can expect her to do so again. She has failed to introduce the discussion in a lively way, mainly because she has not spoken about hijacking! She also failed to exercise control over the communication in the room.

Movement management, or maintaining momentum and smoothness in a lesson, was shown by Kounin to have a far greater association with reductions in unwanted behaviour than any methods used to react to that behaviour. Putting it more simply, prevention is better than attempts to cure.

Seating arrangements

A study carried out in a special school with a group of students aged between twelve and fifteen showed that for academic work there was a marked increase in on-task behaviour, from thirty-five per cent to seventy-five per cent, when children were arranged in rows rather than grouped around tables (Wheldall and Lam, 1987). Previous work had shown similar results with primary school children and recently two studies by Hastings and Schwieso (1994) have revealed the same effect in more detail.

The first study, with Year 5 to 6 children again showed they spent more time on task when seated in rows than in groups, but the different seating patterns did not affect all children in the same way. For those who concentrated well when seated in groups, moving to rows made no appreciable difference, but for the eight most easily distracted children in each of the two classes observed, sitting in rows made a dramatic difference.

> In class A, they were on-task for 72 and 78 per cent of the two phases in rows but for just 38 per cent when seated in groups. In class B, the figures were 72 per cent in rows and 44 and 46 per cent in the group seating phases. Most of these children more than doubled their involvement with work and, taken together, they achieved around the class average when seated in rows.

The second study focused on three boys in a Year 3 to 4 class who were causing serious concern and disruption. The class as a whole was working at 'individual seatwork' tasks for an average of just under half the time, whereas the three boys were out of their seats for more than two-thirds of the time and engaged with their work for less than a quarter. The whole class were then seated in rows for individual work and the class average rose to 78 per cent. More surprisingly,

> the figures for each of the three boys were above this class average and their disruptive effect on the rest of the class decreased considerably. Far from feeling oppressed and trapped in their seats, they thought the new set-up was wonderful.

Hastings and Schwieso go on to argue for flexible seating arrangements which take into account the nature of the activity and the distractibility of the children.

In a study of a class of Year 5 to 6 children, Lucas and Thomas (1990) observed that children working in the same group had similar on-task levels, so that on one table all the children were working most of the time whereas on another they were all mostly off task. Those who have observed children working on individual activities around the same table will confirm how easily one child can distract the whole group. Even a work-related comment requires a response from another child and this can quickly stimulate a general discussion, which, although it fulfils a social function of maintaining relationships, is unrelated to the task in hand and serves to distract the children from concentrating on their work. Lucas went on to describe how she discussed seating arrangements with the children as a part of any activity, and group seating was only chosen for collaborative tasks. For individual working the children seated themselves at tables facing the walls to minimise distraction and came together only at the end of the session to discuss their efforts.

Clearly, the numbers involved, the manoeuvrability of the furniture and the 'geography' of the classroom will all influence how flexible teachers can be with seating arrangements but one should try to minimise distraction when children are working individually. As one commentator suggested in Hastings and Schwieso's article,

> ... the widespread practice of sitting children in the manifestly social context of a group, then asking them to get on with their own work and telling them off for talking, borders on cruelty.

There is an old Norfolk saying concerning the value of apprentice boys to their master.

'One boy is half a man,' that is, his labour equals half that of a man.

'Two boys is half a boy.' When two are together, you have only half the labour of one boy.

'Three boys is no boy at all.'

A cynical observer might suggest that educational research is now revealing the startling fact that children are likely to distract one another.

6 Intervening in Students' Behaviour

So far we have been largely concerned with creating an atmosphere in which students will feel inclined to work and co-operate rather than misbehave, on the principle that prevention is better than cure. Preventing unwanted behaviour requires lively, sensitive teaching and secure, confident behaviour and it is only within this context that students can be expected (or even should be expected) to behave in co-operative ways. Dealing effectively with unwanted behaviour should never serve as a substitute for good teaching but it is an essential skill for all teachers. During one week, ninety-seven per cent of primary and secondary teachers surveyed had to deal with 'Talking out of turn' (e.g. by making remarks, calling out, distracting others by chattering) and over eighty-five per cent with 'Hindering other pupils' (e.g. by distracting them from work, interfering with equipment or materials) (DES, 1989) and it must be accepted that such low-level disruptions are part of one's day-to-day teaching. For the most part teachers prefer to maintain order without resorting to punishments or rewards and this chapter discusses the various factors which make it more likely that students will comply when teachers intervene in their behaviour.

Maintaining a good relationship

Having a good relationship with those we teach makes the process more enjoyable for all concerned and particularly now that students are being regarded by some as 'clients' whose opinions on their schools are becoming increasingly significant, teachers are being encouraged to develop good personal relationships as an important 'new managerial skill' (Reynolds and Packer 1992). This may well bring smiles (or frowns?) to the faces of experienced teachers who do not need telling that if we get on well with students not only do they produce better work but they are more likely to co-operate with us on occasions when we have to correct their behaviour. Tattum (1982) concluded from his study of disruptive students that their behaviour was determined by whether they liked and respected the teacher and not by what consequences could be brought to bear on their actions, and a recent OFSTED report (1/93/NS) made a similar observation. 'Pupils too behaved differently in different settings; on many occasions, their behaviour was directly related to the quality of their relationships with individual teachers and vice versa.' If a student dislikes a teacher he may treat any intervention as a personal attack and evidence that the teacher bears a grudge against him. He may even blatantly misbehave in front of the teacher to display his own power or to provoke a confrontation and the relationship will further deteriorate into a personal battle. On the other hand it is extremely unusual for confrontations to arise between students and teachers who share good friendly relationships.

Teachers who engage in extra-curricular activities benefit from meeting students in more informal settings and consequently have the opportunity to form better personal relationships. Unfortunately, those students who present the most problems are often the least likely to take part in clubs and societies or even attend school regularly. Personal relationships are formed by mutual agreement and if we are held in low esteem by students, attempts to get to know them better might be regarded as prying or ingratiating ourselves. It is evident that some students feel no sense of loyalty to the school community, have abandoned any educational goals they may have had, and purposely set out to disrupt their lessons. The question then is how to prevent such negative attitudes from forming or at least not to make them worse. Coercive approaches such as using threats and punishments are more likely to further alienate such students but attempts to create and foster good relationships in the following ways may help to improve such attitudes.

Solidarity

In 1927, Elton Mayo and his associates from the Harvard Business School began a classic series of experiments at the Hawthorne plant of the Western Electric Company in Chicago (described by Roethlisberger and Dickson, 1939). For many years the company had been concerned with the need to improve the production of telephones, against a background of worker complaint, and had called in a number of experts to advise on the problem. Mayo began by isolating two workrooms, one for a control group where conditions would be left the same, and the other where the illumination would be noticeably varied. Output of components increased measurably in the varied illumination room, but unexpectedly it also rose in the control room where no changes had been introduced. A subsequent experiment showed that if the workers *believed* the lighting was being stepped up daily, though in fact it was not being altered, they commented favourably on the 'increase' in light: if they were led to believe the light was being reduced they said they preferred the 'brighter' conditions. However, the production did not change materially at any stage in this experiment, regardless of the levels of illumination.

Subsequent experiments were carried out on a small group of women operatives producing relays, where various changes in working conditions were introduced which the experimenters believed would be associated with productivity, such as piece work (the more relays produced, the more pay received), rest periods, free hot meals and shorter hours. Over a period of eighteen months the average hourly output rose steadily for each operative, though there were temporary fluctuations associated with domestic and social problems. In the penultimate experiment the operatives agreed to return to the original conditions, working a six-day week without rest pauses for a period of three months, and though the average hourly outputs did decrease slightly, the total output was higher than ever because of the extra hours worked.

In the final experiment lasting seven months, the rest periods were reintro-duced and the average hourly rates for each operative were the highest recorded, together with high levels of job satisfaction. 'During period XIII the group reached one of its highest peaks in morale. This was demonstrated in a number of ways: by pride in their work, trying to beat their former out-put records, helping one another to maintain a high standard . . . *They had become bound together by common sentiments and feelings of loyalty.*' (my emphasis)

It was evident that the changes in physical conditions alone could not account for the improvements in production and morale as a previous exper-iment had included additional benefits. The attitudes of the operatives were also being influenced by:

- the presence of the test room observer who had shown a personal inter-est and discussed their domestic and work-related problems with them;
- an interest and concern being shown for their personal health and well-being and the conditions in which they worked;
- being consulted about each stage of the experiment so that they under-stood the reasons for the changes being introduced and could object if they so wished.

In this way the operatives had been made to feel that they were valued not just as workers but as people who were important to the organisation and to each other, and not just as cogs in a machine.

The work subsequently gave its name to the 'Hawthorne effect' whereby when using people in a psychological experiment one had to take account of the fact that merely by involving them they would be likely to feel special and be inclined to 'make the experiment work', so it became necessary to conceal the true nature of the experiment from them. However, Mayo had shown that a crucial factor in good management is to try to create a sense of solidarity of purpose within an organisation by listening to and consulting with the workforce and making them feel valued. Solidarity involves 'pulling together to achieve or maintain a common front' (Danziger, 1976) and it is a central principle in teacher–student relationships that we should be working *with* rather than against one another. Students should be respected and, as they mature, active partners with teachers, increasingly instrumental in the decisions that affect them, rather than passive recipients of teachers' treat-ment. The Hawthorne principle also applies to the staff of the school, as a sense of common purpose and working together is an essential foundation for solidarity in the whole community. However, if only lip service is paid to consultation and concern for welfare and there are few practical outcomes of benefit to the staff and students, then a sense of solidarity will not be engendered. It is unlikely that the Hawthorne workers would have sustained their efforts without the assurance that the return to no benefits would last only for three months. In the late 1960s a group of factory workers decided to forgo a day's pay each week to assist the country at a time of economic need. Their action was widely publicised by the media and the 'I'm backing Britain' campaign was born, resulting in many workers making similar gestures, but without some evidence of practical benefits to themselves or the wider community, the sense of solidarity was soon dissipated. Our aim should therefore be to demonstrate a genuine concern for the welfare of those with whom we work, both teachers and students, in an attempt to make membership of the community more rewarding and satisfying for all and not simply to produce more 'productive' relationships and academic output. The sense of solidarity epitomised in the Hawthorne effect is a product of genuine concern for the welfare of others in the community and not the cause.

Solidarity is expressed and fostered by:

- staging and supporting social events for the parents, staff, students and other 'membership' groups such as one's form or House;
- supporting sporting and extra curricular activities;
- supporting events which embody the tradition and identity of the school;
- taking a personal interest in one's students;
- sharing aims, loyalties, successes and disappointments with students in the variety of contexts where we share common membership;
- listening to and consulting with students at appropriate times about their work, behaviour and the rules which govern their conduct;
- using inclusive language (we, our, us) when appropriate, for example, 'This lesson we're going to ...', 'Some of us are getting a little overexcited';
- sharing humour and esoteric understandings (see p. 149);
- giving corrective instructions and consequences in a sensitive, relaxed manner, avoiding expressions of personal power and opposition (frowning, pointing, threatening, demanding);
- using detentions constructively to help solve problems;
- implying one expects students to co-operate by giving them time and space to comply with instructions rather than standing over them until they have 'obeyed'. The act of moving away or moving to another matter once the instruction has been given implies that one expects co-operation, though one must follow up if the student does not comply. Rogers (1990) suggests following corrective instructions with 'thanks' instead of

'please', though this requires a rising intonation on the final word 'thanks' which seems more characteristic of the Australian accent and may require some practice. Teachers here sometimes give the mitigated instruction using 'please', then add 'thank you' after a brief pause, which achieves a similar effect;

- resuming normal working relationships after any disciplinary intervention (see p. 167).

Using humour

Humour can also serve to soften corrections and promote positive relationships as sharing a joke implies a degree of social solidarity (Walker and Adelman, 1976). A teacher noticing a student day-dreaming might say in a light hearted manner, 'Sorry Paul, am I disturbing you?' and if Paul accepts the teacher's claim to solidarity and authority he might smile, look a little awkward and give his attention. However, he could challenge the teacher's claim by replying sullenly, 'Yeah' and continuing to look away. This highlights the danger of using humour in this way as the student may interpret it as sarcasm or may simply wish to bring into question the relationship being claimed, by not sharing the joke. The teacher then has to respond to what is clearly more serious disrespectful behaviour and it is all too easy in these instances to become aggressive to avoid looking stupid. On the other hand, genuine humour and relaxed behaviour can keep incidents in proportion and also help to unite the participants.

In one case I heard of, a young female teacher in a school for children with behaviour disorders walked into her class of fourteen-year-olds to find one tall well-built boy brandishing an iron bar in a threatening way at those around him. The atmosphere was extremely tense, but as she walked in she gave him little more than a casual glance and walked unconcerned to her desk. 'Right,' she said, 'Pokers away, pay attention.' For humour to be effective, the teacher must genuinely see the funny side of the situation and not appear to belittle the students who are likely to be very sensitive at such times. In this respect it is probably vital that a good relationship already exists so that one's remarks will not be misinterpreted. If the teacher is disliked, his attempts at humour will probably be treated derisively so before risking it one must be confident of being 'among friends', or at least potential friends, and secure in one's position. When the teacher pretended to be using Larry's face as a model to draw a gargoyle (p. 129) he had to be sure that the student would not interpret it as an attempt to belittle or embarrass him. It is also unwise to try to 'force' humour prematurely as this can give the impression that one is soliciting acceptance or trying to avoid a threatening situation, and is similar to the weak smiles shown by those experiencing social stress. It is therefore important to feel relaxed and secure in one's relationships with students and allow humour to arise naturally.

Friendly greetings and conversations

As one gets to know the students, the developing personal relationships will be expressed in an increasing informality such as in the nature of the subjects discussed and the humour shared. In primary schools, where the class have the same teacher for most of the year, there are usually many opportunities for this to happen but at the secondary level, where contact can be limited to one period a week, individuals can remain largely anonymous. In his survey of a large comprehensive school Badger (1992) found that teachers complained they had insufficient time to have informal meetings and conversations with students to get to know them better and that this contributed towards the behaviour problems in their school.

> Both staff and pupils indicated that lack of time was a major factor linked with behavioural problems. From a pupil point of view a teacher who had time was a 'good one' and by implication less liable to experience disruption. If that time was used to listen to a pupil then so much the better. From a staff point of view time became the most crucial commodity of all. Time to listen, to communicate, to meet, to discuss, to support, to move from lesson to lesson, to prepare lessons, to counsel, to meet parents, to work effectively. Lack of time, above all, is perceived as an all-embracing contributor to behavioural problems throughout the school.

Because of such pressures it is easy to overlook even the friendly greeting and the brief informal chat to individuals and to restrict one's interactions to the subject matter of the lesson, so that one's treatment of students remains at a functional impersonal level. A teacher reflecting on her experience with her GCSE Art class describes how she became aware of the different attitudes she expressed towards two adults who joined the class.

'There were two adults when we first began and I noted that when they came in through the door I would say things, talk about, you know, say, "It's windy today isn't it?" Then I thought, well, I don't say that to the children ... I don't speak to them in that way. I ... There's no reason, there's no law, except it didn't happen when I was at school, that you can't say, "Isn't it windy", "What a nice day", "How's your mum?" You know, "Is your granny alright now?" and things like that as they come through the door, as you would to any visitor into an area over which you preside, and that's made a difference to my teaching ... I've made a more conscious effort to do that.'

As Badger found in his survey, such greetings and personal interest are appreciated by students as they emphasise the familiar and friendly aspects of the relationship rather than the differences in rank. White and Brocking (1983) interviewed students who had left school about their attitudes towards their teachers and many of their comments bear this out.

'They should take a personal interest in you.'

'Being able to talk to teachers is important.'

'You think that the teachers are teachers and they're not people.'

However, if teachers are held in low esteem by their students, such personal interest might be regarded as prying or as attempts to ingratiate themselves.

There is a great deal of evidence to suggest that positive attitudes towards students are associated with fewer discipline problems. For example, 'deviance insulative' teachers (Hargreaves, 1975) were optimistic and assumed their students would behave and co-operate. They liked and respected all students and enjoyed meeting them outside the classroom. Similarly Reynolds and Sullivan (1981) noted the importance of good relationships in incorporating students into the organisation of the school.

> Another means of incorporation into the values and norms of the school was the development of *inter*personal rather than *im*personal relationships between teachers and pupils. Basically, teachers in these incorporative schools attempted to tie pupils into the value-systems of the school and of the adult society by means of developing 'good' personal relationships with them. In effect, the judgement was made in these schools that internalisation of teacher-values was more likely to occur if pupils saw teachers as 'significant others' deserving of respect.

Good relationships are central to effective teaching and co-operative discipline. As one student put it

> The way teachers talk to pupils is important. If a teacher talks at you, you don't really listen, but if you're discussing something on that same sort of level *with* a teacher, you learn much more. (White and Brocking, 1983)

We must, of course, accept the fact that some students may in the short term dislike us for the actions we have to take and should not be tempted to curry favour by compromising the standards of work and behaviour which we expect.

In summary, good relationships are expressed and maintained by:

- maintaining a relaxed manner;
- fostering solidarity with students;
- expressing intimacy where appropriate (for example, by smiling and using a familiar form of a first name);
- using positive evaluations when appropriate;
- using humour where appropriate.

Low-key interventions

In classes where a good co-operative relationship has developed with the teacher, an orderly atmosphere prevails apparently because the students impose their own constraints on their behaviour in the way that most further education and adult audiences do. Either through choice or habit, they help to create a context in which teaching and learning can take place. When the teacher does have cause to correct a student's behaviour, the manner in which this is done expresses the co-operative nature of the relationship rather than the teacher's rank and associated powers. The correction is presented more as a reminder than an order.

In many classes, however, there are students who persistently cause disruption or fail to get on with the work set. Babad *et al.* (1989), whose research is described earlier (p. 90), warn how teachers may unintentionally convey negative attitudes to some students and this is a particular danger when correcting the persistent offender. Anything in the teacher's manner which conveys attitudes such as, 'Not *you* again', 'You'd better stop that or else . . .', or even, 'I'll try to ignore it because I want to avoid a battle', will all reinforce for the student his or her identity as a troublemaker, a role which will then have to be lived up to in the interaction. Negative attitudes also present the teacher as working against the students rather than working with them and the intervention is thus defined as a win/lose situation. On the other hand, the teacher who can treat students *as if* they were normally co-operative, offers them an opportunity to adopt that position by complying. They at least have the chance to present themselves as co-operative, rather than being prejudged or 'labelled' on the basis of previous experience. It may be sensible, therefore, to try to respond with a low-key correction in the first instance of a minor offence though there should be a clear understanding by both student and teacher of what further consequences will follow if this is not heeded.

Withitness

The term *withitness* was coined by Kounin to describe the ability of a teacher to communicate to children 'by her actual behaviour (rather than by simple verbal announcing: "I know what's going on") that she knows what the children are doing, or has the proverbial "eyes in the back of her head".' The concept is concerned with the teacher being able to select the student who is instigating the deviant behaviour (in Kounin's terms, the *target of the desist*) at an early stage before he has had a chance to involve others. If the teacher selects the wrong student – makes a *target* mistake, such as punishing an innocent child – or reprimands for a minor offence while more serious ones are occurring (Mr Howie does just this when he comments on uncovered books yet allows noise and interruptions (see p. 158)), he will fail to communicate 'withitness'. He might also make a *timing* mistake so that the unwanted behaviour had spread to others or increased in seriousness before he intervened.

There are a number of points at which a teacher might intervene to correct a student's behaviour. These would include the moment the child was about to misbehave and any time during or after the misbehaviour but the majority of research suggests that if a teacher intervenes as a child is about to, or just beginning to, misbehave, a repetition of the misbehaviour is less likely than if the child had been allowed to complete the act. There are several possible explanations why early intervention should be more effective, apart from the fact that a child 'caught in the act' is less likely to deny his action. The teacher clearly demonstrates that he is alert, so that the child may feel more liable to detection. The act of interrupting the behaviour is itself a statement of the teacher's control and status in the situation. (In contrast, a child interrupting a teacher might be reminded that such behaviour is inappropriate.) The child may also be denied any reinforcement which would have resulted from completing the act, such as making a friend laugh or engaging others in some disturbance. Early intervention also prevents the spread or escalation of unwanted behaviour, so that the teacher has only to deal with a relatively minor offence. A more esoteric explanation is that the fear of detection becomes associated with the initial action or thought of action, rather than its completion. Gnagey (1975) expresses this view very clearly, 'Teachers who can see deviances developing should stop them before they get started. Otherwise, the fear operates only after the fact.'

One must be careful to exercise withitness with a degree of sensitivity and discretion. For example, though there are many reasons why unwanted behaviour should be nipped in the bud, there may be circumstances when a teacher is able to allow a child to make mistakes and learn from them. It may also sometimes be better for the long-term relationship not to intervene immediately in a public situation but to have a quiet, private word with the student later.

If teachers show withitness, the impression given is that they are alert and will notice when students misbehave. The concept was narrowly defined by Kounin for the purposes of his research, but one could extend the principle to incorporate other aspects of teachers' behaviour. The ability to name children in the class in the early meetings will also suggest an alert awareness, for example. The reverse is very evident when the teacher gives the wrong name, particularly when reprimanding: the impact is totally lost, as the students are able to correct the teacher and regain some initiative in the interaction. Simply naming one student often has more effect than a general reprimand directed at the whole class. Apart from conveying 'withitness', it might also highlight the vulnerability of every individual, whereas a reprimand to the class sustains each student's anonymity, though this may be what one intends.

Remembering to carry through any consequences one had promised also contributes to an impression of being in control or 'withit'. Having instructed a student to remain at the end of a lesson, or promised to deprive a class of a favourite activity, it is vital to remember. Otherwise one gives the impression of being muddle-headed, and students will soon learn to ignore one's threats and instructions. Other aspects of good organisation, such as being in the right place at the right time with the required books and equipment, or anticipating changes in arrangements, such as dental inspections or sports practices, all help to convey the impression of efficiency and 'withitness'.

Non-verbal reminders

As a general rule it is better to say and do as little as possible as it is far better to leave students to infer what they are doing wrong and how they can rectify the situation. I saw a good example of this while watching a group of ten-year-olds taken by an experienced teacher. One boy threw his rubber to a friend and it fell on the floor. As the latter was about to get it, the teacher merely said 'Leave it' and looked at the boy who had thrown it. Rather shamefaced, he went and picked up the rubber and gave it to his friend.

Clear messages can be conveyed by expressive teachers without the use of words, provided of course that the student is looking at them. They are used most appropriately when the 'target' student is the only one who is not complying with a request or condition. For example, the student may be quietly talking instead of working or attending to the teacher, or writing instead of listening to an explanation. They are particularly effective in correcting such behaviour with the minimum of risk of an extended dispute or confrontation, for a number of possible reasons.

- The deliberate omission of words gives the message a sense of being private or covert, implying that the teacher does not wish to make the correction public, to protect the student from embarrassment.
- There is an implication that words are unnecessary because the student *already knows what he or she should be doing* and only needs a gentle reminder. The onus is mainly on the student to comply willingly and the implication is of a shared understanding of the teacher's authority.
- Non-verbal messages, perhaps because they are private in nature and imply mutual trust do not so readily call forth a rejoinder from the student as do verbal corrections.

The teacher first has to establish eye contact with the offending student which can be done by chance, 'catching the student's eye', or by discreetly calling his or her name. Immediately eye contact is established the first gesture that teachers perform is to raise the eyebrows, opening the eyes wider and almost simultaneously tilting the head forward slightly.

The brow raise is universally understood as a greeting when it occurs briefly between people who know one another (Eibl-Eibesfeldt, 1972), but in this context it may serve to 'tune-in' the student to the teacher, indicating 'I am attending to you', as the brow is raised for longer than an 'eyebrow flash'.

143

The student is also clear about the meaning as there is no return of the gesture as would be the case in a greeting. Instead, he or she will remain looking at the teacher to discern the message being expressed, for example that the teacher is beckoning him over, or questioning his behaviour. Teachers often use the brow raise to great effect to control communication during question and answer sessions sometimes even leaning towards a student and extending an open palm, inviting a contribution (see Figure 20, p. 38).

If the student does not comply with this initial brief signal or appears not to understand, the teacher will quickly follow with a more specific gesture, miming the instruction to 'Put it down', 'Turn around', 'Take your feet off the chair', and so on. All this takes place in a matter of seconds and immediately the student begins to comply the teacher will probably signal 'Thanks' in some way and withdraw the gaze.

The brow raise, indicating attention, can be accompanied by other facial expressions which convey the teacher's feelings about what the student is doing. A relaxed smile would express the friendly nature of the intervention, the expectation of compliance and the insignificance of the offence. A frown would clearly show disapproval (Figure 28 on p. 81) where the teacher has been interrupted by a movement at the back of the room. However, such expressions must take account of the existing relationship. Smiling at those who are unfriendly can result from stress and may reveal that one fears conflict: frowning at those who do not accept one's authority can be perceived as provocative. Ideally these expressions should reflect a *shared* understanding of the relationship. A more neutral expression characterises the intervention as detached and professional, leaving the student to consider why he has the teacher's attention.

Activity 9 Non-verbal interventions

These activities can be tried alone but are better carried out with the help of a colleague acting as the student.

1. *The object is to intervene in the event described by calling the student by name and when eye contact is established to convey the message clearly and, if appropriate, to acknowledge the student's compliance, but without speaking.*

    (a) *Student:*   *Talking to neighbour.*
        Teacher: *Convey 'Can I have your attention, please?'*

    (b) *Student:*   *Leaning back on a tilted chair.*
        Teacher: *Convey 'Sit straight in your chair please.'*

    (c) *Student:*   *Using a piece of science apparatus in a silly inappropriate way.*

Teacher: Convey 'Stop that. I'm surprised at you.'

(d) Student: Snatching ruler from a neighbour who objects and resists.
    Teacher: (Use two names) Convey 'Come here, please.'

(e) Student: Out of seat acting the fool as teacher enters the room.
    Teacher: Convey 'What do you think you're doing? Return to your seat.'

(f) Student: Working on the task set.
    Teacher: Convey 'Can I see you for a moment please?'

(g) Student: Chewing
    Teacher: Convey 'In the bin please.'

If you are trying these interventions with colleagues, the 'student' should know the situation but not the intended message from the teacher. The 'student' should always comply but then write down what unspoken message they received, including how they think the 'teacher' felt. Compare the message you intended with the one they received and discuss the possible impressions that such a teacher would give.

2. Intervene in the following situation, using only the student's name, but by varying your tone of voice, facial expression, eye contact and gesture, try to convey the following messages, particularly any emotional component.

The 'student' is fooling around at the back of the room, trying to take his neighbour's book. You are assisting a student at the front when you are alerted by the commotion.

(a) Convey 'Come here please. I'd like a word with you.'
(b) Convey 'Stop that this instant! I'm really angry with you.'
(c) Convey 'What do you think you're doing? I'm surprised at you.'
(d) Convey 'Please don't do that. Be reasonable, please.'
(e) Convey 'Heaven help me – you again! What am I going to do with you?'

Discuss which responses imply that the teacher is in control and which have unhelpful connotations for the teacher's authority.

3. (i) How many ways can you show positive messages such as thanks, admiration, congratulations and pleasurable surprise, without speaking?

    (ii) Think of a suitable phrase or short sentence to accompany each expression.

145

Selective attention

Teachers acquire the habit of looking for unwanted behaviour to show 'withitness', but in attempting to do so they may inadvertently encourage it. Dreikurs (1982) pointed out that one clue to the students' motives being attention seeking is that they comply with the teacher's instructions but then quickly offend again, so it is sometimes better to try to ignore the unwanted behaviour. If the motive is power they will initially refuse to comply and in these cases the act of ignoring may be interpreted by the student as an expression of fear or uncertainty in one's ability to manage the situation, similar to backing down in a confrontation. It is important therefore to appear relaxed and unruffled and clearly show that although one has noticed the behaviour, attention is being deliberately withheld.

Rogers (1990) uses the term 'tactically ignoring' to refer not only to the fact that it is part of a pre-determined plan of action but that it will be used in conjunction with attending to the appropriate behaviour. In this way the student will be aware that the teacher's attention is not forthcoming, not because the behaviour has passed unnoticed, nor that the teacher is simply ignoring *him*, but that it is the specific action which is not being responded to. The principle of planning to ignore particular low-level disruptive behaviours such as calling out, being out-of-seat or being slow to follow instructions, and to attend positively to the 'competing behaviours' of putting hands up, remaining in seat and following instructions promptly, has long been established, particularly at the primary level. Teachers are advised to 'catch them being good', giving selective attention only to students when they are behaving appropriately but to show no reaction, not even a pained glance or a 'give me strength' appeal to the heavens, is not always easy. If one is attempting this strategy it is to be anticipated that the child, on being ignored, will initially increase his attempts to be noticed by escalating the behaviour perhaps with actions too serious or dangerous to ignore. The teacher may then abandon the strategy and publicly chastise the offender which will only serve to consolidate the new, more extreme form of disruption. It is important therefore to have planned what to do in such contingencies. If the student can be quietly removed from the room for a short 'time-out' period (see p. 116) this can be very effective as he is also deprived of the other potential source of attention, his peer group. Montgomery (1989) suggests that young children could remain in the room, but set apart from the others on a time-out cushion or chair for brief periods, as a 'neutral zone for calming down and regaining composure'.

Selective attention can therefore be a useful means of reducing low-level disruptive behaviours and is likely to work best with younger children, and teachers have learned to comment on those who are 'sitting up ready to go', working quietly, or who have 'hands up', to good effect. However, as students grow older such public treatment from teachers is likely to be embarrassing rather than encouraging as it continues to cast the student as a young child.

Inviting co-operation

French and Peskett (1986) found that teachers of infants differed in the way they gave 'pedagogic instructions' from 'control instructions'. The distinction was one of immediate function as they acknowledged that any instruction seeks to exert some control over students. Pedagogic instructions were concerned with the accomplishment of learning tasks and were delivered in straightforward imperative structures, for example, 'Press the little button now', or 'Put them in one by one'. On the other hand, control instructions were marked by a variety of features which attenuated or mitigated the potential impact of the direct imperatives. The simplest of these was the use of 'please' or an added endearment term, for example, 'Peter, stop the talking please' or 'David, sit down love'. Mitigation also occurred in the vocal quality of the control instruction which was sometimes delivered in a friendly or 'jokey' tone. The addition of a positive evaluation such as '... there's a good boy' or a reason, for example, 'Don't do that now otherwise others won't be able to hear', also served to soften the impact. French and Peskett suggested that 'because teachers generally do not use unmitigated control instructions, they are able to hold this option in reserve for occasions when firmness is required.' Following an unheeded mitigated instruction the teacher could use a direct imperative, which would presumably also serve as a reprimand.

Another way of interpreting mitigated control instructions is that they are an attempt to protect the authority agreement by lessening the implications of power in the direct imperative and giving an additional message about the friendly and co-operative nature of the relationship. Expressing solidarity and intimacy function to mitigate the effects of the authority that the teacher is claiming (i.e. the right to correct the behaviour) and give the opportunity for the student to present his compliance as a voluntary, co-operative act. Mitigation is unnecessary with pedagogic instructions as the basis upon which authority is being claimed is clearly the teacher's knowledge of the subject, which is not in question.

Similar ways of making 'directives' appear less obvious have been discussed by Holmes (1983) and it is not surprising to find mitigation occurring with older students, particularly in informally managed classes, though the form it takes varies. One would almost certainly hear vocal mitigation, the use of 'please', and what French and Peskett described as 'request formats', and 'minimisation of adjustments', for example, 'Could you just ...', but not, 'There's a good boy'. A control instruction given in general terms to the whole class also mitigates the impact for the particular culprits, for example, 'Some of us are doing too much chattering and not enough work'. A glance at the offenders shows one is not acting thus out of ignorance.

Holmes pointed out that 'Teachers may avoid ostentatious demonstrations of authority by using explicit directive forms, but children soon learn from experience that the teacher's every wish is their command'. In relation to students' behaviour, therefore, teachers' hints, suggestions, requests and commands are all part of the same continuum as there is an underlying understanding that students are expected to comply. When they do not they, in effect, bring the teachers' authority into question. The milder, mitigated directives give the students the opportunity to co-operate willingly and hence the teacher may avoid emphasising the power difference which is expressed by giving commands to be obeyed. They may also leave a teacher the option of not insisting that the student complies, whereas once a direct imperative has been used, particularly if accompanied by other displays of dominance, this would be seen as backing down. The dilemma faced by teachers is to try to retain an authority relationship, based on co-operation, without jeopardising any firmness with which they may subsequently have to act. Mitigation must be expressed with complete integrity or it is likely to be interpreted as weakness by students, who would then be more likely to resist subsequent attempts to insist on compliance.

Giving positive directions

It is easy to get into the habit of reacting to unwanted behaviour in negative ways such as 'Shush!', 'Don't . . .', 'Stop . . . .', rather than to draw attention to what students should be doing. Rogers (1994a) provides numerous examples of how negative statements can be rephrased in positive forms.

'Don't call out', becomes 'Hands up if you have a question, thanks';

'Don't butt in' becomes 'One at a time, thanks'

and 'Stop running' becomes 'Remember to walk in the corridor, thanks'.

In the same way,

'Shush' becomes 'Remember to use your partner voice, Michael. I can hear every word you're saying' (see p. 195).

A simple positive statement can be very effective as when a teacher noticed that two Year 9 girls were covertly talking instead of listening to his explanation and he quietly said, 'Girls . . . Do your best . . .' and then continued.

Rogers also recommends that teachers should give conditional agreements if possible, rather than refusals, so that

'No, you can't leave until . . .' becomes 'Yes, when you've . . .'. Some teachers use very creative approaches where positive connotations are imparted to instructions which would otherwise be regarded negatively. For example, when students had begun to pack away their books on hearing the bell at the end of the school day, instead of saying,

'Nobody leaves until this work has been copied from the board', the teacher said 'Your ticket for the door is to copy the work on the board'.

On another occasion a student attempting to leave was assuring the sceptical teacher that he really had copied the homework into his diary. The teacher could have asserted,

'Well, you're not leaving this room until I've seen it!', but instead said, 'I'm just going to have to call your bluff on this one, Ricky.'

The expressions we use in giving instructions not only communicate information about what we wish others to do, but can also express the esoteric nature of the relationship we claim to have with them. As mentioned earlier (p. 72), an expression such as 'fags out' instead of 'pay attention' expresses familiar and informal aspects of the relationship and hence mitigates the authority implied in giving the instruction. In the same way, Walker and Adelman (1976) give an example of a student who is able to 'soften' the nature of a teacher's intervention by referring to one of his expressions which had developed into a class joke.

> After one boy, Wilson, had finished reading out his rather obviously skimped piece of work the teacher sighed and said, rather crossly:
>
> *T. Wilson, we'll have to put you away if you don't change your ways and do your home-work. Is that all you've done?*
> *B. Strawberries, strawberries (laughter)*
>
> When we asked why this was funny, we were told that one of the teacher's favourite expressions was 'Like strawberries – good as far as it goes, but it doesn't last nearly long enough.'

Clearly the meaning of such expressions is exclusive to those with the shared experience, so its use expresses this group identity. The teacher had already mitigated the admonishment to the student by threatening to 'put him away', obviously an extreme and unavailable option and probably another of his characteristic expressions. The student would be likely, therefore, to feel some guilt if he did not co-operate with a 'friendly' teacher who was apparently working with, rather than against him.

Some of the terms we use have negative connotations associated with coercion and deterrence and we need to question whether they are now appropriate to describe practices which may have changed. 'Punishment' was a term once in common use but most schools now use 'sanctions', which also has a positive side. Here, the term 'consequences' is used, which more accurately reflects the emphasis on students having to take responsibility for what they choose to do.

Another term which has negative connotations is 'detention', though many would argue that this is still quite appropriate as its function is to deter students from offending. However, if we intend to use detentions constructively to ensure that students complete work, to discuss and practise more acceptable behaviour, and to improve relationships, as suggested later (p. 199), a more neutral term might be better. The aim would not be to invent a euphemism for the same negative event but more accurately to describe a constructive experience.

Asking questions

Everyone finds it difficult to maintain attention on a subject without the occasional times when the mind wanders or we become distracted by another event. When students are talking or day dreaming, or are otherwise occupied instead of working on the task set, the teacher can refocus their attention by asking a work related question such as, 'Hi Mark. How are you getting on?', or 'Any problems Anna?' If they raise a particular problem, one can first remind them what they should do if they are unable to get on, 'Remember to put your hand up (ask me for help) if you can't get on', before dealing with the problem. The initial enquiry is usually sufficient to prompt a return to the task but one can always follow with the reminder to carry on with the work, and how long they have left to complete the task.

Rogers (1989) suggests using 'question and feedback' to break into a 'disruption cycle' and gives the example of dealing with two girls who are talking by starting with a *what* rather than a *why* question.

> *Teacher:* 'What are you doing, Michelle, Denise?'
> *Student:* 'What's it look like?' *(in smart alec tone)*
> *Teacher:* *(not drawn in)* 'Actually it looks like you're talking loudly over here *(feedback)*. What should you be doing?'
> *Student:* 'Dunno!'
> *Teacher:* 'You should be doing your maths. Would you get back to your maths quietly, thanks.'

If the teacher is addressing the class an appropriate question can help to 'tune in' those whose concentration has wandered, though teachers sometimes use them to 'set up' students for a public reprimand by first posing the question and then naming the unwary student.

'Jason . . . Can you tell me?'

The question has been posed with the expectation, not to say hope, that Jason will be totally bemused by this rude awakening and be unable to answer. The teacher can then publicly deliver the familiar mocking rebuke which he himself probably first heard as a student.

'You don't know do you? ... You know why you don't know? ... You weren't listening were you? ... If you don't listen, how do you expect to learn anything?'

Impeccable logic, but designed to humiliate Jason in front of everyone. A more respectful approach would have been first to call him by name, and then, when he attended to ask him a question *that he would probably be able to answer*, which might serve to tune him back into the lesson without showing him up in front of the class.

Incidental corrections

A teacher is reading a story to a class and notices that a student is chewing. While continuing to read she picks up the waste paper bin, takes it over to the student and, on hearing the sweet drop, returns it to the front. A similar instance is described on p. 17 where the teacher removed a pen from a girl's hand and shut her exercise book (see Figure 10). The teacher's attention appeared to be on reading to the class and the 'reminders' to put the sweet in the bin or to listen without writing were carried out as 'asides'. Only a few students nearby would notice what was happening as the reading was uninterrupted.

An incidental matter-of-fact intervention is one in which the teacher is apparently attending to another matter, so that it is carried out almost in an 'absent-minded' manner, not in the sense of forgetful but literally, in that one's mind appears to be on other matters. Within the context of a co-operative relationship it is likely to be very effective for a number of reasons.

- The incident appears only to require minimal attention from the teacher, implying that it is not serious and expressing a clear expectation that the students will comply.
- The interventions usually involve the exercise of unilateral rights towards the student, which expresses the status difference in the relationship.
- The student apparently does not have the attention of the teacher who also takes care not to draw the attention of the class to the event. The interventions are therefore covert and personal and the choice therefore rests with the student whether to comply with minimal embarrassment or to make an issue of the intervention by publicly challenging the teacher.

Some further examples may illustrate these points.

A teacher is helping a student and notices two boys at the other side of the room having a mock fight with their exercise books. She looks up, calls them by name in a matter-of-fact tone, and beckons them over to her. She resumes her work with the student and only when they have come over and waited a few moments does she look up and take them both aside for a quiet word.

Here the teacher allowed only minimal interruption to her work and apparently attended to the boys only when she was ready. She interrupted them, beckoned them over and expected them to wait, albeit briefly, while she finished. Such actions have clear overtones of both the teacher's role and rank as one would certainly not be expected to act in this way towards a superior or even a colleague. Dealing with the boys in a quiet, personal manner emphasised the co-operative nature of the relationship.

An incidental quality is also conveyed by not making the behaviour the main focus of our interaction but by mentioning it in the course of a friendly greeting or conversation. When I was involved with the incident over litter (p. 118), I made this the immediate focus of the interaction whereas I could have walked over, exchanged a greeting and spoken to them about the weather or asked how they were getting on before asking for their help in picking up some of the litter. A teacher may need to speak to a student about a minor matter such as dress or lateness in the same way. Rather than address the matter directly it is both polite and less confrontational first to offer a friendly positive word such as a greeting, ('Jason, Hi. Come and sit here.' (Figure 30)), ('Hello Raj, how's it going?'), a comment about the work, ('Hi Lucy, any problems?'), or any enquiry about a social interest, ('How did the game go on Saturday?'). This emphasises the friendly nature of the relationship before dealing with the reminder about the behaviour, almost as an afterthought ('Where have you been?', 'Have you got your tie with you?').

By first expressing the positive aspects of the relationship in a genuine manner, the teacher distinguishes the student, who is valued, from the behaviour, which needs to be corrected. It is also easier to confront those people we dislike or whom we believe dislike us as by making the positive aspect of the relationship the first focus of the interaction it is harder for the student to object to the subsequent correction. This may seem highly contrived and manipulative but where good relationships already exist teachers would 'naturally' act in this way, perhaps to protect the relationship or simply because they liked the students. It follows that even if the decision to be friendly is consciously taken while dealing with the offence, teachers thereby do not differentiate their relationships to those who normally behave well from those who persistently offend.

An incidental correction is most effective when students accept the teacher's authority as the onus rests with them to co-operate. In a context where the teacher has lost authority one might expect such actions to be challenged,

Figure 30 *'Jason, hi. Come and sit here ... Where have you been?'*

though when they are introduced in an unobtrusive, matter-of-fact manner, even difficult students will sometimes comply without realising it, before belatedly trying to object.

Direct interventions

When low-key interventions fail to have the desired effect or when a teacher judges it to be necessary, a more direct approach should be used but it is still important to try to avoid embarrassing or humiliating the student.

Kounin (1970) called such direct attempts to correct behaviour *desist techniques*, but his research failed to identify any variables which had a significant effect in determining their success. He therefore concluded, 'The techniques of dealing with misbehaviour, as such, are not significant determinants of how well or poorly children behave in classrooms'. On the other hand, it would be true to say that teachers who have established well-ordered classrooms use desist techniques effectively, though they are seldom needed. It is probably in the first meetings that students either learn to respond to or to ignore the teacher, and the manner in which low-key and direct interventions are carried out then may affect classroom management. Their successful use later, however, is possible only in the context of responsive and co-operative behaviour to which they, in turn, contribute.

If an unruly atmosphere has developed, direct interventions may apparently have little or no effect in improving the situation, not because they are being delivered inappropriately but because the teacher's right to deliver them is in question and their frequent use is the consequence of the students' disregard for them. In such circumstances more radical measures are called for, such as the use of progressive consequences as part of an official classroom behaviour policy (see p. 185). It is always important, therefore, to bear in mind those factors which reduce the possibility of emotional confrontations and are more likely to lead to successful outcomes.

Finding the right words

When it is necessary to say something, it is important to think of the actual words one intends to use, because in the heat of the moment it is easy to blurt out the start of a sentence which is impossible to complete sensibly. Perhaps there is a small disturbance in the room as the teacher enters. Appropriate clichés come to mind, such as 'If you think you can behave like that then you're very much mistaken', or 'I don't expect to leave the room for five minutes and find you fooling around when I come back.' What might emerge if the teacher is not careful could be something like this: 'If you expect ... to behave like that when I come into the room ... then ...'. The first few words make it difficult to complete the sentence constructively, and the impact of the reprimand is lost as the teacher stumbles on in an incoherent way. Even if the sentence is completed, it can often be very tortuous – I heard one teacher say: 'Come on … this is not going to be … enough co-operation from you!'

Torode (1976) considered that the actual language used by the teachers he observed was of paramount importance.

> Mr Howie's problems were not, in my estimation, a consequence of his non-verbal communication patterns, his pose, dress or tone of voice. In all these respects he performed precisely the character of the normal teacher if … there is such a thing. The incessant and sometimes violent conflict which characterised his lessons was directly attributable to the teacher's failure to give an enduring definition of the situation while that situation was being enacted.

Giving 'an enduring definition' refers to the ability to present statements of 'external rules' which the teacher enforces in an impersonal but inevitable way. Torode contrasts Mr Howie with his more successful colleague:

> Mr Crammond told them: 'Right now. I think we know the order of events. You've got to get on by yourselves today, and I don't want to see anybody off their seats.' Here the familiar definition is reasserted. The inner picture, the definite *we* is posed as knowing 'the order of events' watched over in the outer picture by the less certain *I*. On the other hand the *you* is portrayed as quite dominated by external necessity. 'You've got to. …' The *I* appears again later in the utterance, again in an indefinite outer picture contemplating a definite factual state of affairs.

This detailed analysis, though interesting, over-emphasises the function of language at the expense of other factors in the situation and would certainly not be relevant to those occasions when non-verbal behaviour alone is used very effectively. The particular language used is only part of the way in which a teacher attempts to give an enduring definition to the situation. Though it can be one factor in conveying impersonal and uncompromising attitudes, it is important to remember that the meaning which is conveyed by any interpersonal communication depends upon the *total* behaviour, so that two teachers could use identical words but achieve entirely different effects (Wragg and Wood, 1984a).

Wood and Schwartz (1977) suggest that *clear directives* – unambiguous instructions, stated in an uncompromising way – are the most effective means that parents can use to ensure that children do as they are told, and the same principle may apply in schools. A teacher's determination will be expressed in the steady focused gaze, serious facial expression, calm unresponsive manner and use of the imperative form for the instruction. As a general guide the directive should specify the student's unwanted behaviour, the effect that it has on you and others, and the behaviour you require, for example,

'Robert ... when you call out others don't get a chance to answer. Put your hand up. *(pause)* Thank you.'

'Jane ... when you wander round the room you distract others. Go back to your seat and carry on with your work.'

If she begins to do so we can say, 'Thank you', but more likely she will indignantly explain, 'I was only borrowing (asking, looking for and so on) ...', and will need to be reminded, 'What should you do if you need help?'. Rogers (1994a) gives excellent practical suggestions for phrasing instructions in appropriate ways and avoiding long and fruitless arguments with students.

For a clear directive to be delivered with complete integrity one must be certain that it is necessary and one has the right to give it as any uncertainty in these respects may be revealed in one's manner. It is also crucial to back up any threats made to students and, though it is now illegal, it is significant that in the earlier example one boy who did leave his seat was immediately 'belted' by Mr Crammond. Failure to back up threats would eventually result in the students ignoring them. Any intermittent and therefore unpredictable punishments would be regarded as unfair because other similar misbehaviour has passed unheeded. Students should quickly learn that one's threats are, in fact, promises.

It is important, therefore, not to say anything that one cannot carry through, and if necessary to plan the words and manner one will use. Taking a few moments to do this instead of reacting immediately to a difficult situation can be time well spent.

Keeping the message brief

It can be a mistake to deliver lengthy reprimands, particularly if they contain an instruction to the class, as the following example from a lesson transcribed from video-tape illustrates:

> The teacher enters the room together with a class of fourteen-year-old students. There is considerable noise and movement in the room and the teacher waits at the front, facing the class, for fifteen seconds before saying: 'All settled where you're going to be? *(1 sec.)* Right, now you can all jolly well go outside and come back into those places as if you were ... *(2½ secs)* ... er *(1 sec.)* ...' *(continues to speak for 4 secs, but this cannot be understood from the tape partly because of the noise of the students going out but also because she spoke more quietly.)* Immediately the instruction to go outside had been given, some students started to move and, while the teacher tried to think of a suitable description, the majority of the class were moving out and the noise was considerable.

The teacher failed to achieve sufficient contact before the lengthy message and also did not control the students' movements adequately. If one fails to anticipate premature movement, as in the example, then the first student to show any intention of leaving his desk should be stopped abruptly. By moving away while the teacher is still talking, students reduce the effect of any reprimand and convey a lack of respect, so instructions must be carefully phrased.

A short reprimand, delivered in a quiet serious manner when the class is silent, is usually quite sufficient to stop unwanted behaviour, but it is tempting to try to 'ram home' the message by saying more. Criticism or justification for one's actions often gives the impression of nagging, and it is far better to discuss the matter with the class or individual later, if necessary. In the example above it might have been better simply to have settled the class and begun the lesson, but having decided to send the students out the teacher need only have instructed them to stand up, and when there was complete silence said, 'You came in *very* noisily ... Now you will *quietly* ... go and line up outside the room. This row.' (Indicate to move.) The quiet delivery, with emphasis on key words, and appropriate pauses while the teacher gazes directly at the students, serve to calm the atmosphere and express disapproval. At the end of the lesson one could remind them of the need to enter classrooms in an orderly manner, and perhaps warn them of the consequences that will follow if they do the same thing again on the next occasion. It would still be a mistake to dwell too long on such a minor matter, however.

A long diatribe in response to unwanted behaviour is rarely necessary and will have the opposite effect to the one intended if the students feel it is unfair. It is hard to understand what Mr Baker felt he was achieving by the following harangue, delivered to a class of thirteen-year-olds (Wragg and Wood, 1984a).

> 'Are you eating? Well stop moving your jaws. Sit still. Some of you should be in strait-jackets. If you don't work then you'll have to copy out of the book. You are going to conform to my standards which are not in any way abnormal. In this life there are some people who want to work, there will be six million unemployed in the 1980s – none of you has convinced me that you are in any way employable. I'm in charge here. I can enforce it and I will. It's as simple as that (bangs fist on table). Sooner or later someone will get physically hurt. Don't push me too far. We're all human, boys and girls alike. You are my family. It's my legal right to punish you. Don't forget that.'

Such a lengthy and exaggerated proclamation of one's power only suggests insecurity and at best the students would have been bored or amused by the outburst. At worst they would have felt angry and insulted. It is also a clear example of what Kounin termed 'behaviour overdwelling' (p. 126) and would only serve to interrupt the momentum of the lesson.

Acting decisively

Badger (1992) in his school survey of students' views found that 'a surprisingly repeated student comment across all years was that 'Teachers doing nothing' contributed to behaviour problems, the implication being that for the teacher not to act decisively on certain incidents increases the likelihood of their recurrence. This does not mean that the most effective measures are assertive and confrontational but that it is a mistake to 'notice' or comment on conduct with evident disapproval or frustration and then to do nothing about it. For example, a teacher might mention that a student is not in his correct seat, or that he has not done his homework. If no further action is taken to put the matter right, given that there is no adequate excuse, this creates the impression either that the offence is trivial and probably permissible, or that the teacher is powerless to do anything about it. Unless one is prepared to go to the trouble of seeing that the offence is corrected, it is better not to notice, though this does have implications for the teacher's 'withitness'. In the following extract from Torode's paper we see Mr Howie making this mistake:

Teacher:	Right, would you turn to page fourteen *please!*
Cannon:	*(Shouts)* Where's Barrie?
Teacher:	Right, would you all stop talking, please? Cannon sit down *(no change in overall level of noise)*. Now, just before we went away . . .
Various Boys:	*(Interrupting)* Are we going away?
Teacher:	*(Continues, ignoring interruption)* We were talking about sets.
Boys:	Sex! Sex!
Teacher:	*(Interrupts uproar)* Scott, why is your book not covered? And Davis, yours as well.
Davis:	I just got it.
Teacher:	You didn't just get it today. The next thing I want to talk about is the interaction of sets.
Cannon:	What was that word you used?

Though this extract contains a number of other mistakes, it was clearly unwise to comment on the uncovered books without seeing that something was done about them. (It also illustrates the students attempting to take control of the communication by interrupting and questioning, and the teacher talking above noise in the room. It is almost certain that Mr Howie's non-verbal and vocal behaviour would have been consistent with the 'loser' image suggested in the transcript.) Also, if one persists with mitigated forms of instruction when they are no longer heeded it can sound like pleading for co-operation and one frequently hears student teachers imploring, 'Will you *please* stop the talking!', or making ambiguous statements such as, 'There's too much noise in here' which does not specify exactly what is required.

In a further example, transcribed from video tape, there is similar indecisive action from the teacher with a Year 6 boy. The class has cleared away their previous activity in readiness for an assembly to follow. The teacher has called them to attend but many of the children are still talking. However, she begins.

Figure 31 *'Oh dear . . . I can't carry on . . .'*

Teacher:	The sharing assembly ... *(talking does not subside)* The sharing assembly ... *(as she again speaks over the noise, one boy, Mark, stands up and throws his orange in the air and catches it)* If you ... *(Mark remains standing in full view of the class, holding his orange)* Oh dear! ... I can't carry on ... Mark, I've got to stop ... please, sit down. *(not said with any conviction.)*
Mark:	*(Rudely)* I ain't got a chair! Graham took it.
Teacher:	*(With apparent surprise)* Oh dear ... Well ... *(the ancillary helper places a chair behind Mark, having anticipated the event)* Thank you very much. *(Mark remains standing and the boy seated next to him speaks to him)*
Student 1:	I didn't nick your orange.
Mark:	Yes, you did. *(Another boy calls over)*
Student 2:	Sit down now, Mark.
Mark:	No! *(In a 'Why should I?' tone)* *(Mark's neighbour then pushes him down into his seat and the teacher immediately takes this as her opportunity to resume)*
Teacher:	Right. If you would ... *(Mark is already out of his seat again and walking across the room but the teacher chooses to ignore this and continues without a pause)* like to read the story you have written in the sharing assembly ... *(one girl interrupts)*
Student 3:	What story?
Teacher:	The one you wrote yesterday. *(Hands go up, some call out. Mark is at the back of the room talking to another boy.)*

One can infer from this short extract that the teacher has difficulty in managing the class and is reluctant to risk asserting herself. She therefore talks above their noise, gives way to interruptions and answers calling out, all of which reinforce her ineffectual position. In this case it would have been difficult to ignore Mark's behaviour but the action she took was very indecisive and expressed how she felt that he had control of the situation *(Oh dear! ... I can't carry on. Mark, I've got to stop,* before the weak request, *Please, sit down.)* This was almost a plea for help, to which some of the children, particularly Mark's neighbour, responded, which again emphasised the teacher's weak position. By continuing to speak when Mark again left his seat she conceded that he could do as he wished as she would not risk a direct confrontation.

In both the previous examples many of the children were very challenging, but the teachers' failure to manage the communication almost certainly contributed to the difficulties they had and by not dealing effectively with the behaviour to which they attended they further undermined their positions. When teachers lose confidence in themselves they often make half-hearted attempts to gain control and do not follow through with their actions. In the activity following this chapter a number of options in handling these incidents will be discussed.

Respectful treatment

It is always important to treat students with respect, particularly when expressing disapproval of their behaviour. This is not simply to set a good example but also to reduce the risk of escalating personal confrontations with resentful students.

Two aspects of punishment have been distinguished by Ausubel (1968). One is the 'non-reward' or aversive treatment as a consequence of misbehaviour, the other is 'the penalty for moral infraction which takes the form of blame, rebuke, reproof, chastisement, censure or reprimand'. The latter is conveyed primarily by the teacher's attitude and language as in the following example.

Two Year 9 girls are quietly talking at the back of the room while the teacher is talking to the class, so he responds angrily, 'Will you two shut up. You've been wittering all lesson so far – haven't got a thing done. You won't know anything more at the end of the lesson than you did at the beginning – which is precious little!'. This sarcastic and reproachful manner clearly personalises the intervention as the teacher's attention is directed at the 'deviant person' rather than the 'deviant act' (Hargreaves, 1975).

A teacher could intervene in a respectful way, dealing only with the behaviour or, in addition, chastise the offender. For instance, a child who had been warned that if he wasted time he would have to complete his work during the lunch hour, could be dealt with in either way. A totally impersonal approach would involve the teacher calmly and privately saying, 'I said that if you wasted any more time you would have to do this work during the lunch hour. Come to my room at twelve o'clock and finish it then.' With a personalised approach the teacher would appear much more emotionally involved with what the student had done, and might deliver the same consequence in a threatening and public manner: 'Trust you to waste your time! You have to be different from the others, don't you? Well, I warned you! Come to my room at twelve o'clock sharp and bring your work – what there is of it!' The first treatment simply presents the student with the logical consequences of his action but does not attach any blame to the offender. The message conveyed is that the student has chosen not to work at that time so must make it up later, whereas in the second case there is an additional message that the offender is inherently wicked, which accounts for his behaviour.

If one adopts a reproachful and disrespectful attitude when intervening one may well worsen the situation as a resentful student could seek revenge, accepting the implied identity of 'troublemaker' and behaving accordingly, in an attempt to demonstrate to his peers that he 'couldn't care less' and cannot be intimidated by teachers. Any further outbursts from the teacher simply consolidate this position as the student becomes equally determined not to lose face in front of his friends. Such public confrontations can very quickly get out of control and what Laslett and Smith (1993) describe as the 'escalation-detonation staircase' becomes, in fact, a rising escalator as neither party feels able to back down.

There is, however, some evidence to suggest that blame may subsequently assist younger children to be more critical of their own actions (Aronfreed *et al.*, 1963) and in a survey of nearly 1,800 junior school students, fifty-six per cent believed that 'Telling you off loudly so that everyone can hear' would make them behave better next time, whereas only thirty-three per cent felt that 'Telling you off quietly so that only you can hear' would be most effective (Merrett and Tang 1994). However, the survey did not report how many students remembered receiving such treatment and were speaking from personal experience rather than observing their peers. The fear of 'getting into trouble' probably deters the great majority of young children from misbehaving though many may have had no first-hand experience of it but will have witnessed others 'getting told off', being 'kept in' and having to do extra work. Some are able to avoid such experiences throughout their school career and it could be argued that we do them a disservice if we try to do away with the practice and rely on approaches to encourage personal responsibility and treat children respectfully. It is interesting that 'telling off' did not feature as a strategy for dealing with disruptive behaviour in the Elton Report (DES, 1989) but when I surveyed over 200 secondary teachers, fifty-eight per cent believed it was appropriate to shout at students occasionally and sixty-two per cent claimed they did. Although thirty-three per cent believed one should ideally never shout at students, only four per cent of teachers claimed this to be their practice (see p. 231).

Some teachers intentionally set out to show up their students in order to correct their behaviour and discourage others from similar acts and Sharpe (1993) has recommended that student teachers should be trained to give their students 'a good telling-off'. He advised that, if appropriate, they should stand over the child with folded arms or hands on hips and insist on eye contact, commanding 'Look at me when I'm talking to you!' He goes on to suggest that this might be done publicly, to display the 'Mr Nasty' side of one's nature to the other students so that they choose to co-operate with 'Mr Nice'. This description will be very familiar to any teacher of my generation as every school had at least one 'hit man' or woman, the mention of whose name was sufficient to make the strong tremble. Some teachers still deal with students in this manner and can reduce them to tears but even if we believed it to be desirable, in the present social climate with its emphasis on childrens' rights and accusations of abuse directed at teachers, it is, to put it mildly, risky. Most teachers would consider it unacceptable to rule by fear and intimidation as it effectively reduces students' own responsibility for their actions and also condones behaviour which in other contexts would be regarded as bullying.

It is probably inevitable that we will sometimes rightly show we are angry over a student's behaviour but it is important to try to direct that anger not at the student, but at the unacceptable behaviour. This can be done by directing one's attention to a specific point down and to the side of the student when denouncing the behaviour (*this* is unacceptable) but returning one's gaze when giving reasons in a calmer manner. This is not easy to do, but if one looks and gestures emphatically at the student, the impression given is that the *student* is unacceptable rather than the behaviour which we should try to dissociate from him.

Personalised verbal rebukes bring only short-term relief and merely establish a pattern for future interactions and it is reassuring that O'Leary *et al.* (1970) found that intervening in quiet, inconspicuous ways was more effective than giving loud reprimands. A quiet firm correction is respectful as it keeps the interaction private and minimises the potential embarrassment for the student.

The following extract is transcribed from a video tape and begins at the start of a lesson with a dispute between Year 10 girls over seating in a laboratory. Debbie is standing and arguing with two girls who are already seated as the teacher intervenes.

Debbie:	(*Angrily*) I can sit here can't I? (*Turns and looks at teacher*) She can copy it out.
Girl on front bench:	No, we haven't got a book.
Teacher:	(*Quietly*) Sit (*Pointing to bench behind*) . . . Debbie.
Debbie:	(*Talking to girl on front bench and ignoring teacher.*) Yeah . . . Well if you got a book . . . I could sit there.
Teacher:	(*Handing Debbie a book from the front bench and speaking in a quiet reasonable manner*) I'm surprised at you . . . Go on (*pointing to another seat. There is a pause of 3 seconds during which Debbie tilts her head to the side in a conciliatory manner.*)
Debbie:	(*In a softer, more reasonable tone*) Carol can sit there.
Teacher:	(*Sharply*) Look you're doing different work to everybody else.
Debbie:	(*Returning to a more aggressive manner*) I don't want to sit there on me own with them.
Teacher:	(*Loudly and firmly*) Sit there! (*Debbie moves*). (*Turns to the two girls on the front bench and speaking in a firm tone*) Right, there's your book, there's your book, get on with it.
Debbie:	(*As teacher moves away Debbie goes back to original place and snatches up a book from the bench*) I ain't finished . . . I've got this. (*Takes the book and throws it down on the bench behind, pulls her chair out in a noisy way and sits down.*)
Teacher:	You're a nasty rude girl. (*Class laughs.*)

The teacher managed to get Debbie seated elsewhere but it was clear that she would be unlikely to co-operate much during the lesson. If relationships are not to be worsened by such disputes the teacher should try to ensure that the outcome is 'better for both' (Kilburn, 1978). In the above extract, when the teacher spoke quietly and respectfully to Debbie and implied that her behaviour was uncharacteristic, (I'm surprised at you), she became conciliatory in her manner. Had the teacher continued talking quietly and sympathetically instead of immediately snapping back sharply, Debbie might have been inclined to sit down without a fuss. She was obviously very annoyed about losing her seat and it would have been more sensitive had the teacher acknowledged her feelings and offered a compromise at this point, for example, 'I can see you're upset about this, Debbie. Would you just sit over here for five minutes while I get the lesson started, then I'll come back and sort it out.'

When dealing with the incident over litter in the playground (p. 118), instead of ordering the boy to comply I could have simply picked up the litter myself if he had not accepted the invitation to co-operate but subsequently I could have written a private note to the student on the following lines[1]:

> Dear Darren,
>   This morning at break when I was on playground duty I asked you to pick up some litter and you refused. I had seen you drop it but didn't want to make a fuss over such a small thing. You may have just been having a joke but it was rude and unnecessary.
>   Please help to keep the school tidy by putting litter in the bins.
>
>   Mr Robertson

Such an approach would lose its credibility if used too frequently, but it has the advantage over a personal interview in that the student does not have to respond. In a face to face talk the student might feel that the teacher's motive was to extract an apology which, in fact, would probably be the only satisfactory outcome. With a private note he may subsequently take the initiative and apologise. Obviously there would be many circumstances when the student's attitude called for more immediate action but the principle of showing respect even when being treated rudely is important, provided it is respect for the student's rights and not respect for him as a dangerous opponent.

Respectful treatment involves acknowledging the students' rights by:

- focusing on the behaviour and not the person;
- avoiding dismissive attitudes, for example, 'I don't care if you're going out tonight, that's not my problem.';
- avoiding intentionally embarrassing or hurtful treatment;
- keeping disciplinary interventions as private as possible;
- offering a compromise if possible;
- listening to the student's point of view, at an appropriate time;
- acknowledging their feelings;
- apologising when one has made a mistake.

When students are disrespectful towards teachers it is questionable to demand respect for one's rank ('Stand up straight and look at me when I'm talking to you!') but one should always feel able to say, with justification, 'I don't speak to you like that and I don't expect you to talk to me like that.'

---

[1] I am grateful to Professor Andy Hanson of Chico State University, California for this suggestion.

Personal responsibility

Students should not be encouraged to believe that other people or events are responsible for what they choose to do. Rather, it is important to convey to them, 'You own your own behaviour' (Rogers, 1994a). It should be made clear what the acceptable behaviour is but also that it is not the teacher's responsibility to make the students comply. ('I can give you the map and the route to take, but you are driving the car.')

Langford *et al.* (1994) in a survey of 117 senior secondary school students in Melbourne found that the great majority endorsed rules to guarantee the right of others to learn but there was a small minority who rejected these on the basis of general hostility to schools and teachers. They argued, therefore, that sanctions were necessary to back up the rules as some students not only resisted them in practice but were also opposed to them in principle. It follows then that teachers should take every opportunity to involve students in the decisions that affect their lives, such as in making classroom rules and consequences, but should also ensure that they face up to those consequences that follow from their actions.

When it is necessary to intervene in their behaviour, personal responsibility can be emphasised to students by presenting them with choices rather than telling them what to do. When we make a choice we are to some extent exercising control over the outcomes which affect us. Choices in life are rarely absolutely free as we actually have limited options to choose from and for most of us, 'I did it my way' has a hollow ring. Nevertheless the sense of 'owning' an action, even if this means choosing one of only two alternatives, or simply of how and when the action is carried out, is for most of us preferable to being made to do something when and how we are instructed. In the same way, we prefer to have the opportunity to co-operate (if we choose) rather than obey (because we have to).

It is helpful, therefore, if we can present choices to students about outcomes that *they* can control rather than imply that we can control them by inflicting particular consequences. A student may, therefore, be given a choice as to where they carry out an action ('You can either choose to work quietly here or you will have to sit at the front') or when they carry out an action, ('You can either choose to do the work set now, or come back and complete it at break'), or sometimes be given a choice between two or more options, ('Can you put the bracelet in your bag or on my desk'. 'Will you switch the computer off or shall I?').

It is not unusual, however, for teachers to convey, by their manner and language, that they intend to control the situation for the student. Consider an example where two girls have been recently warned about talking and giggling at the back of the room while the teacher is instructing the class. He reacts angrily.

165

'I've just told you two to stop nattering and pay attention! If I see you talking again Carol, I'm moving you to the front! Do you understand?'

Here the student must obey the teacher or suffer the consequences which he controls. She is being *made* to keep quiet and listen. However, had he calmly said, 'Sharon, ... Carol ... I've spoken to you once about talking. You can either choose to sit quietly and attend, or if you talk again I shall move you to the front, Carol. It's up to you', the threatened consequences are identical, but the teacher's manner and language offer the students a sense of control. If it is possible to deliver such a message quietly and privately to the students this will further enhance the impression that the teacher is not trying to intimidate them into compliance. Rather than convey to the student, 'If you do this, I will do this to you', one should attempt to convey, 'The choice is yours. I can't make you'.

If we eventually have to ask the student to move her seat, withdrawing and attending to another matter offers her some sense of control over when she chooses to move rather than standing over her until she does (though one must always ensure that if the student does not then move, they know the further consequences that will ensue). When she moves, but does so in a sulky, defiant manner, we can allow her this choice rather than publicly calling her back to 'do it properly this time.'

One must take care to speak in a relaxed definite manner when presenting the choice, as a pleading tone can convey a weak, 'Why are you always doing this to me?' attitude and an aggressive manner suggests 'I've had just about enough of you' both of which emphasise the personal conflict with the student rather than the choice being presented. The actual words we use may also give the wiley student an opportunity to manipulate the situation.

A teacher had warned a Year 6 boy about talking and had eventually given him a choice either to work quietly or be moved. When she saw him talking yet again she walked over and announced, 'I see you have chosen to sit at the front, Robert', believing this to be the instruction to move. With studied concentration he replied, 'No, I'm still thinking about it.'

If students are determined to challenge the teacher's authority there is little that can be done to force them to comply but it is essential that they learn to take responsibility for the consequences of their actions. Teachers can encourage personal responsibility by:

- negotiating rules and consequences with students;
- making it clear that it is not their responsibility to control students' behaviour but only to make the consequences which will follow their actions absolutely clear;
- inviting co-operation rather than demanding obedience;
- offering choices to students whenever possible.

Of course, teachers do have a responsibility to protect students and themselves and should always attempt to take control if they feel the behaviour is
dangerous.

Resuming normal relationships

When one has had to intervene to correct a student's behaviour it is important to resume a normal relationship as early as possible, as if nothing has
happened. If the intervention had resulted in an emotional confrontation this
will not be easy as something clearly has happened, and this underlines the
importance of a calm professional manner when intervening.

A simple enquiry as to how the student is managing or if they have any
problems is sufficient, and one should avoid any reference to the previous
incident, though in this example the teacher is able to appreciate the students' co-operation.

> *The Year 10 class are discussing a topic in groups prior to reporting back and the teacher is
> talking to a group at the front of the class.*

'. . . There's a section where you can go and sta. . .'
(He looks up abruptly at a group at the back who are fooling around)

'Uh, Lads . . . You've got about five minutes to complete the task . . . all right?
. . . I just may change my mind and decide that someone else other than the
chairperson will report back . . . Don't leave it to Abu, you're supposed to be
involved as well.'

(Resumes talking to original group)

*(A couple of minutes later, the teacher moves to the back of the room and speaks to the group
next to Abu's)*

'Are you ready to report back? . . . Good'

(Moves to Abu's group)

(Laughing) 'We're getting on to it now, are we? Right *(Looks at their notes)* Yeah,
that's important. How's that one used?'

The friendly co-operative nature of the relationship was expressed in the
relaxed, laughing tone of voice, the use of 'we' rather than 'you' and the positive comment about the work. When I had to reprimand a student during a
lesson, I would subsequently ask a small favour of him (if the opportunity
presented itself), such as to borrow a rubber or ask him to deliver a message. One tends to ask favours from one's friends and such actions were
attempts to restate the co-operative nature of our relationship. Similarly
Wragg and Wood (1984b) observed that after Mr Abel, a well-liked and
respected teacher, had reprimanded two girls he apparently deliberately

went over and spoke to them in a very friendly manner about their experiment.

It is important to avoid the temptation to justify one's action at such times as one can appear ingratiating and apologetic, as if fearing that the student will no longer like us, or regretting the action one has taken. In the following example, the teacher, after some difficulty, has managed to move a Year 6 student from his group to work on his own. As he takes his seat he sulks, 'I'm not writing anything'. Instead of simply stating that he can either choose to do the work set now, or later during his lunch hour, and moving away, the teacher chooses this moment to try to coax him to work, and explain her action.

> *(In a whining tone)* ... 'This is distracting everyone else and it just isn't *fair* on everyone else ... 'cos you know you can do it – you've done good work before. It's just a matter of thinking and concentrating instead of talking all the time ... It's not fair on everybody else ... As soon as you've finished that piece of work you come back and sit down normally with everybody else ... There's no point in sitting there sulking about it, you might just as well do it ... and get on with it ... It's pointless ... Now I'll come back in a minute to see if you've finished.' *(Moves away)*

Throughout this episode, while the teacher spoke, the boy looked down at his work and did nothing, and the teacher's manner took on a 'be reasonable' tone as if pleading to be understood.

It is better not to become involved in a protracted dispute which students may be using to waste further time or to avoid the consequences of their actions, but to express one's authority clearly by repeating the rule or instruction and not necessarily feeling obliged to explain or justify one's actions at the time, in response to resistance. A useful approach, in this respect described by Rogers (1994a), is to *accept* the student's complaint but then repeat the rule or instruction, for example,

'You may think it's unfair but you know our rule (repeat).'

'She may have been talking but I need *you* to (repeat).'

'You may have been joking but you were disrupting the lesson and I need you to (repeat).'

'You may think I'm picking on you but (repeat).'

'I'm sorry you think that but (repeat).'

'Mrs Jones may let you but (repeat).'

'You may think it's boring but that's the work we have set (repeat).'

168

At the very most the teacher might have acknowledged the boy's feelings, ('I understand you feel upset about being moved, but I gave you a choice . . .'), before giving the instruction about the work to be done and moving away, as students are unlikely to be in the frame of mind to listen and be reasonable at such times. It is better to take clear and firm action and accept that students may feel unhappy about such treatment and to return later with an enquiry or comment about the task set. The object should be simply to resume normal relationships and not to solicit friendship. Clearly, the more emotional the confrontation, the more difficult this will be.

Choosing the appropriate intervention

Experienced teachers have usually developed a range of low-key and direct measures to respond to unwanted behaviour from students and use their professional judgement to decide, whether, at one extreme, it would be better to choose not to intervene or, at the other, to state the consequences which will follow if the student chooses to offend further.

Graded or 'stepped' interventions

Rogers (1989) recommended that teachers made a discipline plan based on beginning with the 'least intrusive' measures and progressing by a series of steps to the 'most intrusive' which would involve having the student removed from the room. The teacher would take into account the context of the disruption (where it occurs; are the students working on a task or is the teacher addressing the class) and begin with an appropriate low-key measure, such as tactically ignoring. Each further step would involve a more direct intervention though any step could be repeated at the teacher's discretion, but the student would be presented with a clear choice before any consequences were enforced.

This principle (or 'law of least intervention') of being able to increase the level of seriousness perceived by the student is widely acknowledged, as is adopting a planned response rather than an emotional reaction. However, the way we choose to intervene should take into account the seriousness of the student's behaviour. If our intervention is too 'soft' the impression may be given that we fear a confrontation with a dangerous opponent and do not want to commit ourselves to more definite action; if the intervention is too harsh it can appear that we feel threatened by trivial incidents and need to be on our guard.

The nature of the disruption

A useful guideline is provided by Neill and Caswell (1993) who distinguished 'open' and 'closed' challenges and gave detailed descriptions of the posture, gaze direction and significant student behaviour which characterises each. In a closed challenge there are no attempts by the students to keep their actions covert or avoid being discovered by the teacher. The students, usually a pair, are relaxed and often smiling and they make no attempt to draw others into their interaction as it is not intended to entertain the class or annoy the teacher. Such behaviour would be described as 'wasting time', 'nattering', 'mucking about' or 'fooling around' and the authors suggest that such incidents seldom evolve into disruption which carries a high risk to the teacher's authority. The majority of such incidents that they observed in their video study '. . . died away by themselves without teacher and pupils even having been engaged', but if the children did notice that the teacher was aware of them this was usually sufficient to call them back to their work. They suggest that an actual intervention may be counter productive, so, initially at least, the most that would be called for would be a low-key intervention. In contrast, the open challenge is more serious as it is intended to involve other students or to annoy the teacher but avoid 'getting caught'. The students involved show a high level of 'control checks', that is they frequently glance at the teacher to check they are not being observed or otherwise try to conceal their actions out of the teacher's view. This clearly reveals that the students are fully aware that their behaviour is prohibited and there is frequently a degree of malicious intent as they deliberately try to undermine the teacher's authority by disrupting the order he is trying to maintain. When the teacher intervenes the student may deny any involvement or trivialise the offence to suggest his own innocence and the teachers over-reaction. Interference with other students' work and property is 'only having a laugh' and actual assaults become 'accidents'. If the teacher fails to deal effectively with such behaviour the students may no longer try to conceal their actions, but openly disrupt the lesson and treat any attempts by the teacher to intervene with contempt.

It may be possible in the first meetings to nip such behaviour 'in the bud' with a low-key correction but one must be prepared for such students to persist with their conduct or to resist when corrected, so teachers should have a direct intervention and statement of consequences prepared. In some situations it may be necessary to adopt a classroom behaviour policy involving defined progressive consequences, which will be discussed in the next chapter, but whatever action one chooses it should be taken in a manner which appears calm, controlled, focused and decisive, and totally unruffled by the students' responses.

Easily said, but if one knows at each stage what to do next this can greatly reduce the stress experienced.

Activity 10 Intervening in unwanted behaviour

1. *Consider what might be unhelpful about the way the teacher chooses to intervene in the incidents described and write down a more positive response aimed at returning them to the task. (Assume the students are aged thirteen to fourteen years, though you could also consider whether their age would affect your response). In the following examples the students have been set tasks to do and the teacher is moving round, dealing with individual queries.*

    (i)   *A boy is taking a considerable time sharpening a pencil beside the bin at the front of the room.*

    Teacher: *(In a tired, sarcastic tone) 'Kevin ... Don't you think it would be a good idea if you stopped wasting time and got on with some work for a change?'*

    (ii) *A boy throws a textbook to a friend at a nearby desk.*

    Teacher: *(In a hurt, hard-done-by tone with rising intonation) 'Daviiid! ... Can't you pass the book properly? It'll be no use to anybody when you've finished with it.'*

    (iii) *The teacher notices one girl wearing an earring.*

    Teacher: *(In a hurt, 'be reasonable' tone) 'Sarah ... You know you shouldn't be wearing an earring.'*

    (iv) *Two boys are having a mock battle with exercise books at the back of the room.*

    Teacher: *(Angrily) 'Cut it out, you two! Anymore rubbish like that and you'll both be in detention.'*

    In the following examples the teacher is addressing the class, introducing a topic.

    (v)   *The teacher hears a tapping sound and identifies the source.*

    Teacher: *(Irritated) 'Kathy ... Do you have to keep tapping that pencil while I'm talking?'*

    (vi) *A girl enters late and makes for her seat.*

    Teacher: *(In an accusing tone) 'What time do you call this Jane? The lesson started five minutes ago!'*

    (vii) *A boy is making a paper aeroplane from a handout the teacher has just given out, and is clearly not attending.*

    Teacher: *(Smiling and attempting humour) 'Oi, Brian ... I've just spent five seconds photocopying that for you.'*

    (viii) *The teacher notices that some students have begun to hum, but cannot reliably identify the source.*

    Teacher: *(Angrily) 'OK, who's humming? Darren was that you?'*

2. *In the incidents involving Mr Howie (p. 158) and the boy with an orange (p. 160), what would be more appropriate responses from the teacher?*

171

Suggestions for responses

The following suggestions are intended to give an indication of a more professional low-key way of responding to the incidents, minimising their significance and expressing the solidarity in the teacher-student relationship. They are not meant to be the definitive responses as, in practice, there will be many variables in the situation which the teacher will take into account when dealing with each matter.

1. (i)   The remark characterises Kevin's behaviour as intentionally avoiding the work set. It is publicly given and Kevin might feel obliged to answer back. One might instead give a non-verbal signal to Kevin to return to his seat or walk over and quietly tell him to continue with his work.

   (ii)   The teacher's tone suggests he is not able to be instrumental in directing David's behaviour but can only plead with him to be reasonable. A more direct correction would be more appropriate, for example, 'David . . . Remember to pass the books properly. They are easily damaged.' Alternatively, catch David's eye or politely call his name. When he attends, express non-verbally, 'I'm surprised at you'.

   (iii)   Again this is a weak, frustrated response implying, 'Why do you always do this to me?' The teacher might have first admired the earring then given Sarah the choice to either put it in her bag or on the teacher's desk, reminding her of the school rule about jewellery.

   (iv)   The intervention defines the behaviour as serious and was given as a personal emotional reaction. A more controlled low-key response would be to call them by name and when they attended, to beckon them over and deal calmly and incidentally with the offence, for example, 'What were you doing? Have you completed the work?'

   (v)   The teacher has interrupted her message to the class and made Kathy the focus of attention. A more direct approach might be to remove the pencil from Kathy's hand incidentally, while continuing to address the class, or privately to say, 'Put the pencil down thanks Kathy. The tapping is very distracting'.

   (vi)   The teacher has again interrupted the progress of the lesson and this public remark would immediately put Jane on the defensive. One might first greet Jane and then deal with the lateness in the appropriate way, for example, 'Hello Jane, . . . Take your seat, I'll see you later', or simply indicate that she should sit down. Lateness, particularly if persistent, must still be followed up with logical or 'official' consequences.

   (vii)   The remark suggests the teacher is reluctant to correct Brian's behaviour either because he is a strong opponent or the teacher is afraid of being disliked. A more direct correction would be appropriate, for example, 'Straighten that out Brian. You'll be needing it in a minute'. As he complies one might add, 'Thanks'.

(viii) *One might expect Darren to deny humming as such practice is calculated to frustrate the teacher and is apparently succeeding. An early, professional intervention would be more effective, directed generally at the class, for example, 'I need everyone's attention. The humming is very distracting.' The humming would probably cease as one spoke, giving the opportunity to say, 'Thank you' before continuing, which would discourage the culprits from resuming. The humming could indicate that the class are becoming bored and the activity should be changed.*

In each case it would be essential to plan what one would do or say next if the student continued to offend.

2. Mr Howie
    Mr Howie clearly needs to take control of the communication, perhaps by instructing the class to stand, reminding them of the rules for speaking and the consequences that will follow. Only if he is able to sustain an orderly atmosphere should he 'notice' the uncovered books, though it might be more sensible first to see that the class are underway on a task. He should then deal with the students privately, stating when the books should be covered and the consequences for failing to do so.

    The incident with the orange
    The teacher could have first given Mark a clear choice, for example, 'Mark ... put your orange in your bag or on my desk, please, and take your seat'. When the seat was provided for him, further resistance could have been dealt with in a similar way. 'Mark, I need you to be seated and attending as I am speaking to the class ... (wait and if no compliance) ... You can either choose to sit down now or we shall discuss this during the break ... (wait briefly and resume the message to the class. If Mark delays resuming his seat, see him at break). One should also discourage other students from intervening, for example, 'Graham! ... I am talking to Mark, thank you'.

    Failure to comply with a clear instruction at any point should result in the dispute being 'postponed' until it can be discussed privately. The reader might also try to role play this incident with a partner, using rules and consequences as in activity 11 on page 197.

7 Disciplinary Plans and Schemes

In response to a perceived need to improve standards of behaviour, work and attendance, many schools adopt more systematic approaches by devising plans for teachers to follow in the classroom, as part of a whole school policy involving the structured use of positive and negative consequences for students' work and behaviour. Various published whole school disciplinary schemes, in particular *Assertive Discipline* (Canter and Canter, 1992), are proving popular with some schools as a radical way of dealing with problems of discipline, truancy, poor motivation and low attainment in students. In fact there is little new in the approaches they use, particularly in the emphasis on praise and rewards, and undifferentiated progressive consequences for offences, except that they are integrated into a systematic, coherent school policy. Indeed, some of the practices employed were once widely used in schools but became less popular due to ethical and practical considerations and are now enjoying a new lease of life. All the schemes concentrate to a greater or lesser extent on:

- adopting a planned approach to dealing with student disruption;
- using praise and rewards systematically to promote good behaviour;
- making the policy official;
- using progressive consequences;
- intervening professionally to correct behaviour;
- supporting the classroom teacher.

A planned approach to classroom discipline

Adopting a planned approach to classroom discipline should mean that when offences occur we do not have to consider what course of action to take as the incidents have been anticipated and the action determined, sometimes even down to the words we will use; we simply follow the plan. This can remove a great deal of stress from the situation as, without a plan, in the heat of the moment it is often not possible to think of what to say or do and it is easy then to resort to trying to intimidate the student into compliance, or even to give way. When we know what we have to do next it is easier to remain calm and this could be the major factor in determining the outcome. Better still, if the student also knows the plan, the element of uncertainty is replaced by predictability.

In a school where there are generally good relationships between students and teachers, very few instances of seriously disruptive behaviour and a strong sense of community, a structured formal policy which specifies the teachers' responses to offences would hardly be required and, if it existed, would probably not be remembered by staff and students due to its infrequent use. However, in a school where there are vulnerable teachers due to inexperience or, more seriously, to inadequate social skills, or where there are many students disrupting the lessons of most teachers, a classroom discipline plan as part of a school behaviour policy is essential. In such schools there may still be some teachers who manage well without a plan and have good relationships with the students (though they may well act consistently, suggesting an implicit plan) but they too need to be seen by the students to support the school policy. If only some teachers are seen to be following a plan it could become a mark of weakness, so though some teachers may not need a school behaviour policy, it does need them.

Having a planned approach particularly helps inexperienced teachers who lack confidence in their right to intervene and are uncertain about what they should and should not do. Many years ago on my first teaching practice, I referred a Year 10 student to the Head of Year and though I cannot now remember what he had done, I do remember that after I had sent him out of the room, another student asked, 'Why don't you deal with us yourself, sir?'. If I had been truthful I would have admitted that I didn't know what to do and also wanted to disown the negative side of my role for fear of losing the affection of the class, but I made some excuse about having to refer problems as I was only a student teacher. Had I been given a plan and required to follow it I would not have had the option of making this error.

A classroom discipline plan should empower teachers to deal effectively with those incidents which arise, in the knowledge that they have recourse to whole school support as part of that plan. This implies that the policy should evolve from discussion and agreement among staff regarding the disciplinary practices which operate in the classroom, the systems for removal and referral of students and the line of treatment which will be followed by those staff to whom the students are referred. Teachers sometimes expect that senior staff will severely chastise and punish the students they have referred and feel unsupported if all they receive is a 'Don't do it again and apologise' chat. Senior staff feel equally unhappy at having to support teachers whose practice they do not privately condone, so it is essential that such issues are resolved. Rogers has written at length on developing a discipline plan in his early publication (1989) and subsequently, and his work can be strongly recommended as giving extremely detailed and practical advice.

Giving praise and rewards

Giving praise

Many approaches and schemes concerned with improving students' behaviour and work are based largely on increasing teachers' use of praise with

175

the rationale either to increase self-esteem (Canfield and Wells 1976; Mosley 1993) or to reinforce the desired behaviour (Wheldall and Merrett, 1985; Merrett and Wheldall, 1988, Galvin and Costa, 1994). It has been shown to be more effective and with less undesirable side effects than using punishment, which can develop negative attitudes in students and damage their relationships with teachers.

There are, however, dangers in giving praise inappropriately and the manner in which it is delivered is crucial to the effect it will have on the students' behaviour and attitudes. In contrast to delivering unpleasant consequences to students or correcting their behaviour, where a detached, professional manner is called for, if praise is to be seen as sincere it must involve an emotional reaction from the teacher.

Young children may not notice when praise is insincere but older students increasingly will. A teacher might encourage her young class to attend by saying, 'Well done, Marcus – sitting up straight and ready to listen', which causes him to grow a few inches more and those around him to try to get equal recognition. However, if a teacher took the headteacher aside and said, 'That's the best assembly you've given this term. Well done, keep it up', it would be entirely inappropriate. By claiming the right to evaluate a person's performance or to set them standards, we are casting ourselves in a superordinate position. This may be true, as when addressing young children, but praise should *enhance* the status of the recipient rather than express the status of the giver. When the teacher praises Marcus for sitting up straight the function is clearly to manipulate the behaviour of his peers ('That is what you have to do to please me'). He might briefly experience a sense of pride in being singled out by the teacher, but his status is being enhanced only in relation to the other children, not the teacher. It might be quite appropriate to do this with young children as, provided they want to please the teacher, it 'works', but as they grow older it is more likely to cause embarrassment as it sets them apart from their peers. A teacher must at some stage therefore decide to alter the way 'praise' is delivered and, in doing so, acknowledge, or even *signify* a change in the student's status. For example, Wheldall *et al.* (1986) showed that 'teacher touch' when accompanied by praise could be an effective reinforcer of work and behaviour in four classes of five- to six-year-old infants. The status implications of touch have already been discussed, but in this case it was clearly shown to intensify the effects of normal praise from teachers. However, if one wishes to enhance the status of students as they grow older it might sometimes be more appropriate *not* to touch them when praising as this expresses the superior status of the teacher and the tendency could be to focus the praise on the student rather than the work. By refraining from touching one would also avoid appearing patronising and would show respect towards the student.

When speaking to someone of superior rank it is clearly presumptuous to offer evaluative praise. More likely one would express:

- *admiration*, conveying 'I wish I were able to do as well as you';
- *pleasure*, conveying 'I really enjoyed, . . . was interested in, what you did';
- *gratitude*, conveying 'That was very helpful to me'.

A more accurate description would be that we *appreciate* the actions of our superiors which implies *we react to them* rather than praise their actions which would imply *they will react to us*.

Figure 32 *Non-verbal thanks.*

Appreciation is also focused specifically on the action rather than the person, so in admiring a student's work, for example, 'That's an excellent description. You've really looked carefully at the details of the picture', we accord them greater status relative to ourselves (and give more information) than by saying, 'Good girl, that's a lovely description' in a patronising manner.

Praise, if given publicly, can also embarrass the recipients, particularly if they are being used to set an example to the other students. At the secondary stage we would be unlikely to hear an experienced teacher saying, 'Well done for putting your hand up to answer', or 'Lucy is first with her book open ready to start. Good girl'. Such behaviour would have to be acknowledged privately perhaps with a smile, a 'thumbs up' sign or a private word which would respect the student's co-operation by not misusing it to attempt to manipulate others (see Figure 32). Any attempt to use praise to manipulate should be avoided: if one 'praises' the meagre efforts of a student who has given the task only minimal attention in the hope that he will do more, this can seriously misfire as the student may correctly assess the praise as inaccurate or manipulative and lose respect for the teacher. However, if teachers can show genuine interest in the student's efforts, this can be encouraging though in such circumstances it is always sensible to set realistic work targets backed up by appropriate consequences.

Inappropriate praise may also raise false expectation in students. It is important that they should feel successful but not to the extent that their expectations are unrealistic, as this recent report pointed out.

> When the Educational Testing Service compared students from five countries and six Canadian provinces in maths and science, two-thirds of the American students declared themselves 'good at maths' compared with a mere 23 per cent of Korean children. But it was the Koreans who came out on top, while the Americans were a devastating last, and it is this gap between perception and reality that is causing educators to ask instead of just feeling good, shouldn't our students have something to feel good about?
>
> (Wilce, 1994)

In summary, therefore, though praise may well promote improvements in behaviour and work:

- it may seem patronising and evaluative, implying that the recipient is of lower status than the giver;
- it may cause embarrassment if given publicly;
- it may, if inaccurate or manipulative, lower respect for the giver;
- it may raise false expectations and breed complacency.

Praise, or, more accurately, *appreciation* should:

- be sincere;
- specify and value the behaviour rather than the person;
- involve an emotional reaction such as pleasure, gratitude or admiration.

Rewards

Rewards, in the form of merit points, stickers, stars, certificates, privileges and prizes have also long been a feature of most schools, particularly at the primary level, and they are now being backed up in a more tangible way by vouchers for fast food, tickets for various entertainments or simply hard cash. This more recent practice is a feature of some disciplinary schemes such as *Discipline for Learning* in an attempt to make them more attractive to older students for whom coloured stickers have little value. In conjunction with praise they are given for behaviour and attendance as well as academic achievement and effort, and the systems are usually structured to start with 'low-value', high distribution points or stickers which gain the more valuable merit certificates and letters to parents, which in turn gains the student access to the tangible gifts, vouchers or money.

This emphasis on personal gain has led to much controversy regarding the ethical desirability and practical value of using rewards. The major argument against their use is that they decrease students' intrinsic interest in the subjects so that they work or behave simply as a means to gain the end reward. If the rewards are withdrawn the activity itself loses its value for the student and therefore *Token Rewards may lead to Token Learning* (Levine and Fasnacht, 1974). One can see that the skill required to perform an activity, such as reading, will not be lost simply because rewards are withdrawn but the child might not choose to exercise that skill, i.e. will not read any more books. For this reason rewards have usually been used to *initiate* particular activities or work habits, when the individual's skills are poor and the consequent enjoyment from the activity is low, but then when the activity is established they are phased out and finally praise alone is given.

This was what usually happened 'naturally' in secondary schools operating 'House Points' or similar systems, as by the third form (Year 9) the students were beginning to view the points as 'childish' and staff too saw their distribution as inappropriate. At this stage the motivating force of the tokens was being replaced by the fear of failing examinations (Ausubel, 1968). However, there is no attempt or recommendation in disciplinary schemes to phase out tangible rewards but rather the system is continually kept 'alive' by introducing new vouchers and attractive gifts, so the school gives an explicit commitment to materialistic values for the whole of the students' secondary education. However, as yet there is no evidence to suggest that those who eventually achieve successful careers are any less committed to their work as a result of such experience.

Hamblin *et al.* (1971) also warn of the dangers of giving tokens as *an expected payment* for behaviour or work.

> . . . in a classroom where teachers negotiate a contract every time they want a child to do something, or when the children nag their teacher for pay after

they have worked, the contracting and the nagging as well as the working will become exaggerated. Under such a system children eventually will not do anything without negotiating for pay. Rather, in setting up a token exchange, the goal is to establish a *gift* system where the exchange occurs without having to be requested by the other . . .

Therefore, one must be alert in such systems to the danger of students bargaining their effort, compliance or even attendance for further incentives, or putting it in more familiar terms 'going on strike for more pay'.

Rather than give direct payment for tokens received, many schools use the merits as a means by which the student can enter a monthly draw for the major prizes. This does introduce a chance element similar in some respects to a gift rather than a payment and, as we have seen with the National Lottery, can prove to be an incentive given that the prizes are valued.

Some schools try to overcome the ethical problem of encouraging students to work for personal materialistic gain by allowing them to nominate local charities or good causes (on a house or year basis) and donate points, or rather the money which the school exchanges for the points, to those organisations. On an individual basis, the student's points could earn a voucher for his parents or guardians to use which could be sent to them together with a letter of congratulations from the headteacher. In a sense, the school sponsors each student for work, good behaviour and attendance.

A similar scheme is operated in some primary classrooms where the teacher negotiates with the class a privilege or treat in which they can all partake. Dried peas or marbles are then awarded by the teacher to the students for their work and behaviour and these are put in a jar or pot which, when full, entitles the class to their reward. In this way individual effort is for the benefit of the social group.

With younger children it should not be necessary to introduce vouchers or gifts as many suitable rewards are readily available in schools; Hamblin lists twenty-eight items used by one teacher, including ten minutes' free time for studying, reading or playing educational games, listening to a record, sweeping the floor, and exchanging tokens for pencils, exercise books and other school supplies which the child would normally have been given. One teacher I worked with allowed the children to bring small toys which they no longer wanted so that others could purchase them with tokens in the 'swap shop'. In some cases it may be possible to arrange with parents that certain home privileges, such as watching television or going out, will depend upon school behaviour during the day.

Another teacher I saw had made life-sized plywood cut-out figures of Superman and Superwoman with a hole where the face should be for the child to look through, as in the old seaside photographic scenery. When children earned sufficient points the teacher would photograph them in the model and display one photograph in the class 'Hall of Fame' and another would be sent home to the parents.

Secondary school students are also motivated by appropriate privileges such as being allowed to do things which would normally be forbidden. A class might earn the right to have a 'no uniform day' by reaching an attendance target or merit points total, and outings, parties and 'free choice' afternoons where students can bring their computer games, videos and CDs can be used in the same way. On a day-to-day basis the same principle can operate. For example, Mr Cramond (in Torode, 1976) allowed a five-minute break at the end of each lesson during which students were permitted to talk among themselves. It is, then, more likely that they would have controlled impulses to talk at other times, particularly as they also ran the risk of losing the privilege.

When using tokens and rewards it is important that all students have an equal chance of receiving them, so that effort and improvement should be acknowledged as well as achievement. Teachers should also all distribute approximately the same number of points each week as this will be seen as fair practice by the students. It will also to a large extent determine which behaviour merits a point, as the number of points to be distributed will govern the frequency with which they are given.

Such systems require that teachers define what is and is not accepted and they therefore determine how students should behave and what they should learn. In a more democratic community could it not be argued that the students, in turn, should have some influence over how they are taught and should therefore be able to reward their teachers? A teacher might, for example, receive points from students for:

- starting the lesson on time;
- giving an interesting lesson;
- explaining a topic thoroughly;
- marking their work thoroughly and on time;
- being polite and friendly;
- not shouting;
- looking smart,

and all points so gained could contribute to their House or Year totals. Many teachers would regard this as patronising and unacceptable but by considering such reciprocal treatment from students it can highlight the nature of the relationship which is being claimed and the undesirable attitudes it can foster from students who do not accept the subordinate position. Teachers might not want students to feel that they exerted some control over how they taught, or to believe that they were teaching well 'because of the points'. However, when the points are 'real' as in performance related pay we would not want our efforts to pass unnoticed.

Making the policy official

Human transactions have been compared to playing games by Berne (1964) and later by Ernst (1972) in relation to student–teacher interactions and it is interesting to speculate how students could be thought of as playing 'The Learning Game' in schools. The object of the game is to succeed in learning and the skills required are those which promote effective study, such as motivation, effort, concentration, problem solving and effective communication with the teacher and one another. The opponents are not the other students, though in a sense those who achieve most could be thought of as winning the learning game. The real opponents are those attitudes which stop students 'scoring' their personal learning goals.

If we take this analogy a little further, before we could think of playing any game we would need to know the rules that governed our behaviour and the consequences of breaking those rules. Rules and consequences must be understood and are not negotiable during a game. In Association football, if a defender deliberately handles the ball in his own penalty area the consequence will be that the referee awards a penalty kick to the opponents. If the offender pleaded with the referee to overlook the offence or only give a 'throw in' on the grounds that he momentarily forgot the rule and promised not to do it again, it would be to no avail. The job of the referee is to officiate during the game and when players dispute their decisions it is rarely the rules and consequences which are in question but whether or not they are being applied *fairly*. This does not mean that rules and consequences are fixed and immutable. They can be altered to improve the game at a time set aside for that purpose *but not while the game is in progress.*

In order for school and classroom rules to acquire an official status there are at least two necessary conditions. Firstly, the rules and consequences should be established, preferably in consultation with the students as this will enhance the sense of solidarity rather than opposition. They must also be learned and understood by everyone playing or associated with the learning game, which means not only publicising them to students, parents, teachers, and governors and displaying them prominently around the school, but also explicitly *teaching and explaining* them to students and checking that they have been learned and understood. To be of practical use the system of consequences must be relatively simple so that it can be easily learned and applied by teachers and consequently learned by students. In some schools even the staff are unsure of what procedures should follow certain offences. One may deal with an offence personally, another refer it to the head of year, another to the deputy head. Of course, teachers should be allowed to exercise discretion and choose what they consider to be more appropriate courses of action but they should be aware of what the official policies are.

Secondly, the staff will be expected to be reasonably consistent in applying the rules and consequences both individually and with one another. Students have a right to expect that all teachers in the school will operate broadly the same set of rules impartially and not have their own particular idiosyncrasies. It would be bizarre for a referee not only to award a penalty but to tie the offender's legs together for ten minutes for good measure ('. . . and let that be a lesson to you!'). Yet some teachers can be relied upon to overlook offences which others treat seriously or a teacher may react harshly one day and not the next. Students learn that they can be late for Mr A but not for Mrs B, forget homework for Mr C but not Ms D and be wary of offending Mr E if he's having one of his 'bad days'.

There are generally five or six classroom rules which, in those schemes with a strong behaviourist influence, are stated in stark unequivocal terms, for example:

1. Follow instructions the first time given
2. Raise hands to be called upon before speaking
3. Stay in seat
4. Keep hands, feet and objects to yourself
5. No swearing or teasing

(Canter, 1990)

There is usually an attempt to phrase rules positively (Do rather than Don't) and many teachers prefer to use polite, though more ambiguous, phrasing so that rules 4 and 5 above would be expressed in terms of treating others and their property with respect.

The process of making rules and consequences seen to be official is worth following as it should ensure that they are known and understood by everyone (including the staff!), and demonstrate that the school gives a high priority to student behaviour. It can be summarised as follows:

1. Establish clear rules and consequences, preferably in consultation with students.
2. Display 'our' rules and consequences prominently in the classroom and around the school and publicise them to parents and governors.
3. Teach the rules, consequences and the underlying rationale to the students and periodically check to see that they have been learned and remembered.

'Official' schemes have a number of advantages:

Students know where they stand – Outcomes are predictable for students so that they can make informed decisions about the risks they run when offending or challenging the teacher. In a 'loose' system, a teacher is often uncertain what to do next if a student persists in offending and consequently threatens, 'If I have to speak to you again . . . you'll be *in serious trouble*' (and I hope I can think of something . . .). With an 'official' system everybody knows what will follow the next time the student offends.

183

Teachers can remain calm – A teacher who does not know what to do in response to an offence experiences stress and frustration and so may resort to attempts to intimidate the offender with aggressive threats, and the incident can quickly escalate into a serious personal confrontation. Teachers feel more secure when they know the next step they must take and therefore find it easier to remain calm; the student is less likely to perceive the intervention as a personal attack. A referee would be considered unprofessional if he berated an offender for committing a foul but a teacher may well show strong disapproval of a serious offence provided it is clear that it is the *behaviour* which is unacceptable and not the student.

Predictable consequences are seen as fair – If teachers are inconsistent the consequences are unpredictable for students. A teacher's response may on one occasion be seen as derisory and on another as an excessive over-reaction, and one teacher may be regarded as 'soft' and another as strict. When consequences are consistent and predictable they are more likely to be regarded by students as inevitable and fair.

Teachers are regarded as behaving professionally – A teacher who intervenes in a calm, decisive manner and who delivers predictable consequences is more likely to be perceived as responding professionally rather than reacting personally. Neill and Caswell (1993) point out that 'Rules, whether they are imposed from outside or you formulate them specifically for your own classroom, can be used to depersonalise confrontations between child and teacher. Effective teachers present rules as something above both teacher and child which both have to obey, or as a bargain which both have to keep to.' Teachers may sometimes decide to take mitigating circumstances into account and 'bend' the rules in the student's favour, but the rules are still in force though the teacher has *colluded* with the student to break them.

It may not always be appropriate to operate the official systems which form part of the school's behaviour policy simply as a matter of course, without taking into account the particular circumstances which prevail.

Co-operative groups

If we return to the game analogy, we have all had the experience of playing friendly games without a referee. There is a tacit agreement to play by the rules and to accept any penalties that might arise. In a well-ordered and motivated class where a good relationship has developed with the teacher, the learning game is played in this way as the teacher seldom has to step into the role of 'professional referee' and can enjoy simply playing the game. If such a co-operative relationship exists, the imposition of an impersonal official system would certainly be a retrograde step, being seen as unnecessary and damaging to the trust which had been built up between the teacher and students. Likewise, if a peaceful and orderly demonstration were subjected to conspicuous, strict and impersonal marshalling by the police it might well provoke the very behaviour it had intended to discourage. It is probably better, therefore, to use the familiar low-key measures consistent with co-operative relationships until such time as they are clearly ineffective and only then to announce that the official consequences will operate as students have not heeded the 'warnings'. This transition should be clearly marked, perhaps by displaying a sign stating 'Official Consequences Now Apply' or another visual display which the students understand, such as 'Condition Red'.

Mitigating circumstances

There will also be occasions when students act foolishly and uncharacteristically due to personal, domestic or health problems and teachers must have the discretion to act as they think appropriate rather than adhere rigidly to the system. Professional teachers have wider responsibilities than referees and are expected to take mitigating circumstances into consideration and no school policy should deny them this right.

Progressive consequences

Instead of varying the level of intrusion in a series of steps so that the instructions to the student become increasingly focused and explicit, one can step up the severity of the consequences of successive rule breaking in a series of usually five levels. At the early levels the consequences are not severe which makes it more likely that they will be accepted by the offenders and will not be so readily perceived as an oppositional attempt to control their behaviour by force.

Level 1 Usually the student is first given a 'verbal warning' and for subsequent interventions the teacher simply informs the student of the level reached without discussion, or lengthy explanations.

Level 2 If any second offence occurs, not necessarily a repetition of the first, the teacher informs the student that his name has been noted, or a 'written' warning has been given. Canter and Canter (1992) now recommend that the teacher carries a clip-board for this purpose as the previous practice of publicly displaying the student's name on the blackboard sometimes provoked a 'See if I care' attitude and a further challenge to the teacher to demonstrate to the other students that they were not to be so easily intimidated, a practice which has been described as 'assertive disruption'.

Level 3, 4 and 5 A tick is placed against the student's name for each of a further three offences during any one session.

There are specified consequences for the student at each level, for example,

Level 1   No consequences

Level 2   Five minutes' detention
Level 3   Fifteen minutes' detention
Level 4   Thirty minutes' detention
Level 5   Thirty minutes' detention and interview with head of year.

Obviously schools may determine their own consequences, for example it could be that all students who behaved appropriately during a session would receive a merit point so a verbal warning at level 1 would mean the loss of that point. Canter recommends that at level 4 the teacher telephones the parent that evening to inform them what has happened and at level 5 the student is sent to the school's principal, but these actions would probably be regarded as premature in our system. The main consequence is the increasing period of detention which, although not a severe outcome for the student, has a 'nuisance' value which is avoidable. The increasing consequences are not differentiated to relate to the nature of the offence so that whereas two students who were disrupting a lesson by talking together might otherwise receive an increasingly intrusive intervention resulting in a choice and the related consequence of being moved to separate seats, in this system their names would simply be continually recorded at the appropriate levels.

Some regard this as an insensitive 'mechanistic' approach which does not serve an educative function but it is very similar to the practice of 'giving lines' which was once probably the most commonly used punishment in schools. The more you offended, the more lines you had to do, regardless of the nature of the offences, though there was a superficial attempt to relate crime and punishment in what one had to write ('I must not ... waste time in lessons; ... be rude to the teacher; ... call out in lessons', or, for the student with multiple offences '... misbehave in school'). The system was also backed up by more serious consequences, such as the dreaded 'order mark' (I never got this far but I know someone who did ...), which, if you got three in a week, resulted in having to be 'on report', and one's parents being informed. (Oh, the shame ...) Those were the days! ... and are again it seems. However, the detention can be used constructively to perform an educative function rather than simply to act as a deterrent (see p. 199).

In addition to the advantages which follow from creating an 'official' system progressive consequences are:

- *easy to operate* – there is no need to plan a variety of ways of intervening, to use the most appropriate language for directives and choices, or to relate consequences logically to offences;
- *quick* – the teacher does not engage in lengthy or frequent interactions over problems of behaviour and consequently teaching suffers little interruption.

Systems involving progressive consequences have been successful in producing more orderly groups but, it is suggested, not without cost as they can:

186

- *mask inadequacies in teaching* – they can be used to suppress problems which would otherwise arise as a result of boring and uncommitted teaching;
- *discourage interaction* – students may be reluctant to risk their contributions being regarded as inappropriate so 'keep their heads down';
- *be seen as insensitive* by students. The educative function of discipline is neglected as offences are not investigated and consequences are not related. 'If we remove from the teacher the element of consideration of the circumstances which led to the misdemeanour, we create the likelihood that pupils will feel a sense of injustice' (Robinson and Maines, 1994).

Perhaps with this in mind, Canter suggests that students should write a note to the teacher if they wish to discuss what has happened.

Intervening professionally

The most carefully planned structured behavioural policies will be unsuccessful if teachers deal with students in unprofessional, personal ways. Aggressive behaviour relies on making students comply because they are fearful of the teacher; weak and indecisive behaviour can encourage students to challenge the teacher further. Therefore, when we intervene it is important to avoid giving any signs that we believe we are in a battle or that our actions are motivated by personal feelings towards the student. The term 'professional' is used here rather than assertive as it places the emphasis on the role relationship between teacher and student rather than on the personal behaviour of the teacher. Lee Canter, the author of *Assertive Discipline*, describes the attitudes behind assertive behaviour in very personal terms.

> Assertive teachers take the following stand in their classrooms: 'I will tolerate no pupil stopping me from teaching. I will tolerate no pupil preventing another pupil from learning. I will tolerate no pupil engaging in any behaviour that is not in his/her own best interest and in the best interest of others. And most important, whenever a pupil chooses to behave appropriately, I will immediately recognise and reinforce that behaviour'.
>
> (Canter, 1990)

Though most teachers would agree with these principles, the tone in which they are stated is questionable, and it is not surprising that *Assertive Discipline* has been described as the 'Dirty Harry approach' (Slee, 1995). Effective teachers present themselves as acting in a professional capacity, protecting students' right to learn, and this image will be enhanced if the rules and consequences are well understood by students and teachers, but, as Canter implies, the teachers' manner must also convey that they are certain about the validity of their actions. This certainty will derive primarily from three sources:

- Being clear about one's *right* to intervene.
- Being sure that one's intervention is *fair*.
- Being clear about the extent of one's *power*.

The right to intervene

When I ask teachers what they would do if they saw a student dropping litter in the playground, the great majority consider it their responsibility to intervene. Students are likely to perceive the intervention as legitimate and, if they do not comply, the teacher has some control over the subsequent consequences. Teachers know 'who they are' and can also expect students to know this.

In contrast, if you were walking in the high street of your local town and you saw someone dropping litter on the pavement would you intervene and ask them to put it in the litter bin? When I ask teachers this question the great majority say they would do nothing, and those who would intervene would be put off if the offender appeared aggressive or drunk. If he or she were of primary school age, or known to them as a student, they would be more likely to intervene. Dropping litter is a civil offence and, in theory, every citizen has the legal right to intervene if they see litter being dropped. However, in this country it would be unusual for a member of the public to do so and if they did they would probably only tentatively suggest, 'Excuse me, but I think you dropped this'. This reluctance to act is not because they care less about litter in the street than in the playground but because they are uncertain about the reaction they would receive. Will the offender question their right to intervene? 'Who do you think you are, a litter warden or something? Haven't you got anything better to do? . . .'.

If a teacher's authority is in question, students may also imply, 'Who do you think you are?' in response to an instruction. I observed a young student teacher taking a music lesson with a Year 10 group. One of the students was unconsciously rolling his music score around his finger as he spoke to his neighbour.

'James,' said the student teacher, 'don't roll your music score up into a telescope!'

Immediately four or five of the 'lads' rolled up their music scores and pretended to peer through them at each other. The 'joke' was very brief and shared by the somewhat embarrassed student teacher and they then quickly complied. It was not the *manner* in which the intervention was carried out that prompted the reaction, it was *who* was doing it. Had the regular class teacher said the same thing, the thought of such a response probably would not have entered the students' heads. However, when the instruction came from someone they perceived as close to their own age and clearly inexperienced they felt able to demonstrate, in the nicest possible way, their own relative status.[1]

I could stand up in a Year 7 class and state firmly, 'It's getting a little noisy' and expect the noise to subside, albeit briefly, whereas if I stood up and said the same thing in the staffroom I would get the, 'Who do you think you are?' reaction from the teachers.

On what occasions, then, can teachers be certain that they have a right to intervene and that their intervention can be justified to the students? When a student's behaviour affects one's capacity to perform one's *role*, that is to teach effectively and create conditions in which students can learn, we should be in no doubt whatsoever that it is not simply our right but our *responsibility* to intervene. However, when the behaviour fails to acknowledge our *rank* we are on less certain ground (see p. 55). An obvious example of this would be when a student fails to stand up straight or look at the teacher when being reprimanded. In such cases it might be better to take Rogers' advice and 'tactically ignore' this secondary behaviour and deal with the primary offence that brought the student to you (Rogers, 1990). This is not to say that students should not be expected to show respectful behaviour towards teachers but that the extent that this occurs will vary in schools with different traditions, whereas the rights required to perform the role are universal. The basis on which one can justify respect for one's rank is becoming less obvious, as status differences in our society lessen.

Fair interventions

Students will often try to question the fairness of any actions that teachers take when intervening. This can be done explicitly,

'Oh, that's not *fair*'

or by suggesting the teacher is inconsistent or prejudiced,

'She was talking just now! You didn't say anything to her did you?'

'Why are you always picking on me?'

or by arguing that the teacher has over-reacted,

'Oh, we were only having a joke'

or by claiming innocence, accusing the teacher of wrongful accusation,

---

[1] With hindsight, the instruction would have been better phrased as a clear directive, 'James, . . . put your score down, thanks', or given non-verbally.

'I didn't do anything! It was him!'

or accusing the teacher of being unreasonable,

'Mrs Jones always lets us . . .'

'What do we have to do this for? It's boring.'[2]

We can therefore discourage accusations of unfairness by

- acting consistently;
- avoiding wrongly accusing students;
- ensuring rules and consequences are clearly understood beforehand.

Of course, if students are convinced of our unfairness they may still fail to comply and the dispute could degenerate into a power battle. When we intervene, our manner must clearly convey to the student a certainty not only about our rights, ('You know it is my responsibility to intervene') but also about our fairness, ('You know you should/should not . . .'). Implying these shared common understandings also presents the solidarity in the relationship.

The extent of one's power

Power is the ability to control outcomes for others both positively and negatively (see Chapter 2). If you were in a bank and suddenly three masked men burst in brandishing shotguns and screaming at everyone to get down on the floor, you would have a legal right to make a citizen's arrest. It would also be reasonable to assume that the robbers were fully aware that their actions were illegal. You could, therefore, with full confidence in the legality and justice of your action, walk up to one of the robbers and state firmly,

'You know you shouldn't be doing this. I am making a citizen's arrest and want you to accompany me to the police station.'

What would obviously determine the outcome of such a foolhardy intervention would be the balance of *power*. One can be highly assertive or professional in one's manner but if the other person has more power and chooses to use it, they can determine the outcome.

As Dreikurs (1982) pointed out, students may also challenge teachers on the basis of power by refusing to comply, telling the teacher, 'You can't make me'.

---

[2] By bringing into question one's fairness, it is reasonable to infer that the student has accepted the teacher's right to intervene. If we asked someone in the street to pick up their litter we would hardly expect them to reply, 'She dropped a bit just now and you didn't say anything to her, did you?'

They are absolutely right. If a student is determined on a particular course of action a teacher does not have the power to make him do otherwise. We cannot make students stay in their seats, do the work set, stop calling out or even leave the room if they decide not to comply. All we can do is make it clearly understood what consequences will inevitably follow from the choices they make. Teachers cannot control students' behaviour but the institutional powers we have give us some control over the outcomes which will follow that behaviour and it is an important lesson for students to learn that *only they control their own behaviour but they must also take responsibility for the consequences that follow.*

The *manner* in which teachers respond to such challenges from students is crucial if an escalating confrontation is to be avoided. The teacher must neither back down or become angry. The non-verbal message must be absolutely clear to the student that the teacher does not feel threatened by, or is trying to threaten, the student. One should sustain eye contact, be close without invading personal space, use open-handed palm-down gestures, speak calmly and, above all, try to remain relaxed. (Easily said . . .).

Speaking in threatening, 'Don't you dare!', or taunting 'Make my day' tones, glaring and frowning at students, standing over them with one or both hands on hips and maintaining tense postures, all contribute to the intervention being perceived as a personal threat and are highly provocative as students soon learn that teachers cannot back up such challenges with commensurate action. Neill (1988) also points out another weakness in taking such a stance. From his research into conflicts between animals he points out that if one opponent is much stronger than the other, even a slight threat will be enough to drive the weaker opponent away. He argues, therefore, that '. . . a teacher who fiercely threatens her pupils is signalling that they represent opponents whose abilities are matched to hers.' In other words the teacher would be defining the student's behaviour as a real challenge to her authority. Neill goes on to argue that because threats imply preparedness actually to attack the opponent, the teacher risks manoeuvring herself into a position she cannot sustain in the face of continued resistance from the student. She cannot legally use violence and has no harsh punishments to back up her threats, and therefore is relying on an element of bluff. As students grow older it is not surprising that they therefore view such treatment from teachers as challenging and provocative: even when they do submit to the bluff they are likely to feel hostile and resentful and an emotional confrontation is the more likely outcome.

It is now generally agreed that a threatening manner is undesirable and counter-productive. Canter, for example, recommends delivering consequences in a quiet, firm, caring manner, and if students become angry, teachers should become calmer. With older students he recommends that teachers should 'move out', that is take the student aside from the others as it is better to avoid having such disputes publicly. If a student seems determined to challenge, one should postpone the discussion until it can be continued without an audience.

In summary, therefore, a professional manner is relaxed but formal and should convey clearly to the student the following hidden messages:

- I am not threatened by you;
- I am not threatening you;
- We both know it is my responsibility to intervene;
- We both know what you should be doing.

Supporting the classroom teacher

Removing students from the classroom

It may sometimes be necessary to have students removed from the classroom, either for a short time-out period or as an extreme measure for persistent or serious disruption. In the latter case it is usually the last resort for the teacher who may have already tried to isolate the student within the classroom.

It was once not uncommon for students to be ordered out of the room during an emotional confrontation with the teacher but this practice is now discouraged. If the confrontation had become serious, students were not likely to leave without some resistance and when they did they were free to roam the school causing further disturbance or even abscond.

When removing a student from the room it is therefore important to:

- have the assistance of another member of staff who has not been involved in any build-up to the removal;
- make sure the student is supervised while out of the room;
- have a contingency plan for the rare occasions when the student refuses to leave.

Some teachers make informal arrangements to help each other by collecting students and having them in their own rooms for an agreed period of time. A messenger would be sent asking the teacher to come and remove the student and this would be done quietly, with as little fuss as possible. One clearly does not want to undermine the authority of the classroom teacher when removing a student, giving the impression that you and not they have control of the situation. Nor is it helpful to treat the student disrespectfully when asking them to accompany you as the advantage of being neutral in the situation would be lost.

In some schools there is a room supervised by teachers on a rota basis where students can be sent with their work, accompanied by a fellow student who would then return to the class teacher with verification of a safe delivery.

In the event of a recalcitrant student still refusing to leave, Dubelle and Hoffman (1984), (cited in Albert, 1989) suggest that every school should have a 'Who Squad' made up of strong and willing staff who could be summoned to make sure the student leaves. They are so called because on entering the room they demand, 'WHO?' This might seem appealing to some long-suffering teachers but it would confirm students' belief that they are in a battle with teachers and that 'might is right'. A less adversarial approach is suggested by Canter (1992) who recommends that every school should have a disciplinary team made up of two or more senior members of staff, who could be sent for in such circumstances. When they arrive the teacher would take the rest of the class out, to leave the student alone in the room with them. This would avoid any suggestion that force would be used.

Systems of referral

With persistent or more serious problems it is necessary to refer to other staff in the school for their help. This could be the start of the process which ultimately results in the student being excluded from the school so great care should be taken to ensure that the system itself does not consolidate or even aggravate the problem, as Galloway *et al.* (1982) concluded from their research.

> The 'official channels' often seemed to carry a built-in escalation clause. If you were going to seek help or support from a colleague, you sought it from a senior colleague, at least at middle management level. In turn this led to a related problem. First it created a climate in which teachers felt they could refer a pupil *to* a colleague, with the implication – which the colleague often resented – that she would investigate and deal with the problem. This seemed to contrast with the climate in other schools which encouraged teachers to discuss problem pupils *with* colleagues, with the implication that the teacher might be able to deal with it herself. A logical result was that relatively minor issues could escalate from a dispute between a subject teacher and pupil to a confrontation between the head and the pupil, culminating in exclusion or suspension.

Galloway goes on to suggest that this devalued the role of the form tutor in playing an important part in the students' pastoral care.

In cases where teachers and students are unable to resolve their disputes to their mutual satisfaction, a system which refers the problem upwards in the staff hierarchy emphasises the 'power' aspect of the relationship, and senior teachers become the heavy artillery called upon when teachers are losing battles. In a system where the problem is considered to be in the *relationship*, both parties would consult a counsellor or conciliator and teachers might be less inclined to characterise their relationships with students as being based on power.

At this initial stage it is preferable that the meeting between the student, teacher and third party, perhaps the form tutor, should be relaxed and informal, even with some refreshment provided. This would express solidarity with the student while attempting to resolve *the problem* (not necessarily the *student's* problem at this stage) by agreeing on future action or using approaches which will be discussed in the next chapter. However, if students do not fulfil their part of the agreement or if their offence is more serious, interviews at later stages in the system should reflect this and become increasingly formal, involving senior staff and parents. At the final stage, where exclusion is being considered, the head teacher, parents, representatives from the school's governors and other interested outside agencies, such as the educational psychologist, would be involved.

The way students' misconduct is dealt with within a school will reflect, and to some extent determine, the attitudes and relationships which develop between teachers and students and even among the staff themselves. The disciplinary system which a school devises should take into account the degree of seriousness attached to different offences such as abusive swearing, bullying and physical violence, which will determine the stage at which the student enters the process, and also the most appropriate panel to deal with the matter at each stage. Persistent, cumulative or increasingly serious offences will determine the student's progress through the stages (usually no more than four 'levels') and the system should not be presented as a coercive institutional response intended to force compliance but as a problem-solving mechanism whose reluctant but ultimate 'no alternative' solution is exclusion.

Targeting specific problems

If a school has a particular problem, such as truancy or bullying, it can be helpful to make a determined effort to alter students' practice and attitudes in a similar way to the police targeting a particular crime, such as car theft.

The staff must be seen to be taking the matter seriously by discussing the problem and the possible solutions with the students or their representatives, and agreeing a plan of action to combat it. For example, if truancy had become a part of the school culture, the plan might involve attendance checks not only at the start of the morning and afternoon sessions, but before each lesson. Any unexplained absences would be painstakingly followed up with phone calls or visits to the home to check that the absence was legitimate and outside agencies would be enlisted to deal with persistent offenders. At the same time, good attendance, on an individual, class and house basis would be rewarded with privileges and prizes. In this way one can alter a practice, and perhaps attitudes, which have become established over a period of time and though not eradicate it, reduce it to manageable proportions before tackling the next problem.

Many schools have developed specific policies to deal with the more serious problems of bullying, truancy and physical violence but the same approach could be adopted towards more commonplace issues such as noise levels, punctuality, school uniform and litter. Students should be involved in constructing the policy and the process of making it official described on page 183 can be followed. For example, Robertson and Webb (1995) devised a school 'voice level' policy for a primary school, to teach children the appropriate volume to use in different contexts. Five colour coded levels were agreed:

1. SILENCE (Blue)
    We talk only in 'emergencies' so we don't disturb other people working. Put your hand up to ask the teacher.
2. PARTNER VOICE (Green)
    Only the person we are speaking to can hear what we are saying.
3. TABLE VOICE (Yellow)
    One person at a time speaks and the others on the table listen. Only the people on our table can hear what we are saying.
4. CLASS VOICE (Orange)
    One person at a time in the class speaks and the others listen. Everyone in the class can hear what we are saying when we use this voice level.
5. PLAYGROUND VOICE (Red)
    We use this voice to call people who are a long way away.

The rationale justified the different voice levels, which were then taught to and practised by the children, who designed charts which were displayed in the classrooms and around the school. Before each session the appropriate level was agreed on and the class chart set accordingly. Teachers tried to use positive corrections such as, 'Use your partner voice please, Anne, I can hear what you're saying', which served to reinforce the system rather than the more ambiguous, 'Keep the noise down' or 'Shush'. When they still failed to comply they were brought back during their lunch hour for a short 'practice session' (not a 'punishment') so that the policy also included logical consequences.

If the system were to be used at the secondary stage, three levels such as *silence, personal* (or *private) voice*, and *public voice* would be more appropriate. Although it may be unfashionable to say so, it is probably a good thing to train children to work on their own and in silence on some occasions. Kendon (1967) suggested that research into information processing supported the hypothesis that the human brain is capable of dealing with only limited amounts of information at a time. For the same reason that a speaker will look away from his listener as he organises his next utterance, it may be that in order to develop our own ability to solve problems or think creatively we need the minimum of distraction, so that we can become completely absorbed in our own thoughts. Some people prefer a background of sound such as music, but that probably does not demand their attention.

Most people work better in silence on tasks requiring cognitive processes and, were this not the case, it is unlikely that libraries would have evolved as places where there is quiet and little distraction.

Observations in schools by Rutter *et al.* (1979) support this view, 'Lessons in the successful schools more frequently included periods of quiet work when the teachers expected the pupils to work in silence'. Even talking which is apparently concerned with a given problem may not necessarily be helpful in reaching a solution. Instead it may be 'an effective time-waster, providing an alternative activity to solving the task' (Bruce, 1973).

For certain tasks, then, children might be required to work in silence so that some demands are made on their own resources. In practice, though, and particularly with younger children, it is rare to see a student sitting quietly wrestling with a problem and really making an effort to puzzle out a solution. If the next step is not obvious or the next idea immediately forthcoming, it is all too easy for him to ask someone else or to leave it, rather than make a sustained effort to think for himself. Children must be given the experience of success through striving, as this is a major factor in deriving satisfaction from work. As Carol put it, 'You can't talk in Mr Marks' lesson, you just have to work ... so after a while you work, and you enjoy it because you're learning a lot' (Furlong, 1976). A voice level policy would clearly differentiate for the student those occasions when silent, independent working was desirable from those where private or public discussion was required.

In relation to punctuality the rationale could be arrived at by discussing such questions as:

* who is inconvenienced by your being late? If we are late for a train we suffer the inconvenience, whereas being late for an appointment inconveniences others;
* are there contexts where it is acceptable to arrive late? People often turn up late to a party but not for a job interview.

In relation to school uniform the rationale would take into account why people wear uniforms and what is implied by a refusal to wear one. Does a soldier (policeman, traffic warden) feel more like a soldier in or out of uniform? (i.e. to what extent does it express one's role?). Do some jobs such as bank manager have unofficial uniforms? Is it always appropriate to wear jeans?

The school policy and the consequences for failing to adhere to it could then be agreed but its success would depend on the consistency and enthusiasm with which it was operated by the whole staff.

Activity 11 Structured interventions

The following account was given by a teacher in a unit for emotionally and behaviourally disordered students.

Year 9 student arrives and goes into other room before class time – starts playing on the computer with others. Is requested to go to own room for the beginning of session by both own personal tutor and tutors in the computer room. Responds rudely, refusing. Is given repeated request and refuses/ignores. Is given final request with warning that it will not be repeated. Computer switched off to terminate game by tutor. Student goes through to other room, sits down with back to table, drops work on floor and refuses to participate by muttering abuse – trying to engage other students in side dialogues, then withdraws with a hunch.

Once other students are working and lesson under way, tutor reapproaches and student tokenistically responds by picking up work sheet off floor and going through the motions of the work activity in minimalist, non-engaged manner, responding with rude comments at every approach or intervention from tutor. This rude/abusive behaviour can be instantly aggravated to aggressive and very hostile behaviour directed at the tutor in an intense way, if tutor 'pushes' activity or requests too assertively at any point.

In pairs, role play the incident at the computer then in the classroom under the following conditions. If at any time you feel it appropriate to praise the student you should do so.

(i)   *In the manner you think would most likely produce such a reaction from the student.*

(ii) *In a reasonable and friendly manner beginning with a low-key intervention, then a direct intervention and, if necessary, presenting a choice to comply or to incur the consequences you devise.*

(iii) *Write the following 'class rules' clearly and display them on the wall.*

CLASS RULES

1. **BE PUNCTUAL FOR YOUR LESSONS AND BRING THE CORRECT EQUIPMENT**

2. **FOLLOW TEACHERS' INSTRUCTIONS WITHOUT ARGUMENT**

3. **TREAT OTHER STUDENTS AND TEACHERS AND THEIR PROPERTY CONSIDERATELY**

4. **COMMUNICATE IN AN ORDERLY WAY.**

On another sheet, write the following progressive consequences and display them.

If you do not follow our class rules the teacher will give you a verbal warning, but if you continue,
1. **You will receive a written warning.**
2. **You will receive a 10 minute supervision.**
3. **You will receive a 20 minute supervision.**
4. **You will receive a 30 minute supervision.**
5. **You will receive a 30 minute supervision and your parents will be interviewed.**

Assume the student has been party to the negotiating of the rules and consequences and role play the incident in a professional manner issuing the consequences as appropriate by marking a sheet which you carry.

8 Fixing the Problem

Fix the problem not the blame

Various approaches and techniques have been proposed to help teachers to resolve behaviour problems. They are all potentially time consuming for the busy teacher who will need to work with individuals or small groups during lunch breaks or at the end of the school day, as opportunities to speak privately to students during one's teaching, even to discuss their work, are limited.

When students are given a detention, the intention usually is that the experience should be unpleasant so that they work or behave to avoid it in future, but it is probably one of the rare occasions when teachers and students meet together privately and it would surely be better to use the session constructively to try to resolve the problem. Some teachers already do this, and instead of giving a 'detention' they ask the student to 'come back for a little chat' about the matter. Another possibility would be for all teachers to set aside, say, thirty minutes at the end of each day during which they would be available to any student who wished to discuss problems they were having. The teacher could then ask to see particular students during this *supervision time* instead of putting them 'in detention', which has coercive overtones. If the teacher has not asked anyone to attend, the time could be used for preparation and marking in case a student turns up unexpectedly to discuss a problem.

The object of such sessions is to resolve the problem and the various approaches and methods discussed here give some idea of the ways this might be done. One can focus either on changing the students' attitudes so that they will appreciate the need to change their behaviour, or on teaching different ways of behaving in situations where problems have arisen. Of course, it would seem of little use to achieve a change in behaviour, perhaps by using punishments and rewards, without a corresponding change in attitude as the original behaviour would probably re-emerge when the reinforcements were withdrawn, but the reasoning is that if a person changes the way he behaves towards others, they will respond differently to him, causing him to change his attitudes to them. However, if students have developed strongly negative attitudes towards teachers and school it is unlikely that they would co-operate wholeheartedly in trying to change their behaviour without first changing their attitudes.

The common factor all the approaches share is the time spent working with an individual or group which provides an opportunity to improve those relationships, provided it is not used coercively to try to force students to comply. If the relationship is hostile and does not improve, the student will thwart any attempts teachers make to resolve the problem because they are, in fact, part of it.

Changing attitudes

Reasoning with students

In a survey responded to by over two thousand secondary teachers (DES 1989, The Elton Report), the two strategies rated 'most effective' in 'dealing with difficult classes or pupils' were:

Reasoning with a pupil or pupils outside the classroom setting (32%);
Reasoning with a pupil or pupils in the classroom setting (21%).

These strategies were used by the overwhelming number of teachers (89% and 92% respectively) though some rated them as 'most inefficient' (2% and 12% respectively). As well as possibly confirming the importance of talking privately with students without an audience, the difference between teachers' ratings may also reflect the quality of the discussion. For the most part, teachers are not trained in this area and manage these situations by an appeal to 'common sense' or they attempt to explain decisions and give reasons to justify decisions and rules. Reasoning with students is quite often more an attempt to 'make them see reason', that is to see that they understand the rationale underlying the rules and the teacher's demands, so that they are then more likely to make those demands on themselves.

Unfortunately, understanding the reasons does not guarantee compliance with the rules. Most persistent offenders can give all the reasons why they should not misbehave, as they have heard them many times before. One can only assume that their actions are thoughtless, ungoverned by reason, or that they have other stronger reasons for behaving as they do. If a student feels bored because he takes no interest in a subject, he may fool around, because this is much easier than making the effort to participate in the lesson. The fact that he is wasting other people's time as well as his own does not enter into his decision. He is bored and seeks an easy outlet. It is tempting for the teacher to try reasoning at such times, for example, 'You get out of an activity only what you're prepared to put into it. If you sit on a trampoline waiting for something to happen you'll soon get bored'. However, the student is only interested in 'winning' so will probably retort, 'Yes, but trampolines are fun. This is boring'. A wiser response from the teacher might therefore be, 'You may find it boring, but that's the work we have set. If you don't complete it now you can do so during the lunch hour'. This is not the time for reasoning.

Some teachers are too easily trapped into the 'reasons game' by students whose objective is to argue their way out of trouble if given the opportunity. This exercise can waste a good deal of time and slow down the pace of a lesson as the following extract shows. The teacher is collecting essays from fourteen-year-old students which should have been done during the half-term break from which they have just returned:

Teacher:	That's the third essay you haven't given in! *(Turns to the next student)*. Where's yours?
Student 1:	My what?
Teacher:	Essay.
Student 2:	What essay? *(Teacher does not reply but stares at student)* I wasn't here ... What essay? ... I ...
Teacher:	*(Teacher interrupts)* The one on the fly. You were here, you haven't been away.
Student 2:	Well, why should I spend my holidays doing homework? I've got other things to do like ... I don't want to sit in all holiday doing homework.
Teacher:	So you think you're going to get your exam without doing any work? *(Student looks at teacher and raises head and eyebrows as if he hasn't heard)*
Teacher:	Are you going to get your exam without doing any work?
Student 2:	*(Student then looks down at a friend who joins in)* Yeah, but look, Miss. Supposing, right? We haven't done about the fly, right? And you haven't taught us about the fly, right? How can we ...
Teacher:	I told you to use the library. You can't expect to be spoon-fed the whole time. Anyway I'm going to do the fly later on.
Student 2:	But if we went into the exam, like, we couldn't go into the library then, could we? While we're sitting there in the exam they wouldn't ...
Teacher:	That's very silly. You ... just because I give you something that isn't in a text it doesn't mean that you can't go to the library and get the information yourself. Other people have managed to.
Student 1:	Miss! The fly hasn't got nothing to do with human biology though, has it!
Teacher:	So disease hasn't got anything to do with human biology?
Student 2:	Yeah, but that's not the fly.
Teacher:	Well, the fly has got to do with disease because it carries disease.
Student 2:	Er ... Well, it's not in here is it? *(pointing to the textbook)* Anyway, I wasn't here.

It is interesting how the teacher is forced to justify her actions throughout the interaction. From the outset it is evident that the student is not being co-operative but makes the teacher respond to his questions (see p. 35). When he is unable to make a suitable reply to the teacher's point about working to pass the exam, he makes the teacher repeat the question to gain time. He is still unable to counter this point, but is rescued by a friend who raises another objection. The teacher deals with this argument, so the first student raises a further objection concerned with the relevance of the topic. This is explained, so the student returns to the original excuse.

There is a place for such discussions because teachers should be able to justify their actions to students, but it was inappropriate and misleading to do so here. One could argue that the teacher presented a model of reasonable behaviour to the class, but in fact the episode served only to waste time. The issue was fairly clear: the student had not done the work set. If it was important, then it would still have to be done, regardless of whether he was previously absent or not. Reasons are not necessarily excuses, but they can be taken into account in considering any consequences.

It seems from the teacher's first statement that it was not unusual for homework to be disregarded. One could take the view that students must learn to take responsibility for their own private study, and that homework is therefore desirable but not compulsory. There is, though, a risk that if one presents homework on the lines of 'further suggested reading', the impression can be given that one does not really care whether or not the students make progress or do justice to the subject. What is worse is to present it as compulsory and then fail to enforce it, as this gives the impression of being weak and lacking in control.

Reasoning with students should not take place during a lesson but at a time set aside for the purpose or during a 'detention'. There should be an understanding that the main objective is to improve the situation in the future, so students should be able to explain their reasons and have them taken into account if they are valid. The interview should be guided by the principle *'fix the problem, not the blame'* so the first stage would be to establish the specific nature of the problem as seen by those concerned, and then to agree on what action could be taken to resolve it. It could be that the student's behaviour, in the circumstances which prevailed, was quite reasonable or that the teacher's behaviour was unreasonable and played some part in the problem. Only if they cannot reach an agreement about future action should a third party be involved to mediate in the discussion with the understanding that they were not there to help the teacher 'win' but to help to resolve the problem which might mean that the teacher as well as the student changes his behaviour.

It is more usual that the problem is seen as being owned by the student, who will then be sent to a senior teacher to be disciplined in some way. Even when the senior teacher listens to the student's views there is still the implicit understanding that they must justify and support the teacher's action, as in the following example. The Year 10 student has been involved in a minor incident with the head of year, a middle-aged woman, but is mainly being interviewed by her because he said he would not attend a detention given by another teacher to the whole class. The teacher had believed that someone had lit a match during the lesson but no-one owned up to doing it. They are informally seated in her room.

Teacher: How old are you, Graham?
Student: *(Mumbles)*
Teacher: Um?
Student: Fifteen.
Teacher: Fifteen . . . Old enough to know right from wrong.
Student: Umm *(Yes)*
Teacher: Old enough to know when you muck about and when you don't.
Student: *(Nods)*
Teacher: So, therefore, if other people muck about, . . . Graham knows what's required of Graham.
Student: Umm.
Teacher: Now I teach you . . . I had to look at you a couple of times in the lesson . . . Why?
Student: *(Whispering)* For mucking about.
Teacher: For mucking about. Was anybody else in the room mucking about at that time?
Student: That was me at that time. Yeah.
Teacher: . . . And this business of yesterday afternoon with Mr Smith wanting everybody to come back. Tell me what's the adult thing to do in a situation like that?
Student: I don't know, my view's just, I'm just cheesed off with it 'cos I don't find that fair. I think that if, that like someone at the back row had struck, which they did, struck the match then they should keep the back row behind. Why keep the rest of us behind unnecessarily? Just 'cos he thinks we might know summink. We may not know nuffin'.
Teacher: Yes, I agree with that . . . but, . . . perhaps he's looking at the form group and trying to get a form identity – and it's very important that as a group of young people in that form you actually take responsibility for each other.
Student: But if we don't know, if we don't know who done it there's no need to keep us all in is there? . . . And
Teacher: Yes, well . . .
Student: And if that person . . . That person ain't gonna own up to doing it is he?
Teacher: Yes, I can understand what you're saying, Graham, but the responsible way of going about things isn't to shriek at the teacher, 'I ain't coming to detention', is it?
Student: *(Wiping tear)* No.
Teacher: What's the responsible thing to do?
Student: To go to it.
Teacher: Um?
Student: To go to it.
Teacher: To go to it or? What's the other thing you do?
Student: See the teacher.
Teacher: You see the teacher privately and do what?
Student: And tell him you're not going to it.
Teacher: Or you discuss it . . . or you come and see me or you see somebody else . . . and we'll have no more of this nonsense will we? Not in Maths . . . not in Language . . . not in your form period, . . . not in Science not in English, not in any of your subjects.

Student: But if I did say, like a couple of other kids have said they ain't coming back this evening. What would the . . . what would be the views
if I said I wasn't gonna go anyway.

Teacher: Because that's disobedience Graham. You think about it. A part of
the expectations of the school is that you don't disobey teachers.

Whole class detentions are discouraged (DES, 1989) and the Head of Year is
in rather an invidious position, having to defend a practice of which she may
disapprove. Her suggestion that it might have been given to foster a sense of
collective responsibility in the form was unlikely to be the reason the teacher
took the action, which is more akin to taking innocent hostages until one's
demands are met. On the one hand, she is clearly sympathetic to the student's concerns yet is constrained by having to support the teacher's action.

If a difficulty is seen as 'our' problem, then both student and teacher would
go to a third party and it is questionable whether this should be a senior
teacher. Galloway (1982) recommended using form tutors in the first
instance and Glasser (1969) went even further to suggest that times should
be set aside in which students' social behaviour at school could be discussed
by the whole class.

Such procedures can be very time consuming and some would argue that
they simply encourage students to question teachers' decisions instead of
doing as they are told. We do not want to encourage them to argue with
and challenge every reasonable demand made on them but we should
respect their right to be heard when they feel they are being treated unfairly.
Reasoning with students should therefore:

- not take place during normal lesson times;
- allow them to express their views and listen to the teacher's;
- be a problem-solving discussion aimed at reaching agreement. This
  would involve both teachers and students agreeing to try to modify their
  future behaviour;
- involve a third party only if agreement cannot be reached, whose role
  would be to help resolve the problem.

Disclosing the mistaken goal

This approach is suggested by Dreikurs *et al.* (1982) as particularly suitable
with children aged ten and younger and would follow from the teacher's
identification of the 'mistaken goal' of the behaviour, that is to seek attention, power, revenge or to display inadequacy (see p. 110). They argue that
children are often not aware of why they behave as they do until it is
revealed to them.

'Regardless of which of these four goals the child adopts, his behaviour
results from his conviction that it will secure his place in the family or group
in which he functions. The child is usually not aware of the purpose of his

behaviour. It is useless to ask a child, "Why did you do this?" He does not know. He recognises his goal, however, when it is disclosed to him.'

In disclosing the mistaken goal, the teacher should not state, 'When you call out in class you want me to notice you, don't you?', but should instead suggest the motive to the child.

'Could it be that when you call out in class you want me to notice you?', or in the case of 'power',

'Could it be that when you won't do as I ask you in class, you want to show me that I can't make you do anything you don't want to do?' Similarly for revenge,

'Could it be that you scribbled all over your work because you wanted to ... hurt me ... pay me back ... show me how upset you were with me?' And for inadequacy,

'Could it be that when you won't join in with our work you feel you might not do it as well as the others ... are worried about failing ... can't be the best.'

The authors acknowledge that children may not be keen to admit to such motives and that teachers may themselves be mistaken and so should not be afraid to suggest other motives and look for a 'recognition reflex'.

> 'Younger children will either admit that they do the misbehaviour for the reason we have suggested or they give themselves away through some facial or bodily mannerism that we term the *recognition reflex*. This recognition reflex usually expresses itself through a smile, a grin, embarrassed laughter, or a twinkle in the eye. Older children ... betray themselves through their bodily language. Their lips may twitch, their eyes may blink or bat more frequently, they may readjust their seating positions, swing a leg, tap with their fingers, or even wiggle their toes. It takes careful observation of their body language in order for us to know if we have made the right guess.'

In this way the teacher attempts to build a working relationship with the child so that they can reach an agreement on a plan of action involving other acceptable ways in which the child can secure the goal he seeks and a private or 'secret' signal which can be given to the child if he misbehaves as before.

The idea of jointly devising a plan with the child to overcome a particular problem has been developed by Rogers (1994b) who also suggests offering a 'plan helper'. If the child agrees this student (or students) would supplement the teacher's role by reminding and encouraging him about his plan in the course of the daily work.

Reframing

This technique derives from the ecosystemic approach described by Upton and Cooper (1990) and in more everyday terms by Provis (1992). It is similar in principle to Dreikurs' in that it seeks to reveal the goals served by the behaviour and how appropriate those goals are for the student, and to identify more effective means of achieving them.

The technique of reframing involves redefining oppositional behaviour in terms which lead both teacher and perpetrator to view the behaviour as a co-operative act rather than as antagonistic. In fact, many teachers when not 'in role' may already take a different view of students' misbehaviour. I sometimes show a video extract of a group of Year 9 students who become aware that they are being filmed in the playground. One boy immediately pushes his mates aside and arrogantly gestures rudely into the lens, much to the amusement of his mates (see Figure 33). Teachers who view this also frequently laugh, not because they find it humorous but more with a surprised 'cheeky devil' reaction. Nevertheless, the experience for them could not be described as unpleasant as the gesture made what would have been a dull extract memorable, but they all agree that had they been present on the scene *as a teacher*, they would have had to express disapproval. Free from that constraint they might regard it as 'a healthy disregard for authority'.

Essentially, this is what reframing requires teachers to do, that is to adopt more positive explanations of the behaviour and to share these with the student. For example, in the above incident there are several positive aspects about the behaviour:

- it was an active reaction to what could be regarded as an intrusion of the students' privacy, rather than to stand around passively, looking awkward;
- it showed the confidence to take risks, even though a little foolhardily;
- it enlivened the moment for the other students, causing some excitement. (Their response could be one of the factors reinforcing such behaviour.)

Most teachers do not want to produce over-compliant students and this boy is certainly not one. By acknowledging and valuing these qualities we express our solidarity with the person *behind* the behaviour and start from a point where we are working with rather than against them. One could go on to discuss other ways in which those qualities could be expressed, as we would not want him to feel justified and proud of telling every school visitor to 'get stuffed!' He might, for example have taken the initiative to introduce himself to the camera operator, asking what the purpose of the filming was and on whose behalf it was being done, and then introduce his friends. He might thus learn to express his initiative and confidence in more socially acceptable ways.

Figure 33 *Expressive communication?*

Cooper and Upton (1992) go so far as to suggest that the behaviour itself, such as talking-out-of-turn, once interpreted not as an unhelpful interruption but as an attempt to seek clarification from the teacher, should then be encouraged. The student will then either abandon it because he does not wish to co-operate with the teacher, or make his contributions more constructive in accordance with the favourable interpretation. In order to change the way others treat us it is usually necessary first to change the way we treat them, and one step towards this is to change our attitudes to what they are doing. Albert (1989) recommends that we change our perception of 'weaknesses' to regard them as 'strengths'.

> We may think of Sebastion as 'stubborn' until we check a thesaurus and find such positive synonyms as 'steadfast', 'resolute', and 'persistent'. If we start thinking of Sebastion's behaviour in these terms, our perceptions can change for the better. We even might begin thinking of Sebastion as a regular Rock of Gibraltar!

Reframing, then, can be helpful in establishing a level of understanding with students about the positive qualities underlying their behaviour, not with the motive, 'You can't do that any more because it doesn't upset me', but so that they will work with the teacher to apply those qualities in more constructive ways.

Exchanging roles

When I was an educational psychologist I used to visit a residential school for students with behavioural disorders. The headteacher was nearing retirement and appeared to cope with all eventualities in a calm, unflappable manner, which was reflected in the well-ordered and friendly atmosphere in the school. A Year 8 boy, whose behaviour in mainstream schools had been extremely disruptive, had recently been admitted to his school and I asked how he was getting on. The head told me that on arrival the boy had run around his room jumping on the furniture and making strange animal noises. He calmly watched this without comment until the boy had stopped and then he got up himself and began to run round jumping on chairs and making strange noises. He resumed his seat and asked what the boy thought of him.

I would not recommend anyone to try this, as, apart from damaging the furniture, there was a danger that the boy would have felt that the head was ridiculing him, but it can be very enlightening to view one's own behaviour and to some extent experience the effect that it has on others, which is the basis of exchanging roles.

At first sight the approach might seem to be directed at changing behaviour but it is intended to bring about a change in attitudes by letting each person try to act out and defend the other's position. By having to do this the hope is that they will both begin to appreciate the other person's perspective and see the need for compromise. It does call for some dramatic flair on the teacher's part and for a degree of co-operation from the student as they must both try to re-enact the incident that caused the problem. In doing so, both the teacher and student may be made aware that some of the things they do and the manner in which they do them can be very provocative and con- tribute to the problem. It is very important that the student agrees to the exercise and that the teacher does not exaggerate the behaviour in an attempt to show how stupid and childish it is, as this would only generate resentment. The object is that they should both try to agree to behave in ways which are more acceptable to the other, to avoid conflicts occurring, though students must understand that teachers' role is to teach and they will consequently still be required to do the work set.

Rogers (1994b) describes how he uses a similar technique he calls 'Mirroring' with younger children, in conjunction with picture illustrations of both the undesirable and desirable behaviours.

> 'Ben was a residential student in a school for emotionally and behaviourally disturbed students. He was very loud when talking at his table and loud when calling out to the teacher. I began the first session by explaining that he was very loud in class and that this was concerning the other students because ... Then I quietly asked if I could show him what I meant. 'Yeah, if yer like!' He grinned, responding to what I'd hoped was my positive body language. 'Look, you be your mate, Brian, I'll sit next to you here, OK? Now let me give you a demo.' I asked very loudly for one of the pencils I'd put on the table (Ben was often inappropriately loud in conversational talk). I then modelled how he called out to get teacher attention by clicking my fingers. I winked, 'Is that right, Ben?' He grinned (boys often do). 'That's what I see you doing, Ben.' Here I'd returned to my normal voice. We then went on to make a plan to talk in a quieter voice in class, and get the teacher's attention appropriately. I did this by showing him a picture of him speaking in an inappropriately loud voice and calling out with his hand up. A second picture was added showing him speaking in a quieter voice (conversationally) and putting his hand up without calling out. I then modelled the new (target) behaviour which became his plan.'

In this variation the child does not have to play a role but is essentially an observer of himself 'in the mirror'. The teacher would not be made aware, however, of any aspect of his own behaviour which might be contributing to the problem, but it would be unlikely that young children could adequately portray this, even if they were aware of it.

One can sense, in Rogers' description, the skills required by teachers using this and other therapeutic methods, to express solidarity with the student and persuade them to take an objective view of the problem in an unthreat- ened, non-defensive way.

209

Changing behaviour

Students control themselves

If people's attitudes towards a particular practice or goal are favourable, but in their everyday behaviour they often fall short of their own ideals, they can be given help to help themselves. There must be a genuine desire to change one's behaviour and those who have a specific goal to aim for, such as losing weight, or passing an examination, are ideal candidates as the benefits of exercising self-control will be evident. If one also has to discuss one's progress with an adviser who is taking a personal interest, helping to set realistic goals and reminding one of the need to be strict with oneself, this can be an added incentive.

A student who was having difficulty in studying for an examination would first identify what he regarded as rewards. These could range from having a cup of coffee to going out with friends. Each reward would then have to be earned by doing a predetermined amount of work and, if this was not accomplished, he would have to deprive himself of the reward. Clearly for this to be successful considerable will power or, more accurately, 'won't power' is required. It is all too easy to slip back into the self-delusion that one will feel more like working after a cup of coffee, bath or other relaxation. If someone else can be persuaded to dispense the rewards, this can be helpful, as there is less opportunity to cheat.

An unusual approach to helping students exercise self-control requires them merely to keep records of their own behaviour. This method has been shown to be effective for teenage students both in America (Broden *et al.*, 1971) and in an ordinary school in England (McNamara and Heard, 1976). One method of recording required students to keep a tally of every occasion that they behaved inappropriately, and another required them to record whether they were studying or not, whenever they thought about it. The latter method would not, therefore, give a reliable measure of the actual number of inappropriate acts, because some might pass unrecorded by the student. Teachers and outside observers were therefore used to confirm that recordings were truthful and accurate.

Both methods resulted in considerable improvements in behaviour for most of the students participating, but McNamara and Heard found that recording every instance of inappropriate behaviour produced a superior rate of improvement. Unfortunately, the numbers involved in the studies were small (in Broden *et al.* only two took part), so it is difficult to draw reliable conclusions, but this is obviously an approach which merits further investigation. The sheer simplicity of the scheme would make it easy to introduce with a few students in a school without impinging on the work of the others.

One can only speculate as to why the students' behaviour should have

210

improved when they were asked to record it. The results could be explained as a form of the Hawthorne effect (the suggestion that merely showing an interest in the subjects of an experiment, making them feel special and listening to their views, may influence their behaviour in the desired direction), but McNamara and Heard offered another possible interpretation:

> At the commonsense level, making the pupil record his own behaviour may encourage him to be aware of what he is doing. Such a strategy is probably very effective with the inconsequential, non-reflective pupil who 'acts first and thinks afterwards' – the child who is not maliciously disruptive but who none the less disrupts the class because he lacks the ability to organise himself and his work.

The very act of recording probably interrupts the inappropriate behaviour which would subsequently have to be resumed, and this pause would give an opportunity for the reflection that the authors suggest takes place. (There are also similarities with the practice of confessing one's sins.) However, if self-recording became common practice in schools, familiarity might breed contempt. It would be so easy for students to falsify their recording, as two girls did in the McNamara and Heard study. The authors warn, therefore, that 'while self-recording is no panacea for secondary school problems, it might well be an additional and useful strategy in the teacher's repertoire of techniques for coping with some problem behaviour of some pupils'.

The main objective in dealing with unwanted behaviour is to encourage the student to behave or work appropriately in the future and, in the absence of someone in authority, to exercise self-control. Cheyne and Walters (1970) point out that self-control may be mediated emotionally, because the student fears the consequences of being caught, or cognitively, in that the child understands that his actions are not compatible with a rule which he accepts. Emotional control would, therefore, seem to derive from aversive treatments, resulting from the teacher's use of power, whereas cognitive control is dependent upon a reasoned appraisal of the situation and is more consistent with an authority agreement. One must also consider the role of habit training in promoting self-control, as it may be that some students behave appropriately simply because they have learned to.

However, if teachers merely wait for children to understand and accept that they should behave appropriately then they may be waiting a very long time. One unco-operative child can ruin a lesson for the whole class and approaches which rely on the voluntary exercise of self-control may be inappropriate in the initial stages as they can be easily manipulated.

Contracts with students

Contracts, or formal agreements between students and teachers, are most commonly used as a last resort to prevent suspension or as a pre-condition to the student returning to school after exclusion. The parents may need to be involved in negotiating the contract whereby the student agrees to con-

211

form to particularly specified behaviours, such as not being late on more than one occasion during a fortnight or not being involved in any physical violence, on the understanding that if they 'break' the contract they will be subject to the agreed consequences. If students see that it is in their interests to negotiate such agreements they can also be used before a serious crisis has arisen. For their part of the agreement they might be required to work harder or behave better, to specified standards, in return for particular privi- leges such as extra curricular activities, outside educational visits or any rea- sonable concession which the school can offer. A teacher might, for example, agree not to shout at students if this is raised as an issue. What is important is that the agreed behaviours are clearly specified in terms of their nature and frequency. The following account illustrates this approach and some of the difficulties involved:

Jane was in her second year of an upper school when the headteacher referred her to me for disruptive behaviour. In discussing the circumstances with the staff, it emerged that only a few were actually allowing her to attend their lessons and she was on the point of being suspended from school. She had caused a rumpus in the library and thrown a transistor radio across the room, had stuck chewing gum into a boy's hair and committed other similar disruptive acts. She was frequently late for lessons, and when questioned by the teacher would often get abusive and storm out of the room, sometimes locking herself in the toilet. The surprising thing was that she seemed to want to remain at the school. She was very seldom absent and, when sent home for misbehaviour, would return to wait for her friends at the gate. We therefore made an agreement with her. She would lose one point each time she was late for a lesson, did not bring the proper equipment, or disrupted the lesson. She could gain a point by working well during a lesson. The con- cession from the school was that she would not be suspended unless her weekly total of points lost exceeded ten. They were also conceding, there- fore, that she could continue with her misbehaviour provided she was able to earn enough points by working to stay within the ten points limit.

It was more difficult to get the staff to accept this arrangement than Jane. The headteacher did not want to enter into any 'bargains' with a student although, by previously allowing her to miss some lessons, concessions had already been made. A few staff already coped well and did not want to bother with the arrangement. Once the scheme was underway some teachers tried to deduct points as a punishment for any offence; for instance when she was rude to a member of staff in the corridor, two points were deducted. These had to be returned as no agreement had been made in this respect. They also wanted to take off points in a punitive manner – 'Late again! That's another point you've lost!' – when in fact it was essential to behave in a non-provocative manner. If Jane argued that it was not her fault that she was late and so shouldn't lose a point she was quickly informed that she was disrupting the lesson and would lose a further point if she continued. In this way staff were relieved of the considerable anxiety of how to avoid a hostile confrontation with Jane, without appearing to let her do as she pleased. They were able to respond in a calm, non-aggressive manner so that the whole character of the interactions altered. For several weeks Jane kept just within the limit by working hard to make up any necessary points on the final day and thereby avoid suspension. Then a surprising thing happened. She stopped going out with a boy who was also at the school, and this coincided with a change in her behaviour. Why this should have happened is difficult to imagine, but she began to behave in a much more acceptable way, sometimes ending the week with a positive total of points. This marked a turning point for her, as, although she never became a model student, she was able to be contained within the school without the help of a contract in subsequent years.

One can argue that the contract alone did not bring about the change in Jane's behaviour. The arrangement involved her receiving daily individual attention from a sympathetic teacher to discuss her progress, and this may have had a beneficial effect. One could equally argue that such attention would perpetuate the bad conduct, because it would inevitably be discontinued once she had improved. The contract obviously had no direct effects on any personal problems she had which may have predisposed her towards such behaviour. The most noticeable change which resulted from the arrangement, however, was in the nature of the interactions between Jane and certain members of staff. The contract enabled the staff to remain calm and non-provocative in response to her behaviour, as well as requiring them to reward her efforts. She was therefore not able, or did not feel the need, to escalate the situation in the way she had done previously.

If one has a particularly disruptive student there is no harm in discussing what he values, or would like changed, in the school. It might be possible to reach some agreement whereby both parties have something to gain, and future interactions could be much more benign as a result.

The notion of a contract may also be useful in making older students aware of their own responsibility for creating a context in which learning can take place. In cases where a teacher has lost all control in a class it might be possible to offer to make the lessons more interesting in return for their co-operation and attention. The content and proposed method could be discussed beforehand so that the class become more actively involved in the process. This would probably only be appropriate with older secondary students as such negotiation after 'defeat' would acknowledge that the teacher had lost authority and had no power to retrieve the situation. It might also require the services of a neutral support teacher to mediate and monitor the agreement to see that both sides honoured the contract, though there would still be no guarantee that the students would co-operate even if the teaching improved.

213

Students train teachers

In the previous example, in order to change Jane's behaviour, the teachers had first to change their own. This principle has been demonstrated in reverse by Graubard and Rosenberg (reported by Gray, 1974) who taught problem children how to make their teachers behave better towards them! As one might expect, the researchers found that students who were frequently in trouble often complained that teachers were unfairly picking on them. Sure enough, when careful records of interactions were kept by the students and trained observers, a high level of negative comment from the teachers was found, although on many occasions the students failed to recognise the teachers' positive behaviour or misinterpreted it as hostile. Unbeknown to the teachers, the researchers selected seven children, aged between twelve and fifteen, from a class considered 'incorrigible', and instructed them in ways in which they could make the teachers treat them more positively and, using videotapes, taught them to make more accurate judgments of the teachers' behaviour.

Jess, one of the seven selected, was a particularly violent fourteen-year-old, who had apparently knocked other students unconscious with chairs and beer bottles and had been suspended for forty days for hitting a principal with a stick. He and the other six were trained to ask teachers for help, and then reward them with a smile and remarks such as, 'You really help me to learn when you're nice to me', and, if the teacher offered any words of encouragement, 'It makes me feel good when you praise me.' The smiles proved something of a problem for Jess. What actually emerged was a menacing leer, but with video-tape sessions he was taught to give a charming grin. Another technique in which they were instructed was the 'Ah-hah reaction'. If the student felt he had understood a teacher's explanation, he would say that he did *not* understand. When the teacher got half way through the second personal explanation, he would exclaim 'Ah-hah! Now I understand! I could never get that before!' This technique was aimed at giving the teacher a feeling of accomplishment and making him like the student.

The research demonstrated that during each of the five weeks of the project the teachers became more positive towards the students concerned. It is interesting that later, when the teachers were told about the experiment, many of them felt it was the students who had changed, rather than themselves. Just as Jane's teachers had first to alter their behaviour to bring about a change in interactions, so Jess and the others had to alter their behaviour for the teacher to relate differently to them.

9 Checklist for Successful Teaching

The checklist summarises some of the features of classroom interaction and practice which are significant in teacher-student relationships. Teaching situations differ considerably but an observer might use the list flexibly to focus on aspects of lesson content and organisation, teacher self-presentation and classroom management skills. These are clearly interrelated and overlapping areas which will be evident from an examination of the factors listed under each heading in the checklist.

For clarity and ease of reference the list is divided into factors concerned more with preventing unwanted behaviour, and features of dealing with problems that have arisen, and these are referenced to the appropriate points in the text.

Preventing unwanted behaviour

1. Teaching is more likely to be successful if:
   - lessons have an overall theme. Aims should be considered and one's teaching should have continuity (p. 57);
   - each lesson has specific objectives (p. 57);
   - work is thoroughly prepared (p. 93);
   - the choice of work is appropriate to the age and ability of the students (p. 57);
   - the work makes intellectual demands on the students (p. 122);
   - marking is regular and thorough (p. 121);
   - the form of presentation and the activities undertaken are varied (p. 57).

   Effective teaching provides the major basis for one's claim to be in authority.

2. When teaching, the students' attention can be better sustained by:
   - standing prominently in the room (p. 94);
   - engaging in eye contact with individual students (pp. 26–33);
   - demonstrating one's involvement with the subject: enhancing the meaning with vocal variations reinforced by bodily movements and facial expressions (pp. 88–9);
   - looking for and responding to feedback from students (p. 96);
   - moving closer to those who do not appear to be attending (p. 16).

3. Opportunities for unwanted behaviour can be reduced by:
   - arranging seating and layout of the classroom appropriate to the activity (p. 131–3);

- ensuring a prompt and brisk start (p. 127);
- introducing the main theme clearly. Avoid dealing with side issues, unnecessary repetition of points already understood and interrupting one's teaching with lengthy reprimands or justifications of one's action (pp. 126–8);
- ensuring there are no noticeable breaks in the lesson which could have been avoided (pp. 128–31);
- not attending to individuals or small groups at the expense of the whole class (p. 126–7);
- allowing time to conclude the lesson in an organised and orderly manner (p. 127).

Such measures reduce the opportunities for students to misbehave. Reasoning and justification of one's actions should take place at times set aside for the purpose, rather than providing students with an alternative to work (p. 200–3).

4. Questioning is more likely to increase motivation and conceptual development if:
   - the questions are intriguing and thought provoking and require students to reflect on their views and observations (p. 99–100);
   - students are encouraged to express their views and opinions openly as they will then be more inclined to justify them (p. 99–100);
   - the questions are not asked as if they are tests (p. 98);
   - the teacher asks follow-up questions, involves other students, sometimes withholds answers and acts as devil's advocate (p. 99–100);
   - all answers are treated as acceptable and, if appropriate, as valuable (p. 98).

5. Questioning can give rise to management problems in large groups if:
   - the answers require some time for thought and are given at length (p. 100–1);
   - the teacher does not indicate clearly who 'has the floor' or forgets to call on those who wish to contribute (p. 37);
   - the teacher fails to ask short factual questions with pace or directs them to only a few students. They should be used to keep a group alert and accountable and to check understanding and train of thought (p. 100–3);
   - the teacher does not ensure that everyone attends to the answers given (p. 100).

If questions are used appropriately, students are more likely to attend or participate actively than if they were simply expected to listen. However, if such sessions are not properly managed they can become noisy and uncontrolled and the teacher is then faced with restoring order.

6. Confidence in one's authority will be expressed by:
    - using the territory of the room freely and, when necessary, entering students' personal space in an unthreatening, indirect manner (p. 11–16);
    - using a steady, unthreatening gaze when talking to students or a 'questioning', silent gaze when 'noticing' unwanted behaviour (p. 31);
    - initiating and ending interactions with students (p. 35–41);
    - implying that you expect students to comply voluntarily with your instructions (p. 137, 151);
    - choosing forms of address (p. 42–6);
    - asking students questions and evaluating their answers (p. 98);
    - trying to remain relaxed even when feeling threatened or angry. Avoid behaviour which is self-comforting, self-protective or self-grooming (p. 3–6, 184, 191);
    - taking the initiative in interactions. Choose when and if you will respond in giving eye contact, replying to questions, resisting interruptions and returning smiles (p. 35–41);
    - avoiding battles over your rank, for example, 'Stand up straight when you're talking to me!' (p. 55–7).

    Such measures contribute to establishing that one's authority is legitimate and are helpful in the early relationships with students.

7. Praise is essential in promoting effort and desirable behaviour but if it is not given sensitively:
    - it may cause embarrassment, especially if given publicly (p. 178);
    - it can sound patronising, implying that the student is of lower rank or ability. One should not imply that the student is 'well trained' as this reflects praise on the trainer (p. 176);
    - it could be seen as an attempt to manipulate students either as a means of persuading them to comply or to do a disagreeable task or to use them as an example to others (p. 176);
    - it could breed complacency in the student if the praise is not really warranted (p. 178).

    Praise should be sincere and appreciative of specific behaviour or work. It should express admiration, gratitude or pleasure and enhance the status of the student relative to the teacher.

Dealing with unwanted behaviour

8. One should prepare for disciplinary interventions by:
    - planning interventions from the least to the most intrusive or defining progressive consequences (p. 169, 174, 185–7);
    - planning what one will do or say and how it will be done or said.

Anticipate the likely replies and actions that students will use to delay or avoid compliance and plan one's own responses (p. 154–6, 174–5);

- using related or logical consequences of students' behaviour rather than arbitrary punishments (unless progressive consequences have been defined) (p. 165);
- discussing mutual support with other staff, particularly for removal of students from the classroom (p. 192–4).

9. Emphasise students' responsibility for their own behaviour by:
   - discussing with them which rules should operate in the classroom and why, and what consequences should follow when rules are not complied with (p. 113, 165–7);
   - mitigating control instructions to invite co-operation (p. 147–8);
   - offering a choice regarding the logical consequences of failing to comply, rather than implying they can be forced to obey (p. 166).

10. Forceful, dominant behaviour expresses personal power and is conveyed by:
    - invading the student's personal space (p. 14);
    - bodily facing the student (p. 11);
    - glaring at the student with a menacing expression (p. 27–8);
    - towering over the student (p. 14–16);
    - giving commands in a threatening tone of voice (p. 70);
    - not moving when speaking (p. 94);
    - raising one's voice (p. 72).

Such behaviour is a form of bullying and may result in hostile compliance or an emotional confrontation and will probably worsen relationships with students.

11. Teachers will be less likely to contribute to unwanted behaviour by:
    - not following it with rewarding attention (p. 111–12);
    - discouraging peer group attention (p. 112);
    - avoiding an emotional outburst (p. 119–20);
    - making it easier and more rewarding for students to do the work set than to avoid it (p. 120–2).

12. To lessen the coercive connotations of interventions and hence appeal to students to co-operate, they can be mitigated by:
    - addressing them anonymously to the whole group (p. 147);
    - delivering them quietly or privately to individuals (p. 161–2);
    - using 'please', a polite tone of voice and relaxed manner (p. 147);
    - phrasing them as questions or hints, though not with a pleading tone of voice (p. 146–7).

Such measures give students the opportunity to express their compliance as a co-operative act.

13. Direct interventions which interrupt students' activities carry more impact if:
    - they are given only when really necessary (p. 71);
    - contact is achieved before the message is given. Students should be silent and attentive. (p. 71–2);
    - they are brief and coherent (p. 156–7);
    - they are phrased as clear directives stating what we wish or need students to do rather than stop doing (p. 148, 155);
    - direct, focused behaviour and open-hand, palm-down gestures are used (p. 46–50).

    Such measures express a firm, professional response rather than an emotional personal reaction.

14. Confrontations and disputes with students are more likely to be resolved successfully for both teacher and student if:
    - a co-operative relationship already exists (p. 134–5, 152);
    - the teacher focuses on the behaviour and not the person (p. 161–3);
    - they are not carried out publicly (p. 162);
    - the teacher does not use dominant threatening behaviour or show avoidance (p. 191–2);
    - respect is shown towards the student. Avoid trying to embarrass, humiliate or belittle students (p. 160–4);
    - the students' feelings are acknowledged (p. 164, 169);
    - a compromise can be offered (p. 164, 202);
    - a calm atmosphere is maintained (p. 191). Any anger shown should not be used to intimidate students;
    - the tension can be relieved with genuine humour (p. 138).

    After any dispute normal relationships should be re-established as soon as possible without appearing to ingratiate oneself (p. 167).

15. Corrective measures are more likely to be successful in changing students' attitudes or behaviour if:
    - any negotiation is carried out as informally as circumstances will allow (p. 193–4);
    - discussion is focused on how to 'fix the problem' rather than to assign the blame (p. 199);
    - they are perceived by students to be agreed rather than imposed on them (p. 200–4);
    - they are seen as predictable or fair (p. 184, 189).

Activity 12 Rate your own teaching

The following questionnaire was given to over two hundred teachers in six secondary schools in England and Wales. If you would like to compare your views and practice with their's, complete each of the three sections, and for each item tick the box you think that, ideally, should represent your practice, then put a cross in the box which describes your actual practice. On some items this could be the same box.

Using the instructions for scoring you should then total your actual scores for each section and for the full questionnaire and compare these with the secondary teachers in the survey. You can also compare your actual and ideal score for each item to see, in detail, how your views and practice compare.

The activity could be carried out anonymously by all teachers in a department or school to examine the range of views and practice with a view to stimulating discussion and ultimately improving consistency between staff.

SECTION A Teaching One's Subject

Tick the box you think applies to you

		NEVER	OCCASIONALLY	QUITE OFTEN	FREQUENTLY	ALWAYS	INAPPROPRIATE
1	I plan or revise my lessons on the basis of presenting challenge and interest to the students	☐	☐	☐	☐	☐	☐
2	I find my own lessons interesting and worthwhile	☐	☐	☐	☐	☐	☐
3	I vary the type of activity in which students engage	☐	☐	☐	☐	☐	☐
4	I have a clear idea what I expect students to be learning from my sessions (not simply what they should be doing)	☐	☐	☐	☐	☐	☐
5	Students become enthusiastic about my subject and produce more work than I require of them	☐	☐	☐	☐	☐	☐
6	I mark the students' work thoroughly, giving as much helpful feedback as I can	☐	☐	☐	☐	☐	☐
7	I keep thorough records of each student's progress and have a good idea of individual needs	☐	☐	☐	☐	☐	☐
8	I see that the work I set is satisfactorily completed by the students	☐	☐	☐	☐	☐	☐

SECTION B Relationships with Students

Tick the box you think applies to you

	NEVER	OCCASIONALLY	QUITE OFTEN	FREQUENTLY	ALWAYS	INAPPROPRIATE
1 I take a personal interest in the students I teach and know something of their outside interests and background	☐	☐	☐	☐	☐	☐
2 I focus on positive aspects of their work and behaviour and generally try to be encouraging	☐	☐	☐	☐	☐	☐
3 Students can make me laugh and I enjoy sharing a joke with them	☐	☐	☐	☐	☐	☐
4 I talk about my own experiences and interests with students	☐	☐	☐	☐	☐	☐
5 Students who have left school come back to let me know how they are getting on	☐	☐	☐	☐	☐	☐
6 Students smile at me or initiate greetings with me as I move around the school	☐	☐	☐	☐	☐	☐
7 Students talk to me informally and ask my opinions or advice about 'non-school' matters	☐	☐	☐	☐	☐	☐
8 I take part in extra curricular activities	☐	☐	☐	☐	☐	☐

SECTION C General Discipline

Tick the box you think applies to you

		NEVER	OCCASIONALLY	QUITE OFTEN	FREQUENTLY	ALWAYS	INAPPROPRIATE
1	I have to raise my voice to be heard above the class talk	☐	☐	☐	☐	☐	☐
2	Questions and answer sessions get disorderly as students call out or talk among themselves	☐	☐	☐	☐	☐	☐
3	I shout at students who are not attending or who are misbehaving	☐	☐	☐	☐	☐	☐
4	I get angry with students and show it	☐	☐	☐	☐	☐	☐
5	I have to use punishments	☐	☐	☐	☐	☐	☐
6	I get into confrontation situations with students about their work or behaviour	☐	☐	☐	☐	☐	☐
7	I allow certain students to do little work, provided they are quiet	☐	☐	☐	☐	☐	☐
8	I avoid enforcing some school rules with some students	☐	☐	☐	☐	☐	☐

Scoring

For Sections A and B score 1 for 'Never', 2 for 'Occasionally', 3 for 'Quite Often', 4 for 'Frequently', 5 for 'Always'.

For Section C score 1 for 'Always', 2 for 'Frequently', 3 for 'Quite Often', 4 for 'Occasionally', 5 for 'Never'.

Total your scores for each section and for the grand total A + B + C.

My interpretations of the scores are, of course, only speculative and not based on interviewing teachers.

SECTION A Teaching One's Subject

Less than 20
Only one per cent of teachers scored in this range. You are probably overworked and thoroughly demoralised, but, if not, a serious review of practice is called for and you certainly need some help and advice.

20–25
Seventeen per cent of teachers scored in this range. You are probably feeling the pressures of work and may have too many commitments, both professional and private, which take your time.

26–32
Fifty-seven per cent of teachers scored in this range. You have rated yourself as did the great majority of the sample, though if you scored at the lower end of the range you are probably still dissatisfied with your teaching to some extent.

33–37
Twenty-three per cent of teachers scored in this range. When rating 'ideal' practice, the majority of scores came in this range, so your practice is what most teachers aspire to reach.

38–40
Two per cent of teachers scored in this range. You are either an example to us all, or are being less than honest with yourself. Incidentally, no teacher in the sample scored 39 or 40.

SECTION B Relationships with Students

Less than 18
Three per cent of teachers scored in this range. You have very formal and distant relationships with students. This could reflect the ethos of the school in

which you teach or you might feel that school would be a better place if it were not for the students.

18–23
Twenty-five per cent of teachers scored in this range. Your relationships with students are likely to be formal and work-centred and you are not a great fan of PSE. If not, you may feel you are failing to get to know students as well as you might wish.

24–30
Forty-seven per cent of teachers scored in this range. You probably see your pastoral role as important and do your best to get to know students well, given the limited time that you teach them and the other demands on your time.

31–36
Twenty-three per cent of teachers scored in this range though this was the 'ideal' choice for the majority of teachers. You probably have fairly informal relationships with your students and enjoy their company.

37–40
Two per cent of teachers scored in this range. You probably consider your relationships with students to be the major reason for your teaching. Are you always clear about your role as teacher or might you sometimes identify too closely with them?

SECTION C General Discipline

Less than 18
One per cent of teachers scored in this range. You are likely to feel very demoralised and are fighting for survival. Newly qualified teachers are most vulnerable and need support in the induction year. If you have not done so already, ask for some help.

18–22
Five per cent of teachers scored in this range. Your days are very hectic and tiring. It is probable that you don't get a great deal of satisfaction from teaching your subject, though you might consider you have good relationships with students.

23–28
Twenty per cent of teachers scored in this range. Lively might be the appropriate adjective to describe your days and you probably need your rest at the weekend. Perhaps things are better with the younger classes, though you could just be teaching in a difficult situation.

29–34

Sixty-three per cent of teachers scored in this range. This is a relatively high range of scores for the large majority of teachers compared with sections A and B and suggests that most teachers are not experiencing serious problems of discipline, contrary perhaps to popular belief.

35–40

Eleven per cent of teachers scored in this range. Count yourself fortunate, or give yourself a pat on the back! This was the ideal for the majority of teachers.

Total overall score

Less than 66

Two per cent of teachers scored in this range. There are probably very few satisfactions for you in teaching at the moment. Professional help, a change of school or even profession, might be the solution.

66–79

Seventeen per cent of teachers scored in this range. Teaching may be very stressful and you probably need more hours in the day to complete your work.

80–95

Sixty-three per cent of teachers scored in this range. You have the satisfaction of knowing that almost two-thirds of the sample have rated themselves in a similar way, though your particular stresses and satisfactions may differ.

96–109

Seventeen per cent of teachers scored in this range. This was the 'ideal' range for the majority of teachers, so you probably feel very satisfied with your efforts.

110–120

One per cent of teachers scored in this range. You probably wear your underpants outside your trousers or skirt and can leap tall buildings with a single bound.

The following sections give an item analysis of the responses, if you are interested in comparing your answers in detail to the teachers in the survey, or if you have been unable to complete a section due to an inappropriate item.

SECTION A Teaching One's Subject

1. *I plan or revise my lessons on the basis of presenting challenge and interest to the students.*

	N	O	QO	F	A
Actual %	(1)	(4)	(31)	(50)	(14)
Ideal %	(0)	(1)	(4)	(28)	(67)

Do teachers present the same sessions over and over again or do they revise the work? A score of 4 puts you with fifty per cent of the teachers and only fourteen per cent would have scored 5, the ideal for the two-thirds of the group.

2. *I find my own lessons interesting and worthwhile.*

	N	O	QO	F	A
Actual %	(0)	(7)	(45)	(42)	(6)
Ideal %	(0)	(0)	(2)	(30)	(68)

If we enjoy teaching there is probably more chance that the students will also enjoy it, but difficult classes, over-familiarity with the work, pressure of work and many other things could affect our enjoyment. A score of 3 or 4 was typical for most of the teachers surveyed though, once again, two-thirds believed 'always' to be the ideal.

3. *I vary the type of activity in which students engage.*

	N	O	QO	F	A
Actual %	(0)	(8)	(31)	(41)	(20)
Ideal %	(0)	(2)	(10)	(44)	(44)

One way of recapturing attention is to vary the type of activity so that lessons do not become over predictable and tedious. Most teachers scored 3 or 4 on this item and, looking at the 'ideal', many felt that there could be too much variety perhaps at the expense of helpful routines or sustained periods of concentration.

4. *I have a clear idea of what I expect students to be learning from my sessions (not simply what they should be doing).*

	N	O	QO	F	A
Actual %	(1)	(2)	(15)	(42)	(40)
Ideal %	(0)	(1)	(1)	(8)	(90)

Keeping students busy and ensuring that they are learning something are not necessarily the same things and ninety per cent of the teachers felt that the latter should be the ideal. Most teachers rated themselves as either 4 or 5 on this item.

5. Students become enthusiastic about my subject and produce more work than I require of them.

	N	O	QO	F	A
Actual %	(2)	(42)	(37)	(17)	(2)
Ideal %	(0)	(3)	(18)	(46)	(33)

Good teaching doesn't simply impart knowledge, at its best it can be inspiring. Students who produce extra work are likely to be expressing their interest for your subject though they might be reflecting parental pressure. Only a third of teachers believed this should always be the ideal, perhaps because experience of real situations persuaded the others that even in their wildest dreams this would not always be possible. Most teachers rated themselves below their own ideals on this item, scoring 2 or 3.

6. I mark the students' work thoroughly, giving as much helpful feedback as I can.

	N	O	QO	F	A
Actual %	(1)	(7)	(31)	(38)	(23)
Ideal %	(0)	(1)	(1)	(20)	(78)

Not an appropriate item for teachers of some subjects, but a strong agreement among most that this should always be the ideal. Probably due to pressures of work many fell short of their ideals, scoring 3 or 4.

7. I keep thorough records of each student's progress and have a good idea of individual needs.

	N	O	QO	F	A
Actual %	(1)	(9)	(32)	(35)	(23)
Ideal %	(0)	(0)	(2)	(18)	(80)

Again, many teachers fell short of what the great majority considered to be the ideal, presumably because they did not have the time to keep such records. The distributions are very similar to the previous item, as one might expect, most teachers scoring either 3 or 4.

8. I see that the work I set is satisfactorily completed by the students.

	N	O	QO	F	A
Actual %	(0)	(4)	(24)	(46)	(26)
Ideal %	(0)	(1)	(1)	(10)	(88)

A very strong agreement among teachers that this should always be the ideal, but most scored themselves as 4. Ensuring that work set is always satisfactorily completed can be very time consuming and wearing but probably saves time in the long run as students learn they can't get away with it in your case.

SECTION B Relationships with Students

1. I take a personal interest in the students I teach and know something of their outside interests and background.

	N	O	QO	F	A
Actual %	(1)	(11)	(26)	(47)	(15)
Ideal %	(1)	(2)	(7)	(40)	(50)

It surprised me that more teachers did not consider 'always' to be the ideal, than the fifty per cent who did. The majority rated themselves as 4, matching the ideal of forty per cent.

2. I focus on positive aspects of their work and behaviour and generally try to be encouraging.

	N	O	QO	F	A
Actual %	(1)	(3)	(19)	(49)	(28)
Ideal %	(1)	(1)	(1)	(30)	(67)

There was a fairly close relationship between what teachers felt to be ideal and what they judged to be happening, with nearly half of them rating themselves as 4. Most schemes to improve students' work and behaviour place great emphasis on positive treatment.

3. Students can make me laugh and I enjoy sharing a joke with them.

	N	O	QO	F	A
Actual %	(1)	(16)	(20)	(39)	(24)
Ideal %	(1)	(11)	(22)	(36)	(30)

This item produced a wide range of opinion on what the ideal should be and the distribution of 'actual' responses were very similar, the majority choosing 4.

4. I talk about my own experiences and interests with students.

	N	O	QO	F	A
Actual %	(1)	(35)	(23)	(30)	(11)
Ideal %	(1)	(28)	(29)	(30)	(12)

Ideal and actual responses to this item were remarkably similar with most
choices distributed between 2, 3 and 4. The results could reflect differences
in practice between teachers on the desirability of informal relationships with
students, shown in the tendency for the 'actual' responses to peak at
'occasionally' and 'frequently'.

5. Students who have left school come back to let me know how they are
    getting on.

	N	O	QO	F	A
Actual %	(4)	(47)	(24)	(24)	(1)
Ideal %	(2)	(19)	(37)	(32)	(10)

    When teachers have known students throughout their secondary schooling
    this is clearly more likely to happen so this item will affect teachers
    differently, depending on how long they have taught at the school. However,
    there were mixed views on the desirability of such practice shown in the
    range of 'ideal' responses. In practice the majority of teachers rated
    themselves as 2.

6. Students smile at me or initiate greetings with me as I move around the
    school.

	N	O	QO	F	A
Actual %	(0)	(2)	(22)	(57)	(19)
Ideal %	(1)	(1)	(14)	(50)	(34)

    When I accompany a teacher around a school I am aware that some have
    many friendly exchanges with students, whereas others pass unnoticed. The
    majority of teachers felt that friendly exchanges were desirable most of the
    time and in practice this seemed to be happening as most rated themselves
    as 4.

7. Students talk to me informally and ask my opinions about 'non-school'
    matters.

	N	O	QO	F	A
Actual %	(1)	(20)	(36)	(38)	(5)
Ideal %	(1)	(10)	(33)	(43)	(13)

    This item is likely to be related to item 4 and the distribution of results is
    broadly similar.

8. *I take part in extra curricular activities.*

	N	O	QO	F	A
Actual %	(7)	(41)	(20)	(20)	(12)
Ideal %	(1)	(9)	(34)	(37)	(19)

Many things could affect responses to this item, such as a teacher's age, domestic situation and the extent that the school encourages such activities. Most teachers rated themselves as 2 but felt ideally there should be greater participation.

SECTION C General Discipline

1. *I have to raise my voice to be heard above the class talk.*

	N	O	QO	F	A
Actual %	(1)	(52)	(28)	(14)	(5)
Ideal %	(36)	(56)	(7)	(1)	(0)

In spite of good intentions not to do this, many teachers slip into this practice. The majority of teachers rated themselves as 'occasionally' a score of 4, and also felt this was the ideal.

2. *Question and answer sessions get disorderly as students call out or talk among themselves.*

	N	O	QO	F	A
Actual %	(8)	(62)	(17)	(10)	(3)
Ideal %	(60)	(39)	(0)	(1)	(0)

Attempts to involve a class in discussion are sometimes difficult to manage and can sometimes get disorderly. However, the large majority of teachers rated themselves as 4, though ideally felt that this should never happen.

3. *I shout at students who are not attending or who are misbehaving.*

	N	O	QO	F	A
Actual %	(4)	(62)	(25)	(8)	(1)
Ideal %	(33)	(58)	(7)	(1)	(1)

The majority of teachers rated themselves as 4 on this item and the distribution was similar to that on item 2. However, the majority also rated 4 as the ideal, contrary to the message being expressed in this and many other current texts.

4. *I get angry with students and show it.*

	N	O	QO	F	A
Actual %	(10)	(75)	(10)	(4)	(1)
Ideal %	(44)	(54)	(1)	(1)	(0)

With the stress of dealing with difficult students it is not surprising that seventy-five per cent of teachers said this happened occasionally, though it is perhaps unexpected that more than half felt this to be ideal.

5. *I have to use punishments.*

	N	O	QO	F	A
Actual %	(0)	(67)	(19)	(10)	(4)
Ideal %	(17)	(72)	(7)	(3)	(1)

Teachers with co-operative classes rarely have to use punishments and the great majority of teachers rated themselves as using them only occasionally, which was also viewed as the ideal by most.

6. *I get into confrontation situations with students about their work and behaviour.*

	N	O	QO	F	A
Actual %	(20)	(69)	(9)	(1)	(1)
Ideal %	(62)	(37)	(1)	(0)	(0)

The majority acknowledged that they occasionally got into confrontations, rating themselves as 4, but there was a clear majority who believed that ideally this should not happen.

7. *I allow certain students to do little work, provided they are quiet.*

	N	O	QO	F	A
Actual %	(36)	(53)	(6)	(4)	(1)
Ideal %	(78)	(19)	(1)	(1)	(1)

A teacher might do this to avoid a confrontation with a student or to concentrate on those who co-operate. However, it probably only reinforces the unhelpful attitudes in those students who get away with doing little work and so in the long-term is counter-productive. There was a clear expression of this understanding from seventy-eight per cent of the teachers, though a majority acknowledged doing it occasionally.

8. *I avoid enforcing some school rules with some students.*

	N	O	QO	F	A
Actual %	(31)	(59)	(7)	(2)	(1)
Ideal %	(69)	(27)	(3)	(1)	(0)

A related item to the previous one, probably sharing the same explanations, and the similar distributions of choices reflects this. A majority of teachers did this occasionally, but even more believed that ideally this should not happen.

References

ALBERT, LINDA (1989) *A Teachers' Guide to Co-operative Discipline*, American Guidance Service.

ARGYLE, M. and COOK, M. (1976) *Gaze and Mutual Gaze*, Cambridge University Press.

ARGYLE, M. (1975) *Bodily Communication*, Methuen.

ARONFREED, J. (1968) *Conduct and Conscience*, Academic Press.

ARONFREED, J., CUTLICK, R. A. and FAGAN, S. A. (1963) 'Cognitive structure, punishment and nurturance in the experimental inductions of self-criticism', *Child Development*, **34**, 281–94.

AUSTIN, J. L. (1962) *How to do things with words*, Oxford University Press.

AUSUBEL, D. P. (1968) *Educational Psychology: A Cognitive View*, Holt, Rinehart and Winston.

BABAD, E., BERNIERI, F. and ROSENTHAL, R. (1989) 'When less information is more informative: diagnosing teacher expectations from brief samples of behaviour', *British Journal of Educational Psychology*, **59**, 281–95.

BADGER, B. (1992) 'Changing a Disruptive School' in REYNOLDS, D. and CUTTANCE, P. (eds) *op. cit.*

BALL, S. J. (1980) 'Initial Encounters in the Classroom and the Process of Establishment' in WOODS, P. (ed.) *Pupil Strategies*, Croom Helm.

BARNES, D., BRITTON, J. and ROSEN, H. (1969) *Language, the Learner and the School*, Penguin.

BERNE, ERIC (1964) *Games People Play*, Penguin Books.

BIEHLER, R. F. (1978) *Psychology Applied to Teaching*, 3rd edn, Houghton Mifflin.

BIRDWHISTELL, RAY L. (1973) *Kinesics and Context: Essays on Body-Motion Communication*, Penguin Books.

BRAZIL, D. (1976) 'The Teacher's Use of Intonation', *Educational Review*, **28**, 180–9.

BRODEN, R. M. (1971) 'The effects of self-recording on the classroom behaviour of two eighth grade students', *Journal of Applied Behaviour Analysis*, **4**, 277–85.

BROWN, G. A. and EDMONDSON, R. (1984) 'Asking Questions' in WRAGG, E. C. *Classroom Teaching Skills*, Croom Helm.

BRUCE, D. (1973) 'Language and Cognition', *Cambridge Journal of Education*, **3**, 1, 2–11.

BUZAN, T. (1971) *Speed Memory*, David & Charles.

CANFIELD, J. and WELLS, H. (1976) *100 Ways to Enhance Self-Concept in the Classroom*, Prentice Hall.

CANTER, LEE (1990) 'Assertive Discipline' in SCHERER, M. *et al.* (1990) *op. cit.*

CHEYNE, J. A. and WALTERS, R. H. (1970) 'Punishment and Prohibition' in CRAIK, K. (ed.), *New Directions in Psychology 4*, Holt, Rinehart and Winston.

CONDON, W. S. (1976) 'An Analysis of Behavioural Organisation', *Sign Language Studies*, **13**, 285–318.

COOK, J. (1975) 'Easing behaviour problems', *Special Education: Forward Trends*, **2**, 1, 15–17.

COOPER, P. and UPTON, G. (1992) 'An ecosystemic approach to classroom behaviour problems' in WHELDALL, K. (ed) *op. cit.*

COULBY, D. and HARPER, T. (1985) *Preventing Classroom Disruption*, Croom Helm.

DES (1989) *Discipline in Schools* (The Elton Report), London, HMSO.

DANZIGER, K. (1976) *Interpersonal Communication*, Pergamon.

DAVIES, B. (1983) 'The Role Pupils Play in the Social Construction of Classroom Order', *British Journal of Sociology of Education*, **4**, 1, 55–69.

DELAMONT, SARAH (1983) *Interaction in the Classroom* (2nd edn), Methuen.

Discipline for Learning, Course and materials supplied by Teaching and Learning Associates, Bristol.

DREIKURS, R., GRUNWALD, B. and PEPPER, F. (1982) *Maintaining Sanity in the Classroom* (2nd edn), Harper & Row.

DUBELLE, S. and HOFFMAN, C. (1984) *Misbehavin': Solving the Disciplinary Puzzle for Education*, Technomic Publishing Co.

EIBL-EIBESFELDT (1972) 'Similarities and Differences Between Cultures in Expressive Movements' in WEITZ, S., *op. cit.*

ELLYSON, S. L. and DOVIDIO, J. F. (eds) (1985) *Power, Dominance and Non-verbal Behaviour*, Springer-Verlag.

ERNST, KEN (1972) *Games Students Play*, Celestial Arts.

EXLINE, R. V. and YELLIN, A. (1969) 'Eye contact as a sign between man and monkey' Symposium on non-verbal communication, Nineteenth International Congress of Psychology, London, reported in EXLINE, R. V. (1972) *op. cit.*

EXLINE, R. V. (1972) 'Visual Interaction: The Glances of Power and Preference', Nebraska Symposium on Motivation, pp. 163–206, University of Lincoln Press.

EXLINE, R. V. (1985) 'Multichannel Transmission of Nonverbal Behaviour and the Perception of Powerful Men: The Presidential Debates of 1976' in ELLYSON, S. L. and DOVIDIO, J. F. *op. cit.*

FESTINGER, L. (1961) 'The psychological effects of insufficient rewards', *American Psychologist*, **16**, 1–11.

FLANDERS, N. A. (1968) 'Interaction analysis and inservice training', *Journal of Experimental Education*, **37**, 126–32.

FRENCH, P. J. and PESKETT, R. (1986) 'Control Instructions in the Infant Classroom', *Educational Research*, **28**, 3, 210–19.

FURLONG, V. (1976) 'Interaction Sets in the Classroom: Towards a Study of Pupil Knowledge', in STUBBS, M. and DELAMONT, S. *op. cit.*

GALLOWAY, C. M. (1979) 'Teaching and Non-Verbal Behaviour' in WOLFGANG, A. (ed.) *Non-Verbal Behaviour: Applications and Cultural Implications*, Academic Press.

GALLOWAY, D., BALL, T., BLOOMFIELD, D. and SYED, R. (1982) *Schools and disruptive pupils*, Longman.

GALVIN, P. and COSTA, P. (1994) *Developing a Behaviour Policy and Putting it into Practice*, Positive Behaviour Service, Leeds City Council.

GANNAWAY, H. (1976) 'Making Sense of School' in STUBBS, M. and DELAMONT, S. *op. cit.*

GILLHAM, B. (ed.) (1981) *Problem Behaviour in the Secondary School*, Croom Helm.

GLASSER, W. (1969) *Schools Without Failure*, Harper and Row.

GNAGEY, W. J. (1975) *Maintaining Discipline in Classroom Instruction*, Macmillan.

GNAGEY, W. J. (1960) 'Effects on classmates of a deviant student's power and response to a teacher-exerted control technique', *Journal of Educational Psychology*, **51**, 1–9.

GOFFMAN, E. (1959) *Presentation of Self in Everday Life*, Penguin.

GRAY, F. (1974) 'Little Brother is Changing You', *Psychology Today* (March).

HALL, R. V., AXELROD, S., FOUNDOPOULOS, M. *et al.* (1971) 'The effective use of punishments to modify behaviour in the classroom', *Educational Technology*, **11**, 4, 24–6.

HAMBLIN, R. L, BUCKHOLDT, D., FERRITOR, D., KOZLOFF, M. and BLACKWELL, L. (1971) *The Humanisation Process*, John Wiley.

HARGREAVES, D. H. (1967) *Social Relations in a Secondary School*, Routledge and Kegan Paul.

HARGREAVES, D. H. (1972) *Interpersonal Relations and Education*, Routledge and Kegan Paul.

HARGREAVES, D. H. (1984) 'Teachers' Questions: open, closed and half-open', *Educational Research*, **26**, 1, 46–51.

HARGREAVES, D. H., HESTER, S. K. and MELLOR, F. J. (1975) *Deviance in Classrooms*, Routledge and Kegan Paul.

HARRIS, C. S., THACKRAY, R. I. and SCHOENBERGER, R. W. (1966) 'Blink rate as a function of induced muscular tension and manifest anxiety', *Perpetual Motor Skills*, **22**, 155–60.

HARROP, A. (1974) 'A behavioural workshop for the management of classroom problems', *British Journal of In-Service Education*, **1**, 1, 47–50.

HASTINGS, N. and SCHWIESO, J. (1994) 'Kindly Take Your Seats', *TES* 21st October.

HINDE, R. A. (1979) *Towards Understanding Relationships*, Academic Press.

HOLMES, J. (1983) 'The structures of teachers' directives' in RICHARDS, J. C. and SCHMIDT, R. W. (eds) *Language and Communication*, Longman.

HOWELL, S. (1981) 'Rules not Words' in HEELAS, P. and LOCK, A. (eds) *Indigenous Psychologies*, Academic Press.

KENDON, A. (1972) 'Some Relationships Between Body Motion and Speech' in SIEGMAN, A. W. and POPE, B. *Studies in Dyadic Communication*, Pergamon.

KENDON, A. (1967) 'Some functions of gaze-direction in social interaction', *Acta Psychologica*, **26**, 22–47.

KENDON, A. (1983) 'Gesture and Speech: How they interact' in WIEMANN, J. M. and HARRISON, R. P. *Non-verbal Interaction*, Sage Publications.

KILBURN, J. (1978) 'Better for Both – thoughts on teacher–pupil interaction', *Education 3–13*, **6**, 2, 9–11.

KOUNIN, J. S. and OBRADOVIC, S. (1968) 'Managing emotionally disturbed children in regular classrooms: a replication and extension', *The Journal of Special Education*, **2**, 2, 129–35.

KOUNIN, J. S. (1970) *Discipline and Group Management in Classrooms*, Holt, Rinehart and Winston.

LANGFORD, P. E., LOVEGROVE, H. and LOVEGROVE, M. N. (1994) 'Do Senior Secondary Students Possess the Moral Maturity to Negotiate Class Rules?', *Journal of Moral Education*, **23**, 4; 387–407.

LASLETT, R. and SMITH, C. J. (1993) *Effective Classroom Management*, 2nd edn, Routledge.

LEPPER, M. R., GREENE, D. and NISBETT, R. E. (1973) 'Undermining children's intrinsic interest with extrinsic reward: A test of the "over justification" hypothesis', *Journal of Personality and Social Psychology*, **28**, 129–37.

LEWIS, D. (1978) *The Secret Language of Your Child*, Souvenir Press.

LUCAS, D. and THOMAS, G. (1990) 'The "Geography" of Classroom Learning', *British Journal of Special Education*, **17**, 1, 31–4.

MAHONEY, M. J. and THORENSEN, C. E. (1972) 'Behavioural self-control – power to the person', *Educational Researcher*, **1**, 5–7.

MARLAND, M. (1975) *The Craft of the Classroom: a Survival Guide*, Heinemann Educational Books.

MCNAMARA, E. and HEARD, C. (1976) 'Self-control through self-recording', *Special Education: Forward Trends*, **3**, 2, 21–30.

MEDNICK, S. A., GABRIELLI, W. F. and HUTCHINGS, B. (1987) 'Genetic factors in the etiology of crime' in MEDNICK, S. A., MOFFITT, T. E. and STACK, S. A. *The Causes of Crime*, Cambridge University Press.

MEHRABIAN, A. (1972) *Non-verbal Communication*, Aldine Atherton.

MERRETT, F. and WHELDALL, K. (1988) *The Behavioural Approach to Teaching with Secondary Aged Children (BATSAC) Training Package*, Birmingham: Positive Products.

MERRETT, F. and TANG, W. M. (1994) 'The attitudes of British primary school pupils to praise, rewards, punishments and reprimands', *British Journal of Educational Psychology*, **64**, 91–103.

MILLS, I. (1975) 'Can the human brain cope?' *New Scientist* (16th October 138–40).

MOIR, A. and JESSEL, D. (1995) *A Mind To Crime*, Michael Joseph.

MONTGOMERY, D. (1989) *Managing Behaviour Problems*, Hodder & Stoughton.

MOSLEY, JENNY (1993) *Turn your school around: Circle time approach to the development of self-esteem and positive behaviour in the primary staffroom, classroom and playground*, Learning Development Aids.

NEILL, S. R. ST. J. (1987) 'Non-verbal Communication – Implications for Teachers' in MARTINSSON, B. G. (ed.) *On Communication*, **4** (SIC13), University of Linkoping.

NEILL, S. R. ST. J. (1988) 'Non-verbal Communication – Its Significance for the Pastoral Specialist', *Pastoral Care in Education*, **6**, 7–14.

O'LEARY, K. D., KAUFMAN, K. F., KASS, R. E. and DRABMAN, R. S. (1970) 'The effects of loud and soft reprimands on the behaviour of disruptive students', *Exceptional Children*, **37** (October), 145–55.

OFSTED (1/93/NS) *Education for Disaffected Pupils*, HMSO.

PARTINGTON, J. A. and HINCHLIFFE, G. (1979) 'Some aspects of classroom management', *British Journal of Teacher Education*, **53**, 231–41.

PIK, R. (1981) 'Confrontation Situations and Teacher-support Systems' in GILLHAM, B. *op. cit.*

PRESLAND, J. (1978) 'Behaviour modification – theory and practice', *Education 3–13*, **6**, 1, 43–6.

PROVIS, M. (1992) *Dealing with Difficulty: A Systems Approach to Problem Behaviour*, Hodder & Stoughton.

REYNOLDS, D. and CUTTANCE, P. (eds) (1992) *School Effectiveness. Research, Policy and Practice*, Cassell.

REYNOLDS, D. and PACKER, A. (1992) 'School Effectiveness and School Improvement' in REYNOLDS, D. and CUTTNACE, P. (eds) *op. cit.*

REYNOLDS, D. and SULLIVAN, M. (1981) 'The Effects of School: A Radical Faith, Re-stated' in GILLHAM, B. *op. cit.*

RICHARDS, JIM (1994) ' "Subject Expertise" and It's Deployment in Primary Schools: A Discussion Paper', *Education 3–13* March.

ROBERTSON, J. and WEBB, N. (1995) 'Rainbow shades to tone it down', *TES* June 30th.

ROBERTSON, J. (1978) 'Enthusiastic Teaching: Sustaining Pupils' Attention', *Association of Educational Psychologists' Journal*, **4**, 8, 28–36.

ROETHLISBERGER, F. J. and DICKSON, W. J. (1939) *Management and the Worker*, Harvard University Press.

ROGERS, B. (1990) *You Know the Fair Rule*, Longman.

ROGERS, B. (1994a) *The Language of Discipline: A Practical Approach to Classroom Management*, Northcote House.

ROGERS, B. (1994b) *Behaviour Recovery: A Programme for Behaviourally Disordered Students in Mainstream Schools*, ACER Camberwell Victoria.

ROGERS, W. (1989) *Making a Discipline Plan*, Nelson, Melbourne.

ROSENBURG, H. (1976) 'Modifying teachers' behaviour', *Special Education: Forward Trends*, **3**, 2, 8–9.

ROSENSHINE, B. (1970) 'Enthusiastic teaching: a research review', *School Review*, **78**, 4, 499–514.

ROSENTHAL, R. and JACOBSON, L. (1968) *Pygmalion in the Classroom*, New York. Holt, Rinehart and Winston.

ROSS, A. (1978) 'The lecture theatre is a world of entertainment', *TES* (23 June).

RUTTER, M., MAUGHAN, B., MORTIMORE, P. and OUSTON, J. (1979) *Fifteen Thousand Hours*, Open Books.

RYAN, K. (1970) *Don't Smile 'til Christmas*, Chicago Press.

SCHERER, M., GERSCH, I. and FRY, L. (eds) (1990) *Meeting Disruptive Behaviour*, Macmillan.

SHARPE, KEITH (1993) 'A good telling-off: the disciplinary interview in initial teacher training', *Primary Teaching Studies*, Summer 16–22.

SKINNER, B. F. (1971) *Beyond Freedom and Dignity*, Penguin.

SLEE, ROGER (1995) *Changing Theories and Practices of Discipline*, The Falmer Press.

SMITH, H. A. (1979) 'Non-verbal communication in teaching', *Review of Educational Research*, **49**, 4, 631–72.

SOLOMON, R. L. (1964) 'Punishment', *American Psychologist*, **19**, 4, 239–52.

SPADY, G. (1973) 'Authority, Conflict and Teacher Effectiveness', *Educational Researcher*, **2**, 4–10.

STRONGMAN, K. T. and CHAMPNESS, B. G. (1968) 'Dominance hierarchies and conflict in eye contact', *Acta Psychologica*, **28**, 376–86.

STUBBS, M. and DELAMONT, S. (1976) *Explorations in Classroom Observation*, John Wiley and Sons.

STUBBS, M. (1976) 'Keeping in Touch: Some Functions of Teacher-talk', in STUBBS, M. and DELAMONT, S. *op. cit.*

TANNER, L. N. (1978) *Classroom Discipline for Effective Teaching and Learning*, Holt, Rinehart and Winston.

TATTUM, D. (1982) *Disruptive Pupils in Schools and Units*, Wiley.

THOMAS, A., CHESS, S. and BIRCH, H. G. (1968) *Temperament and Behaviour Disorders in Children*, New York University Press.

THOMAS, W. I. (1931) *The Unadjusted Girl*, Little Brown & Co.

TORODE, B. (1976) 'Teachers' Talk and Classroom Discipline' in STUBBS, M. and DELAMONT, S. *op. cit.*

TURNER, B. (1973) *Discipline in Schools*, Ward Lock Educational.

UPTON, G. and COOPER, P. (1990) 'A new perspective on behaviour problems in schools: the ecosystemic approach', *Maladjustment and Therapeutic Education*, **8**, 1, 3–18.

WADD, K. (1973) 'Classroom Power in Discipline in Schools', in TURNER, B. *op. cit.*

WALKER, R. and ADELMAN, C. (1976) 'Strawberries' in STUBBS, M. and DELAMONT, S. *op. cit.*

WATSON, O. M. and GRAVES, T. D. (1966) 'Quantitative research in proxemic behaviour', *American Anthropology*, **68**, 971–85.

WEBER, M. (1958) From Max Weber: *Essays in Sociology*, GERTH, H. and MILL, C. W. (eds), New York. Oxford University Press.

WEINRAUB, M. and PUTNEY, E. (1978) 'The effects of height on infants' social responses to unfamiliar persons', *Child Development*, **49**, 3, 598–603.

WEITZ, S. (1974) *Non-verbal Communication*, Oxford University Press.

WHELDALL, K. and LAM, Y. Y. (1987) 'Rows Versus Tables II. The Effects of Classroom Seating Arrangements on Classroom Disruption Rate, On-task Behaviour and Teacher Behaviour in Three Special School Classes', *Educational Psychology*, **7**, 4, 303–12.

WHELDALL, K. and MERRETT, F. (1985) 'The Behavioural Approach to Teaching Package for Use in Primary and Middle Schools, (BAT-PACK)', Birmingham Positive Products.

WHELDALL, K. (ed.) (1992) *Discipline in Schools. Psychological Perspectives on the Elton Report*, Routledge.

WHELDALL, K., BEVAN, K. and SHORTALL, K. (1986) 'A Touch of Reinforcement: the effects of contingent teacher touch on the classroom behaviour of young children', *Educational Review*, **38**, 3, 207–16.

WHITE, R. and BROCKING, D. (1983) *Tales Out Of School*, Routledge and Kegan Paul.

WILCE, HILARY (1994) 'Spare the praise, save the child', *TES*, 25.3.94.

WOOD, P. and SCHWARTZ, B. (1977) *How to get your children to do what you want them to do*, Prentice-Hall.

WRAGG, E. C. and WOOD, E. K. (1984a) 'Teachers' First Encounters with their Classes' in WRAGG, E. C. *op. cit.*

WRAGG, E. C. and WOOD, E. K. (1984b) 'Pupils' Appraisals of Teaching' in WRAGG, E. C. *op. cit.*

WRAGG, E. C. (1981) *Class Management and Control: A Teaching Skills Workbook*, Macmillan.

WRAGG, E. C. (ed.) (1984) *Classroom Teaching Skills*, Croom Helm.

WRIGHT, D. (1973) 'The Punishment of Children', in TURNER, B. *op. cit.*